Origins of the Iroquois League

The Iroquois and Their Neighbors
Christopher Vecsey, *Series Editor*

Origins *of the* Iroquois League

Narratives, Symbols, and Archaeology

Anthony Wonderley
and Martha L. Sempowski

Syracuse University Press

Copyright © 2019 by Syracuse University Press
Syracuse, New York 13244-5290

All Rights Reserved

First Edition 2019

22 23 24 25 26 27   7 6 5 4 3 2

∞ The paper used in this publication meets the minimum requirements
of the American National Standard for Information Sciences—Permanence of Paper
for Printed Library Materials, ANSI Z39.48-1992.

For a listing of books published and distributed by Syracuse University Press,
visit https://press.syr.edu.

ISBN: 978-0-8156-3660-1 (hardcover)
      978-0-8156-3667-0 (paperback)
      978-0-8156-5492-6 (e-book)

Library of Congress Cataloging-in-Publication Data

Names: Wonderley, Anthony Wayne, 1949– author. | Sempowski, Martha Lou, 1942– author.
Title: Origins of the Iroquois League : narratives, symbols, and archaeology / Anthony Wonderley
    and Martha L. Sempowski.
Other titles: Iroquois and their neighbors.
Description: First edition. | Syracuse : Syracuse University Press, 2019. | Series: The Iroquois
    and their neighbors | Includes bibliographical references and index. | Summary: "This is
    a scholarly work of anthropological archaeology in which Wonderley and Sempowski use
    their combined scholarship to shine a spotlight on what are perhaps the most significant yet
    neglected issues in the Iroquois past: When and how did historically known tribes begin to
    coalesce, what factors allowed the success of those population amalgamations, and when did
    the League of the Iroquois achieve its final form?"—Provided by publisher.
Identifiers: LCCN 2019036263 (print) | LCCN 2019036264 (ebook) | ISBN 9780815636601
    (hardcover) | ISBN 9780815636670 (paperback) | ISBN 9780815654926 (epub)
Subjects: LCSH: Five Nations—History. | Iroquois Indians—History.
Classification: LCC E99.I7 W845 2019 (print) | LCC E99.I7 (ebook) |
    DDC 974.7004/9755—dc23
LC record available at https://lccn.loc.gov/2019036263
LC ebook record available at https://lccn.loc.gov/2019036264

Manufactured in the United States of America

The authors dedicate this work with love to their grandchildren:

From Wonderley: To Emily Olivia and Thomas Wayne —long may you run.

From Sempowski: To Brian, Michelle, Benjamin, and Julia —who inspire hope for the future.

Contents

Illustrations

Figures

Maps

Tables

Acknowledgments

Many thanks to Syracuse University Press and especially to editors Suzanne E. Guiod and Alison M. Shay, as well as to two anonymous reviewers who made this (as much as they could) a better book.

Knowing that they stand on the shoulders of many scholars, the authors owe a particular debt of gratitude to William Engelbrecht, William Fenton, George Hamell, Robert Kuhn, Peter Pratt, Daniel Richter, Lorraine Saunders, Anthony Wallace, and Charles Wray.

The authors also thank David Danglis for reformatting and standardizing the maps and, in the process, making them better.

Wonderley Acknowledgments

I am immensely grateful for work and opportunities with the Oneida Indian Nation and to fellowship there with colleagues Birdie Burdick, S. J. Capecelatro, Pam Fahey, Steve McSloy, Brian Patterson, and Margaret Splain.

I surely appreciate the knowledge and companionship extended to me by archaeological friends Monte Bennett, Gerald Hayes, Richard Hosbach, and Daryl Wonderly (Chenango chapter, New York State Archaeological Association).

I thank the artists who drew artifacts illustrated here: Daniyel Faulkner (figures 1–3, 13, 15a) and Julia Meyerson (figures 14 and 15b). To Martha Sempowski, *mil gracias*—for collaboration, encouragement, and help generously proffered along the immense journey that, finally, has become this book.

Sempowski Acknowledgments

My association with the Rochester Museum & Science Center during its halcyon days of archaeological research, conferences, and publications has been unusually rewarding. The Seneca Archaeology Research Project that formed after Charles Wray's death became the basis for collaboration with an exceptional group of colleagues—namely, Lorraine P. Saunders, Gian Carlo Cervone, Patricia Miller, Kathleen Allen, Annette Nohe, Dale Knapp, and Ralph Brown. Charles F. Hayes III, director of the RMSC Research Division, lent institutional support to the project's efforts. I am also grateful to the Rock Foundation Inc., the National Endowment for the Humanities, and the National Science Foundation for their financial support of the research and publications. My thanks also go to the project's fine renderer of artifacts, artist Gene Mackay (figures 4–6, 9, 12).

My contributions to this book are based on long-term research carried out through the Seneca Project, but owe a huge debt to the remarkable insights provided by my co-author, Anthony Wonderley.

Finally, I would like to acknowledge the patience and forbearance of my spouse, John Sempowski, who was always willing to listen critically.

Origins of the Iroquois League

Introduction

The League of the Iroquois, the most famous Native government in North America, dominated intertribal diplomacy of the Northeast and influenced the course of American colonial history for nearly two centuries. The age and early development of the alliance, however, have long been in dispute. This volume addresses what happened before written history—when tribes coalesced, when intertribal alliances presaging the League were forged, when the alliance assumed its familiar Five Nations form—and what factors may have underlain and perhaps helped to propel these developments.

This, the first book-length treatment of the topic, weaves together the perspectives and approaches of two anthropological archaeologists synthesizing archaeological evidence from eastern and western ends of Iroquois (Haudenosaunee) territory as well as symbolic material and mythic narratives pertaining to the Iroquois League. This collaborative effort, with its combination of different regional interests and distinct research approaches and styles, creates an unanticipated interpretive synergy. The results and conclusions provide a testament to the value of this wide, multifaceted approach to the complex issues surrounding the origins of the Iroquois League.

To introduce the topic of the League's origins, we first describe salient features of the Iroquois way of life, then summarize the course of Iroquois history during the seventeenth and eighteenth centuries. The basic corpus of written material and main lines of research about the League are briefly sketched. Next, we review the archaeological evidence recognized up to the present for the formation of

1

tribes and tribal alliances. While acknowledging some recent dissatisfaction with the term *tribe*, we define what we mean by that term and advocate its use here (see detailed discussion below, "Tribes and Confederacy in the Archaeological Record" and "The Trouble with Tribes"). There follows a preview of content in the book. Finally, we outline the basis on which each of the authors dates developments in eastern and western reaches of the League of the Iroquois.

Iroquois Life and Culture: Some Baseline Considerations[1]

Throughout the Northeast about AD 1600, speakers of Iroquoian languages lived in small, widely dispersed groupings in present-day southern Ontario, New York, and northern Pennsylvania. Clusters of individual tribes or tribal alliances included the Susquehannas in present-day Pennsylvania; the Wenros along the southern edge of Lake Ontario west of Rochester, New York; the Eries in western New York west of the Genesee River; the Neutrals in southwestern Ontario west of the Niagara River; and the Hurons and Petuns of Ontario near the Georgian Bay.

A little earlier, the St. Lawrence Iroquoians had resided along the river of the same name as well as in present-day Jefferson County, New York (chapters 2 and 4). All around these Iroquoian groups were speakers of various Algonquian languages.

The Iroquois proper were speakers of five, fairly closely related languages in upstate New York. East to west, the five tribes, or nations, were the Mohawks, Oneidas, Onondagas, Cayugas, and Senecas. These, of course, were the charter members of the alliance most frequently called the League of the Iroquois (also Five Nations Confederacy, Iroquois Confederacy). Estimates of their early seventeenth-century population have ranged between twenty thousand and thirty

---

1. Introductions to the subject include Engelbrecht (2003), Shannon (2008), and Snow (1994). The most comprehensive historical summaries are those of Fenton (1998), Parmenter (2010), Richter (1992), and A. Wallace (1972).

Map 1. Iroquoian groups in New York and Ontario, early 1600s (Wonderley 2009, map 3).

thousand people (Fenton 1998, 21; Richter 1992, 17; Snow 1994, 110; Trigger 2000, 21).

Their homeland—referred to here as Iroquoia—comprised two physiographic zones. Bordering the southern shore of Lake Ontario was a lowland plain extending eastward down the valley of the Mohawk River. Uplifted perhaps one thousand feet above the lake lowlands was the Allegheny Plateau—a sedimentary formation heavily dissected by northward-flowing streams. When impounded in the glacial past, several of these watercourses had formed the Finger Lakes. Soils were appropriate to the digging-stick technology employed to raise maize, the principal food of the Iroquois.

The surrounding forests were filled with hemlock, American beech, and white pine in the lower sections; oak, maple, and white ash in the higher. In addition to furnishing bark and wood for house and palisade construction, the forests contained a wide range of wild foods, including several kinds of berries, butternuts, and walnuts. These woods, furthermore, were home to white-tailed deer, whose remains account for about three-quarters of the identifiable mammal bones in the archaeological assemblages of Iroquoian sites. The Iroquois could obtain a variety of fish from the lakes and streams: eels, salmon, trout, pike, perch, bass, walleye, bullhead, and catfish.

The larger settlements were surrounded by stockades made from two or more lines of upright stakes, twelve to twenty feet high, among which bark and branches were interwoven. The palisaded perimeters and the generally high locations of the settlements testify to the threat of violence from intervillage feuding. The goal of such fighting was to incorporate into the home group an enemy for each individual lost from one's own community. An enemy's scalp counted in such a tally but one could also bring home a living prisoner. Such a captive might be figuratively adopted, then tortured and executed in a public rite in which the community absorbed the captive's spirit by eating his or her flesh. Alternatively, the prisoner really was adopted to replace a deceased family member by assuming that person's name, rights, and responsibilities. In such a fashion, the deceased was metaphorically brought back to life, a principle of symbolic resurrection akin to the "raising up" of League sachems in the League of the Iroquois.

Settlement clusters and tribal territories were widely separated from each other at least partly for defensive reasons. An archaeological tendency has been to assume that endemic violence is the result of demographic pressure or competition over some scarce resource. That makes little sense in the Iroquoian situation where, in fact, a cultural approach has long been quietly favored by, among others, Bruce Trigger:

> A modified version of John Witthoft's (1959:32–36) theory of the origin of Iroquoian warfare suggests that it was an indirect response to the development of horticulture. As hunting became less important for subsistence, warfare, which had always been practiced to a limited degree in connection with blood feud, provided a substitute means for men to acquire personal prestige and establish a role for

themselves in the political lives of their communities. The need for this prestige necessitated having enemies and stimulated the spiraling pattern of bloodshed that became an integral part of the Iroquoian way of life. (Trigger 1981, 34)

A stockaded village might be at least three acres in extent and contain a thousand or more inhabitants living in longhouses made from elm-bark shingles set on a framework of saplings and logs (Gehring and Starna 1988, 13). Almost twenty feet in height and width, such a residence resembled an enormous Quonset hut sixty to two hundred feet long depending on how many families lived within. The greater part of the building was divided into apartments twelve to twenty-five feet long. On one side, the living area was open to the central aisle running the length of the house. On the other, it was furnished with a bench or sleeping platform attached to an exterior wall. Each apartment was occupied by a nuclear family sharing a hearth or cooking fire with a similar family across the central corridor.

Iroquois villages moved over time—perhaps every twenty years or so—in response to a number of possible factors: deterioration of their domiciles, increasing amounts of vermin within them, declining soil fertility around them, and the patience of women whose job it was to seek firewood at an ever increasing distance from the settlement (Fenton and Moore 1977, 69–70). In consequence, the archaeology of any one tribe focuses on the sites in chronological order reflecting, it is thought, the shifting pattern of village removal and rebuilding.

Beyond the walls of a settlement stretched fields of corn and other domesticated plants. The subsistence regime was a form of garden agriculture anthropologists call swidden or slash-and-burn horticulture. First, a tract of land was burned off. With the underbrush cleared, large trees were girdled with ax strokes and left to die. Teams of women then planted seeds (maize, but also beans and squash) in hillocks. After weeding the area during the summer months, women harvested the crops and prepared them for consumption. Over time and as the yield declined, the plots were rotated. Tending to crops required perhaps six weeks of a woman's time annually.

A gender-based division of labor assigned duties of the village and immediate clearing to women—those of the forest and foreign lands to men (Fenton 1998, 214). Women collected firewood and gathered wild foods. In addition to raising the maize, they prepared the meals and fashioned the fired-clay vessels in which food was cooked. Men cleared new garden plots, constructed houses, and erected palisades. But what they mainly did was hunt, fight, and conduct diplomatic relations with the outside world, a way of life necessitating the absence of men for long periods of time.

The fundamental social unit was not the nuclear arrangement but the extended family reckoned through the mother's line—the matri-lineage. Such a group typically comprised a grandmother and her daughters and grandchildren along with various spouses. Most long-houses probably were home to such a family under the supervision of the senior matron.

These female-centered families belonged, in turn, to a matrilin-eal clan, a grouping of families presumed related through the female line. Each clan owned a set of names as noted in the early eighteenth century by the knowledgeable observer Joseph François Lafitau: "In every family [read: clan] a certain number of ancestral names, both men's and women's are kept. These names are their own and known to be taken of such and such a family." Here again, the practice of recy-cling names is best known in the passing on of sachem names/titles in Iroquois League ritual. "Now it is the custom in each family," Lafitau continued, "to requicken and resuscitate, in some measure, those who, issuing from that family, have made it illustrious. They exalt thus, at the same time, the names of those whom they make live again, and impose on those of their grand nephews destined to represent them. The latter assume more or less importance according as those who had borne their names were more or less important themselves by their qualities, virtues and deeds" (Fenton and Moore 1974, 71).

Clans played an important part in ceremonial activities, espe-cially when grouped in two-party units—moieties—owing recipro-cal obligations to one another. Notions of reciprocity and, indeed, all of the other principles of kinship, suffused the Iroquois League and determined the manner in which it operated (see chapter 6). Additionally, clans were fundamental to political life. Each clan probably had deliberative councils—one composed of senior women, the other of senior men or counselors. Most of the leaders hailed from certain prestigious families looked up to as a kind of aristocracy, and many of the important men held their positions by virtue of appointment by the senior clan matron. The ruling committee of a village or of a tribe or nation (several villages regarding themselves as one people) was basically the clan council extended and writ larger.

Summary of the Iroquois League's History

What, it is often asked, is the historical evidence for the antiquity of the Iroquois League? Meeting with local Iroquois leaders at the main Oneida village in early 1635, the Dutchman Harmen Meyndertsz van den Bogaert was told: "Here it is Mohawk, Oneida, Onondaga, Cayuga, Seneca all over—Iroquois League" (Gehring and Starna 1988, 15–17). This apparently is the earliest documentary reference to the Five Nations Confederacy (Trigger 2000, 488–89; Parmenter 2010, 41–45).

The first description of the Iroquois League as a whole house—that is, one family (see chapter 6)—was conveyed by a Mohawk speaker in 1654. As quoted by the Frenchman Simon Le Moyne, that orator said: "We the five Iroquois Nations compose but one cabin; we maintain but one fire; and we have, from time immemorial, dwelt under one and the same roof." At this point, the source (*The Jesuit Relations*) interposes: "In fact, from the earliest times, these five Iroquois Nations have been called in their own language, which, is Huron, *Hotinnonchiendi*, that is, 'the completed Cabin'" (Thwaites 1896–1901, 41:87–89).[2] The temporal phrases here—"from time immemorial" and "from the earliest

2. Each Iroquoian language, of course, had its own word for the "whole house" or "completed cabin." The one in common use today—Haudenosaunee—derives from Morgan's rendering, in his 1851 book, of the Seneca form (Fenton 1998, 212).

times"—are problematic because they are translations of *de tout temps*, which, in turn, is a rendering of something in Mohawk unknown to us. We only know that the orator—Canaqueese, "the French bastard"— was trying to impress his hearers with the strength, unity, and venerability of the Iroquois Confederacy (Bauchamp 1895a, 217; Fenton 1998, 70, 250; Kelsay 1984, 2; Parmenter 2010, 89; Shannon 2008, 39).

During at least the early 1600s, the Iroquois League "was rife with disunity," the individual tribes often acting independently as each pursued its own interests (Fenton 1998, 10, 494, 716; see Tooker 1978; Trigger 1978, 344). However, the central fact of life for all constituents during the seventeenth century was the growing fur trade, which gave to all "an overriding convergent interest. While the beaver was uncommon in Iroquois country and quickly grew even scarcer in response to increased hunting, the Iroquois soon realized that their separate and collective future depended upon the beaver. To increase their own access to furs, however, they had first to reduce or eliminate the competition of their neighbors" (Wolf 1982, 165).

Guns, acquired in fair numbers from Dutch-held Albany during the 1640s, conferred a substantial military advantage over Native foes (Fenton 1998, 298–99). Obtaining firearms, powder, and shot via trade required beaver pelts, which, for the Iroquois, usually meant encroaching on the hunting territories and trade routes of other Native groups or seizing stocks of furs others had accumulated. Such actions fueled further competition, which, in turn, required more guns, further igniting the rivalry for beaver pelts.

As they fought for pelts, the Iroquois also fought to replenish their numbers in the face of massive death from infectious pathogens brought over from the Old World. Having no defenses against diseases such as smallpox and chicken pox, the Iroquois suffered horribly in epidemics from at least the 1630s through the 1690s. Dean Snow estimates that over 60 percent of the Mohawk population perished in the first smallpox outbreak of 1634, "and population was only 23% of its 1634 size by A.D. 1646" (1996, 179). The Iroquois responded by intensifying the traditional practice of adoption, thereby increasing, at least in the short run, their chances for survival. Taking in foreign people captured in war, the result was an assimilation program of vast proportions (Brandão 1997; Dennis 1993; Jennings 1984, 92–96). A foreign observer among the Oneidas, for example, claimed that in 1668 two-thirds of the tribe were Algonquins and Hurons who had become Iroquois in "temper and inclination" (Thwaites 1896–1901, 51:123). Perhaps the estimate was a conservative one. Another source claimed that "pure-blooded" Iroquois comprised less than 20 percent of the overall population (Parmenter 2010, 124).

For furs and people, then, Iroquois struck out against other Native peoples in the course of the Beaver Wars—a firestorm of violence in which tribes of the Iroquois League destroyed or dispersed the Neutral Confederacy (1647–51), the Huron Confederacy (1648–49), and the Petun or the Tobacco (Tionontaté) tribal alliance (1649–51), all in Ontario—in addition to the Erie Nation or coalition in northern Ohio (1654–56) (Engelbrecht 1991, 2; Fenton 1998, 244–45; Fitzgerald 2001, 37; Garrad 2014, 53). In 1662, the widest-ranging year of hostilities, Iroquois parties attacked Susquehannocks in Pennsylvania; Quapas in the lower Ohio; Abenakis to the northeast; Shawnees to the south; and Sioux, Cree, and Huron refugees to the west and northwest (Parmenter 2010, 155). During the 1670s–1680s, League warriors assaulted Native peoples in the Midwest including the Illinois, Ojibwas, Foxes, Shawnees, and Ottawas (Richter 1992, 144–48).

Hostilities were not directed against Europeans to the east because the interests of all Iroquois tribes lay chiefly with Albany, New York, owned first by the Dutch and, after 1664, by the English. Guns aside, Albany was the primary source for European-made utilitarian goods, such as brass kettles, spun cloth, steel hatchets, and other metal tools. A continuing supply of these goods became a necessity for utilitarian purposes and for use in mortuary ritual (see chapter 6). One researcher reported that about 99 percent of the material recovered from an Oneida village site dating from around 1660 was European in origin (Hosbach 2004, 194). Nearly all the foreign items were more cheaply and plentifully available from the English than from the French, and Albany was the main source of English goods (Fenton 1998, 330; Trelease 1997, 216–17). Further, Iroquois desire for

European-controlled commodities extended into the nonutilitarian realm to include glass and seashell beads—the latter being especially important in League and funerary ceremonies. By the 1630s, wampum distribution was controlled by Euro-Americans (Ceci 1989; Fenton 1998, 298–99; Jennings 1988, 52, 78; Tooker 1978, 421–23), and nearly all of what reached the Iroquois passed through Albany.

Given the strength of commercial ties, peaceful relations with Albany were inevitably and invariably expressed in the idiom of close kinship. The Iroquois became linked to the English as brothers in the Covenant Chain—a series of contracts attaching diverse Native peoples to the Iroquois and the Iroquois to the English at Albany. From about 1677 on, the Iroquois used the arrangement to promote the interests of their League and allied tribes and to reduce conflict between English and Indians. Through mediation, the Iroquois won status and room to maneuver by becoming indispensable to all parties (Jennings 1984; Richter 1992).

In contrast to pacific relationships with the Dutch and English, interactions with the French were tenuous and tense. A state of inter-mittent war between members of the League and New France char-acterized the 1600s. On-again, off-again hostilities culminated in French attacks that destroyed the major settlements of the Senecas in 1687, the Mohawks in 1693, and the Onondagas and Oneidas in 1696.

The Iroquois at that point were exhausted and diminished, their numbers having declined from emigration (more than half of the Mohawks were said to have left New York for the Jesuit reserve of Caughnawaga in Canada), recurrent disease, and constant war (Fen-ton 1998, 329, 357, 364). In 1700, the estimated Iroquois population of about 5,100 was less than a quarter of what it had been in 1630 (Snow 1994, 110). In what has been called the Grand Settlement of 1701, rep-resentatives of the Iroquois League concluded formal treaties in Mon-treal and Albany, which secured peace with France and recognition by both European powers of League neutrality (Brandão and Starna 1996; Wallace 1957). In consequence, members of the League entered the eighteenth century rethinking and refashioning their policies.

The new orientation disposed the Iroquois to make peace with French-sponsored Native groups to the west, and to seek out new foes not obviously aligned with European interests. In consequence, they began looking southward about 1700. For more than fifty years, Iroquois warriors engaged in constant hostilities mainly with the Catawbas but also directed against the Cherokees, Creeks, Choctaws, and others. The southern orientation also resulted in the admission to the Iroquois League, in about 1723, of the Tuscarora tribe of North Carolina. The refugee men, numbering perhaps six hundred, greatly augmented the military capacity of the Iroquois Confederacy, then said to be about 1,800 warriors (Fenton 1998, 383; see Richter 1992, 239). Thereafter, the Iroquois League was known as the Six Nations (Landy 1978, 519).

The essence of the League's policy during the early eighteenth century was to play the English and the French off against one another to the Iroquois' advantage. It was a balancing act requiring aggressive posturing. It was possible, Anthony Wallace thought, only for as long as the Iroquois could credibly threaten violence against the Euro-Americans.

> While the League as such, by the treaties of 1701, remained committed to neutrality between the French and English, groups of warriors—acting according to the code of revenge—could, if offended, at any time assail either [English or French] party. It was always possible, of course, for the British to seduce some Mohawk into service against the French, and the French to persuade some Geneseo Senecas to strike the British, but these breaches of contract served more as an ever-present reminder of the importance of keeping the League itself neutral than as an excuse for terminating the agreement. Thus, without more duplicity than was characteristic of either the British or the French themselves, the League chiefs were able to orchestrate the revenge mechanism of warfare into the contrapuntal melody of extorting political and material gifts from both the French and the English. The importance of this theme in Iroquois life from 1701 to 1755 can hardly be overestimated. It gave them

territorial security, a relatively high material culture, a continued ascendancy over neighboring peoples, and an enormous sense of their own importance. (A. Wallace 1972, 48)

A significant component of the play-off system was to sell land south of New York to the Euro-Americans. During the early eighteenth century, the Iroquois collaborated with Pennsylvania in supervising the Susquehanna River drainage as a resettlement zone for shattered Native groups fleeing enslavement, land loss, and military defeat further south (P. Wallace 1945, 66; Jennings 1984, 35, 304). Cooperation with the English colony brought the Iroquois prestige, goods, and suzerainty over client tribes. The latter groups provided the Iroquois with warriors while serving as a shield to protect Iroquois country from southern raiders (Fenton 1998, 324, 402; Jennings 1984, 290, 312–23, 359–65; Jennings 1988, 324, 402). The partnership was based on the assumption that the Iroquois owned the southern lands by right of conquest over the Susquehannocks in the late seventeenth century (Tooker 1984; P. Wallace 1945, 358). This legalistic premise allowed Pennsylvania to deal with a single, obliging Indian party willing to grant quit claim (extinguish Indian title) to the lands. For that to be, both parties had to maintain the presumption of Iroquois ownership and the Iroquois had to have land to give away (Jennings 1988, 48–50). The sell-off ended, according to Richard Aquila, by the late 1740s, when the Iroquois had nothing left to offer (1997, 193–94).

The larger play-off system began to unravel at the same time (Aquila 1997, 18; Fenton 1998, 400–401). The date 1755, cited earlier by Anthony Wallace, is the approximate point at which neutrality became impossible because of British dominance in the conflict that drove France from North America—the Seven Years' War—which is also commonly referred to as the French and Indian War (1754–63) (Fenton 1998, 13).

Simultaneously, the central fact of Iroquois coexistence with Euro-Americans was altered: land had long since replaced furs as the form of wealth most desired by colonists. Euro-Americans eager to obtain land had arrived at the borders of Iroquoia and, by the

1770s, the eastern tribes were hard-pressed by the expanding English population.

The American Revolutionary War unleashed that expansive impulse that would terminate Iroquois independence. In 1777 the Iroquois League was adjourned, leaving tribes and even individuals to make their own choices about affiliation in the conflict (Fenton 1998, 211). Judging that the British could supply more necessary goods than the impoverished American colony, most Iroquois ended up fighting for the British. Most of the pro-British Iroquois ended the war gathered around the British fort at Niagara.

After the Revolutionary War, two councils coalesced as successors to the Iroquois League and its legacy. Joseph Brant and fellow Mohawks settled in Canada on a tract set aside for them by the British government. About one thousand members of all the tribes comprising the League were represented there along the Grand River of Ontario. Almost immediately (about 1783–84), their leaders reestablished a new League-like council that, until 1924, governed what became today's Six Nations Reserve (Fenton 1998, 602; Weaver 1978). In the new United States of America, a League organization numbering perhaps two thousand was reconstituted near Fort Niagara at Buffalo Creek in Seneca territory (Shannon 2008, 200). That council moved back to ancestral Onondaga land near Syracuse in 1847, where it has long been a reservation government—and more (Blau et al. 1978, 499). In fact, "the idea of the League as an alliance of kindred nations having independent sovereignty," William Fenton observed, "persists to this day among their descendants in New York and Canada" (1978b, 263).

Historiography of the Iroquois League

Fundamental lineaments of knowledge about the Iroquois League were conveyed in written works of four individuals: the Rochester lawyer Lewis Henry Morgan, the Iroquois traditionalists John Arthur Gibson and Seth Newhouse, and the anthropologist William Fenton. What they said comprises a core literature essential to understanding what researchers think about the subject.

Lewis Henry Morgan

Morgan's *League of the Ho-dé-no-sau-nee, Iroquois* (1851) introduced the Iroquois Confederacy to a general reading audience and provided the first anthropological perspective on the subject. The Iroquois League originated, according to Morgan, with some fifty village headmen whose names became permanent offices or titles to be inherited by successors. The hereditary nature of the offices set the titleholders or sachems apart from other chiefs whose standing derived from individual merit (Morgan 1962, 62–66). These sachemships were established at the very beginning. Indeed, the entire institution, as Morgan understood it, "was not of gradual construction, under the suggestions of necessity; but was the result of one protracted effort of legislation" (1962, 60–61). The principal founders of the Iroquois League were Dä-ga-no-we'-dä "and Hä-yo-wen'-hä, his speaker, through whom he laid his plans of government before the council which framed the League" (1962, 101n1). The story of the League's beginnings as Morgan understood it is reviewed in chapter 1 as part of the body of legend and myth known as the Deganawida epic.

Wampum, Morgan indicated, was the material correlate of the founding and operation of the League (1962, 120). The substance known historically and referred to by archaeologists as "true wampum" consisted of beads fashioned from marine shells, then strung or sewn in patterns on to "belts." During the 1600s, the small tubular objects were made by Native peoples of the Long Island Sound region with metal tools. Purple beads were produced from the hardshell quahog, while the far more numerous white beads were fashioned from columellas of whelk. Averaging about 5.5 mm in length and 4 mm in diameter, these objects have a standardized look (Ceci 1989, 63). Wampum, as Morgan understood it, served as the League's record-keeping medium to mnemonically preserve knowledge of laws and transactions (1962, 94, 121). Indeed, the League's oldest records—the injunctions and rules announced by Deganawida—had been talked into strings of wampum "at the time of their [the laws'] enactment" (1962, 120).

Morgan's most important insight was that "the League was established upon the principles, and was designed to be but an elaboration, of the Family Relationships" (1962, 60). The concept of kinship and family relationship was expressed in the League's central metaphor (see chapter 6):

> After the formation of the League, the Iroquois called themselves the *Ho-dé-no-sau-nee*, which signifies "the people of the long house." It grew out of circumstances, that they likened their confederacy to a long house, having partitions and separate fires, after their ancient method of building houses, within which the several nations were sheltered under a common roof . . . The several nations of the Iroquois, united constituted one Family, dwelling together in one Long House; and these ties of family relationship were carried throughout their civil and social system, from individuals to tribes, from tribes to nations, and from the nations to the League itself, and bound them together in one common, indissoluble brotherhood. (Morgan 1962, 51, 60)

Within the metaphorical longhouse, the relationships between the tribes meeting in council were visualized as those of kin divided into two units owing each other familial responsibilities (moieties).

> The Mohawks, Onondagas and Senecas, who, as elsewhere stated, were brother nations to each other, and fathers to the other three, seated themselves upon one side of the fire. On the other side were arranged the Oneidas, Cayugas and Tuscaroras, who, in like manner, were brothers to each other, but children to the three first. By their peculiar customs, if the deceased sachem belonged to either of the three elder nations, he was mourned as a father by the three junior; and it became the duty of the latter to perform the ceremony of lamentation prescribed by their usages for the deceased, and afterwards that of raising up his successor. (Morgan 1962, 118)

The glue of family feeling connecting the tribes of the Iroquois League was membership in the matrilineal clans. Morgan used the word *tribe* where we would say *clan* but, by whatever name, these units were important in ceremonial, social, and political life. What most impressed him was that clans comprised an intertribal network linking people of different nations as close relatives (Morgan 1962, 81–82).

Finally, Morgan drew attention to the strong ritual component of the Iroquois League. The fifty names/titles of sachems were kept fresh in people's memories by reviewing them in the act of "raising up" or installing new sachems—that is, symbolically resuscitating a deceased chief by transferring his title to a new officeholder in the ceremony we call the Condolence Council. All fifty names were retained in memory by recitation in the formal litany of the League called the Roll Call of Chiefs (or "Roll Call of the Founders" or the "Hai Hai") (Morgan 1962, 118–25).

As for the age of the League, Morgan said that, according to Iroquois tradition, the confederacy framed by Deganawida "has come down through many generations to the present age, with scarcely a change" (1962, 61).

John Arthur Gibson and Seth Newhouse

The oral narrative of the Iroquois League's beginnings was laid out most fully by two Native scribes on the Six Nations Reserve in Ontario at the turn of the twentieth century (see chapter 1). John Arthur Gibson and Seth Newhouse synthesized bodies of tradition relating to how the League came about through the endeavors of a prophet ordained to bring peace to a violent world (Fenton 1998, 80–97; Parker 1916; Scott 1912; Woodbury 1992). Their accounts continue to resonate strongly among contemporary Haudenosaunee (Iroquois) people and, in fact, are still the main source of the Deganawida epic for most.

In addition to providing the mythic charter of the Iroquois League, both Gibson and Newhouse synthesized information as to how the League was supposed to function (Fenton 1998, 80–97; Parker 1916; Scott 1912; Woodbury 1992). About half of all their texts feature Deganawida defining the League's rules and regulations, its symbols and metaphors, its office titles and the rite (Condolence Council) for maintaining those titles (Woodbury 1992, xi, xxxiii). All these versions are concerned with protocol and proper ceremonial performance. All inventory fifty sachem titles in close agreement with one another and with Morgan's list. All define roles of the participants, provide rules of order of council proceedings, and transcribe the words of speeches and songs. In effect, this section of the epic is an instruction manual on how things should be done. Both the narrative of the League's formation and the bylaw section of the narrative are assumed to have been passed down from a distant time. Gibson said the Iroquois League began in the year 1390.

William Fenton

The central figure in Iroquoian studies during much of the twentieth century, William Fenton focused on rites and ceremonial structure with the idea that this was the fundamental bedrock stuff of culture. He conducted considerable ethnographic research that included documenting two performances of the Condolence Council (Fenton 1946; Fenton 1998, 163–79).

Fenton also did substantial historical research to determine the antiquity of the League. An obvious test of age was to see whether the roster of fifty sachems provided by Morgan, Gibson, and Newhouse could be traced back in time (Fenton 1998, 98). Toward that end, Fenton combed the documentary record of Euro- and Native American diplomatic interaction from the mid-seventeenth to early nineteenth centuries to identify and date the familiar names (Fenton 1998, table 6). What he found was that only about a dozen could be documented in the 1600s and nearly a third was not present at all. Fenton concluded that a large chunk of the names had appeared in the mid- to late 1700s. He did not, however, focus on that as evidence for change. Instead, Fenton explained the absence of their names to the fact that sachems generally did not do the public speaking recorded at treaty events (Fenton 1998, 11, 714). In the end, he affirmed that "originally, men bearing the titles of its fifty founders composed its grand council" (1998, 494). When Fenton looked back in time, he always did so less as an historian than as an anthropologist disposed to favor "stability over change" (1998, 397).

Fenton also inquired into the antiquity of the Iroquois League's main ceremony through historical study of a portion of the rite called the Three Bare Words. Ethnographically, this refers to a verbal interchange in which a speaker dries the tears, cleans the ears, and removes obstructions from another's throat so that the interlocutor, assumed to be grief-stricken, may return to the normal mode of everyday interaction. Today, the Three Bare Words are familiar from performances of the Condolence Council, the lengthy ceremony to mourn the loss of a League chief and to install his successor. Often called burdens or matters, the three sentiments are first delivered in the rite when visitors arrive at the location of the ceremony. Over an outdoor fire, the hosts welcome the visitors, give thanks that the latter have survived a dangerous journey, and proceed—rhetorically—to comfort the other party with these formulaic words (Fenton 1946, 112–15; Hewitt 1944, 68–69; Michelson 1988, 68; Woodbury 1992, xxxviii–xl). This outdoor segment of the Condolence Council is frequently called the Greeting at the Wood's Edge.

Historically, much the same presentation was the way every interethnic political meeting opened for at least a century and a half. Fenton found the interchange recorded in writing about eighty times between the 1640s and early 1800s (1998, 181). In general, however, what he documented was not literally the Three Bare Words exactly as spoken—that is, not precisely the same in content and order. And, of course, what he was seeing was diplomatic protocol, not performances of the Condolence Council. Nevertheless, the strength of the customary greeting implied the existence of the condolence ritual in the distant past. In the end, Fenton's abiding concern with ritual practice led to the conviction that, while content may change, underlying ceremonial pattern endures (1987, 425; 1991, 207).

One of Fenton's influential insights was that the Iroquois periodize their history into three epochs, each the subject of a key oral tradition (1998, 24, 120–23): the creation myth, the Deganawida epic, and the religious teachings of the Seneca prophet Handsome Lake formulated about 1800 (1998, 24, 120–23). Of the three, the Iroquois League material was the most important to Fenton for understanding Iroquois history. In consequence, he paid close attention to the Grand River chroniclers, publishing one of Newhouse's versions (1949) and translating one of Gibson's (1998, 85–92).

Fenton also compiled all known versions of the oral narrative. In the course of this research, he discovered that the Deganawida epic had no great age. It was, in fact, not recorded or in any way alluded to until the mid-eighteenth century. Why had no one mentioned it prior to that? Fenton seems to attribute the absence of mention to the idea that non-Native people, overwhelmed as they were with practical concerns, were too busy to write it down (1998, 52).

Fenton advanced several interpretive points of view in the course of analyzing the League myth and cheerfully conceded that some might be mutually contradictory (1998, 92n14). His most frequently expressed opinion was that the confederacy assumed its form and function as described in the versions of the Deganawida epic composed about 1900 (1998, 494, 434). The epic, then, was regarded as historically true having been faithfully preserved from a distant time. Fenton also thought, however, that the historical process of the League's formation was likely to have been a gradual affair occurring over a century, between about 1450 and 1550 (1998, 72–73, 129–30).

Tribes and Confederacy in the Archaeological Record

Tribes

The clearest indication that tribes or nations are coming into being is inferred from study of settlement pattern (Wright in Finlayson 1998, xii). The reasoning is that when populations seem to consolidate and draw together into larger village entities, then one can infer "an increasing identification of villages or village clusters as discrete socio-political units" (Niemczycki 1984, 1). In New York, the general picture is that, during the early 1400s, Iroquois villages "were too scattered for nations to have existed as clearly as they did later in the seventeenth century. Divisions above the village itself across the region must have been little more than vaguely recognized linguistic units." But "as the villages began to cluster," Dean Snow reasoned, "some sense of linguistic and political unity must have emerged within such clusters." By about 1525, "large fortified villages were clustered in the hinterlands of the historic Mohawk, Oneida, Onondaga, Cayuga, and Seneca nations, and it is appropriate to speak of them in those terms" (Snow 1994, 48–49).

This scenario was first demonstrated by James Tuck working with Onondaga sites. The Onondaga as a tribe, he concluded, came into being when two previously separate communities located themselves next to one another about 1400–1450 (1978, 326–27). In the Burke and Schoff archaeological sites, "a symbolic alliance between two communities was probably consummated for reasons of mutual defense," Tuck thought. "This can be interpreted as the founding of the Onondaga Nation" (1971b, 215).[3]

Among the Senecas, when two large villages came into existence near one another about 1570–75, they were "assumed to have coexisted in some form of alliance with one another—a settlement pattern characteristic of the historic Seneca." The Adams and Culbertson sites, archaeologists of the Seneca Archaeological Research Project stressed, constitute "the earliest recognizable evidence for the emergence of a group biologically and culturally identifiable as the powerful tribal entity that came to be known as the historic Seneca Iroquois" (Wray et al. 1987, 239; see also chapter 6).[4]

In the east, "a clear Mohawk nationality emerged," according to Snow, as previously independent communities began to merge in new,

---

3. James Bradley seems to agree that the emergence of the Onondaga tribe is associated with the Burke site, which he apparently dates to the late fifteenth century (1987, 2001; see chapter 2).

4. Although it would be unrealistic to propose an exact date for Seneca tribal coalescence, that process appears to have taken place sometime in the third quarter of the sixteenth century (see chapter 6).

defendable locations during the fifteenth century. The outstanding example of the process was the hilltop site of Otstungo, dated by Snow to about 1450–1525 (1995b, 91, 115).[5]

Confederacy

The next level of sociopolitical complexity—the formation of a confederacy—has not been detected from study of settlement pattern, at least in New York, where no further consolidation of villages occurs. Once formed, the apparent tribal clusters remained roughly fifty miles apart (Engelbrecht 1985, 164–67; Trigger 1981, 14). Hence, the League of the Iroquois seems not to register spatially.

In the absence of settlement pattern information, archaeologists can only suppose that the League must have come about some time after tribes were formed. Tuck saw the process of village amalgamation and increasing propinquity as leading ineluctably to a state of increased peaceful communication and, therefore, after tribal formation to the intertribal alliance of the League. Originally, Tuck guessed that occurred during the Garoga phase, presumably meaning the 1500s (1971b, 140). Later, Tuck implied that the League-beginning event was remembered as "Deganawida blotting out the sun as part of the traditional account of the founding of the Iroquois league"—that is, a solar eclipse in 1451 (1978, 326–27).

Snow thought the fortified villages testified to an impulse to end strife—as described in the Deganawida epic—which led to the formation of the League of the Iroquois by 1525 (1994, 49, 58–60). Drawing the opposite conclusion from the same evidence, Robert Funk and Robert Kuhn rejoined that the highly defensive settlements of the

---

5. Robert Kuhn favored a later dating for Otstungo's occupation: 1500–1525 (2004, 150). A pattern of village amalgamation, however, has not been clearly demonstrated in the case of the Oneidas (see chapter 2) or the Cayugas (Niemczycki 1984, 93).

sixteenth-century Mohawk constituted a good indication that the Iroquois League "had not been established" (Funk and Kuhn 2003, 157).

"The archaeological study of confederacies is even more challenging and beset with pitfalls than that of tribes," Bruce Trigger acknowledged. "Yet the subject is of great theoretical importance in view of the unresolved controversy as to whether confederacies were or were not entirely a response to the trading of furs with Europeans along the east coast of North America in the sixteenth century" (1981, 38). Trigger was interested in work in this regard that attempted to move beyond settlement-pattern evidence to detect the formation of confederacies. The best-known effort along these lines was the ceramic research of William Engelbrecht. He hypothesized that the increasing friendly contact resulting from the formation of the confederacy would have produced an increase in the similarity of ceramics within its territory (1974, 1985, 177). However, Engelbrecht's analysis of pottery from about 1550 to 1640 did not identify an event or process interpretable as the formation of the Iroquois League.

Drawing attention to smoking pipes as material correlates of diplomatic activity, Robert Kuhn and Martha Sempowski (2001) pointed out those artifacts may furnish evidence for dating the League of the Iroquois. The appearance, therefore, of Mohawk pipes in the Seneca region about 1600, concurrent with a substantial increase in Seneca use of pipes, may indicate the entry of the Senecas into the League to complete the confederacy in its historically familiar five-nation form (see chapter 6).

Reasoning similarly, Anthony Wonderley (2005a) documented the presence of identical effigy pipes present in the eastern Iroquois region and the St. Lawrence Iroquoian province of Jefferson County, New York, during the late 1400s to early 1500s. The distribution pattern of these distinctive artifacts might well be the archaeological footprint of alliances antedating the five-nation Iroquois League.

That brings us to the present day and the subject of this book. We take up the search for the League by considering what we think are the material clues for tribalization, confederacy formation, and development of the League up to the early 1600s. We explore the roles of cultural, social, and exogenous factors in precipitating and/or facilitating those major developments.

The Trouble with Tribes

Late in the twentieth century, anthropologists debated the appropriateness and usefulness of the term *tribe*. One objection was that the word carried connotative freight as designating a primitive group. Tribes had been conceived as a particular category of social formation more complex than what were called *bands* and less complex than what were called *chiefdoms*. There were evolutionary implications in this because of interest in the overall development of sociocultural complexity over time (Service 1962; Steward 1955). Accusations leveled against such theorizing include the charge that anthropologists thereby treat less complex societies as living fossils or as somehow morally reprehensible. The anthropological point, however, was never to judge worth. Most researchers wish merely to compare a single case to broadly similar social formations in order to learn more than the facts of that one example allow (Sahlins 1968).

A larger issue was a growing suspicion that the tribes anthropologists studied were recent historical phenomena caused by the European expansion in the modern era. If that is so, a *tribe* can tell us nothing about any supposedly pristine, nondisrupted condition prior to, say, AD 1500. In consequence, the word *tribe* was frequently avoided, often by subsuming it into a different term referring to a concept larger than originally intended. Eric Wolf, for example, in *Europe and the People without History*, employed the phrase *kinship mode of production* to designate what had previously been thought of as *tribes* as well as many *bands* and *chiefdoms*. When he came to write about the Iroquois, Wolf resorted to calling the tribes "village clusters" and "named clusters of matrilineages" (1982, 163–65). Such euphemisms represent no advance in clarity when tribal identity has a geographical basis with unquestioned continuity over time.

That is the case in New York, where Iroquois groups tended to remain within distinctive territories over long periods (Trigger 1981,

14, 38). In consequence, using the word *tribe* seems an act of common sense to many anthropological archaeologists (Niemczycki 1984, 79–80; Niemczycki 1987).[6] It seems so to us. *Tribe* is the word we use most frequently to designate the constituent members of the Iroquois League. Each such tribe was a small society of horticultural villagers in which virtually every social relationship was carried out in the idiom and through the relations of kinship. Economics, politics, and religion were not separate institutions, nor is there likely to have been much if any occupational specialization. On the contrary, work was functionally generalized. Subsistence and technological operations were understood by all and could (with greater or lesser competence) be performed by all. Essentially egalitarian and nonhierarchical, each of these social formations had a common language and possessed its own territory (Sahlins 1968; Trigger 1969, 83; Trigger 2000, 6). Furthermore, our term *tribe* describes what seventeenth-century Europeans called a *nation*, by which they meant a Native American ethnic group that spoke the same language, practiced the same customs, and was geographically circumscribed (Dennis 1993, 240; Thwaites 1896–1901, 16:227).

We understand that the social formations in question underwent change over time. However, we believe there is strong evidence for unbroken continuity between the entities we discern in the archaeological record and the members of the Iroquois League first documented in the seventeenth century. The Iroquois tribes as they were known in historic times are, quite simply, of some relative antiquity and they are still in existence today. Present-day Iroquoian tribal groups generally refer to themselves as nations.

Chapter Overview

Chapter 1, "The League Story over Time," contains a detailed study of the Deganawida epic in which we ask: to what extent is the myth

---

6. More recently, John Hart and William Engelbrecht employ the term *ethnic group* for *tribe* and, apparently, for the Erie, Huron, and Neutral Confederacies (Hart 2012; Hart and Engelbrecht 2012; see Engelbrecht 1985, 164–65).

applicable to the archaeological record? In order to answer our question, we tackle a complicated body of oral narrative chronologically and comparatively. The results are, first, a critical survey to establish what facts are posed in multiple narratives; and second, an attempt to better understand those facts by considering them in historical context.

Chapter 2, "An Interaction Sphere of Pipes in Eastern Iroquoia, Late 1400s to Early 1500s," examines evidence for an early (pre-League) alliance among the eastern Iroquois. Although an early such alliance among the eastern Iroquois has long been suspected, substantiating archaeological evidence has been lacking. Now, however, fired-clay smoking pipes incised with pictorial representations provide promising answers. Identical, emotionally resonant images are found in areas known as the homelands of the Mohawk, Oneida, and Onondaga tribes and in the St. Lawrence Iroquoian province of Jefferson County, New York, late in the fifteenth and very early sixteenth centuries. The distribution of these male-associated artifacts is thought to reflect engagement in diplomatic activities. Finding identical pipes in different places implies, at the least, that peaceful interactions obtained among the occupants of those areas. The pipes appear to depict acts of emergence from the earth as described in myths of tribal origin. Referencing such subject matter presumably fostered notions of kinship and relatedness in diplomatic settings. In answer to a long-standing debate in Iroquoian studies, this development of an early League-like coalition occurred in pre-Columbian times. A more surprising outcome is recognition of a fourth member of the alliance—very possibly the principal one—in Jefferson County.

Meanwhile, in the western Finger Lakes area (homeland of the Seneca tribe), as well as elsewhere throughout the Genesee River Valley, another very distinctive form of human effigy smoking pipe occurred in sites dating to the early to mid-1500s, which is discussed in chapter 3, "Smoking Pipes and Alliance-Building in Western Iroquoia." Although stylistically distinct from the eastern examples, these pipes bore imagery similarly evocative of "emergence." As in the east, they make interpretive sense as illustrating myths of tribal origin—tales that are geographically specific to the traditional Seneca homeland. The wide distribution of the pipes, as in the east, may indicate male diplomatic interactions and early alliance-making across the Genesee River Valley.

By its nature, alliance-building on a regional scale entailed heightened violence. Chapter 4, "War along the St. Lawrence, Early to Mid-1500s," details an archaeological record implying that the eastern Iroquois were involved in war with St. Lawrence Iroquoians to the north. Female captives—potterymakers—taken in the fighting probably were brought home to become integrated into the lives of Mohawk, Oneida, and Onondaga villagers. Evidence for this is clearest at Oneida sites in which a distinctive St. Lawrence Iroquoian trait enters into local pottery. The foreign element, a representation of corn, apparently contributed to the depiction of a full-figure humanoid typical of Oneida ceramic art for the next century. Judging from other archaeological indications, groups from Jefferson County may also have joined eastern Iroquois villages as refugees fleeing chronic violence along the St. Lawrence River.

The same period witnessed a relatively small influx of exotic materials from distant sources including marine shells and the first European goods. Whether these trends were related and what they might mean is a recurrent issue in Iroquois archaeology. In chapter 5, "Wampum, Seashells, and Peace," the topic of exotics is considered with reference to the internal dynamics of confederacies. Inwardly, such social formations were peacekeeping operations designed to suppress revenge killings and blood feuds among tribal members. Lacking the ability of state-level societies to coerce agreement, Native Americans developed a set of ritual practices that established amity (fictive kinship) with outsiders (nonrelatives) in ceremonial expressions of sympathy (condolence) and symbolic resuscitation (requickening). Because such rites involved the exchange of highly valued substances, the sudden appearance of exotic items during the early 1500s may signal the accelerating ritual needs of confederacies to maintain, within, their own climates of peace. The most highly valued exotic was marine shell, which, in the form of tubular beads called wampum, became *the* material correlate of condolence and requickening practices during the 1600s. Cultural commitment to wampum must have been swift, to judge by the earliest archaeological and documentary evidence.

In chapter 6, "The Longhouse Metaphor: Its Role in the Growth of the League of the Iroquois," we discuss how nucleation of population into two large villages initiated the historically known configuration of the Seneca tribe about 1570–75. The distinctive human effigy pipes highlighted in chapter 3 disappear and other types of pipes become scarce—implying, perhaps, a lessening of foreign diplomatic interchanges involving smoking. While sixteenth-century graves still include a disproportionate majority of adult females, some of the women are now identifiable (from skeletal analysis and artifactual evidence) as captives or refugees from areas west of the Genesee River.

These ethnically diverse settlements and those of succeeding periods exhibit an increasing elaboration of mortuary ceremonialism with more graves oriented westward and many more furnished with material goods including European items and marine shell. The shell, apparently from the central Atlantic via the corridor of the Susquehanna River, drops off sharply in frequency early in the seventeenth century, suggesting disruption of the southerly trade network. To mourn and console reciprocally at this time and place may literally have been to condole. Encountering what look like the material correlates of condolence leads to the suspicion that reciprocal funerary rituals in these ethnically heterogeneous groups may have served to promote a sense of common kinship—even if fictive—and familial closeness.

In the early 1600s, the assemblages of the Mohawks and Senecas— Iroquois League members most distant from each other—come to resemble each other. For the first time, similar types of artifacts appear and in roughly similar abundance. At both, an extraordinary increase in smoking pipes is also evident, presumably related to an upswing in diplomatic and ceremonial activities. Furthermore, a compositional analysis of Seneca pipes indicates a Mohawk-area clay source for some. Overall, the heightened Mohawk-Seneca interaction strongly suggests the establishment of direct and friendly ties between the two in 1600–1610. That is the archaeological footprint of the Seneca's involvement in the League, the coalescence of the confederacy into its historically familiar form. This development completes a series of events that began over a century earlier with a coalition of the eastern tribes.

Dating Considerations

Precise dating of late fifteenth- and early sixteenth-century sites, and therefore the interpretations linked to them, is highly problematic, especially when comparing sites pertaining to different groups and geographical regions. At best, assigning specific occupation dates to archaeological sites is an inexact science, particularly for relatively recent periods of human history. The late prehistoric and protohistoric periods under study here, prior to the introduction of "dateable" European artifacts into Iroquois sites, present a particular challenge. Ceramic seriation varies from one area of Iroquoia to another, and radiometric dating techniques yield dates with margins of error greater than the likely site occupation intervals for the period discussed here. Thus, it is difficult to arrive at occupation estimates of sufficient specificity for truly reliable chronological comparisons across different areas. Therefore, recognizing that there may be legitimate debate regarding the exact dates assigned to sites in eastern and western Iroquoia, we wish to make explicit the assumptions and evidence underlying the respective site chronologies of the two regions.

The sense of chronology among the eastern Iroquois presented in chapters 2 and 4 is grounded in an Oneida context looking outward to link, comparatively, with dates proposed in neighboring Mohawk and Onondaga regions. The assumption, obviously, is that similar characteristics elsewhere indicate comparable age.

The date for the Nichols Pond site commencing the Oneida sequence (ca. 1450–75) is the informed estimate of Peter Pratt (1976, 107, 148; Pratt and Pratt 1986, 12; Weiskotten 1995). While it is a guess, it is consistent with what we understand to have been happening elsewhere. For example, a type of effigy pipe contemporaneous with Nichols Pond is known from the St. Lawrence Iroquois Roebuck site

(Grenville, Ontario), believed to be from approximately 1450 (Tremblay 2006, 71; Canadian Museum 1998).

In general, there are enough sites present in the Oneida area to account for what looks like a continuous sequence of village movements. The sequence, that is to say, has no obvious gaps as might be revealed by seriational analysis of several material culture traits known to change with time (collars of ceramic pots, for example, of ceramic types, or trends in triangular projectile points). Tracking the changes in these categories establishes not only the relative placement of the sites but also the direction of time's arrow (Bennett and Wonderley forthcoming; Wonderley 2006).

An important milestone in pre-1600s Oneida dating is the Vaillancourt site (estimated 1525–55) which is keyed to very similar-looking assemblages from the Garoga, Klock, and Smith-Pagerie sites in the Mohawk Valley. Robert Funk and Robert Kuhn estimated these stations dated from about 1520 to 1590 (2003, 133). Using accelerator mass spectrometry (AMS) dating, John Hart proposes a longer span of occupation extending from the late 1400s to the late 1580s (2018).

There is a possible chronometric basis to the Vaillancourt estimate. Faced with the fact that all the relevant radiocarbon dates from the Mohawk sites seemed aberrant,[7] Funk and Kuhn noted that some readings coincided precisely with the probable occupation time— if one favored the mean intercept or midpoint date (2003, 128, 133). Mean dates at the Klock site, for example, were 1553 and 1560 (Funk and Kuhn 2003, 48). The same appears to be true for a pair of radiocarbon assays from Vaillancourt. Their midpoints (mean intercepts) are 1540 and 1560 (Wonderley 2006, 9, fig. 5).

The dates of Seneca sites discussed in this volume are based primarily on the site sequence proposed by Charles Wray and Harry Schoff (1953) and Wray (1973)—a construct supported by the identification

---

7. Radiocarbon dating is a method used to determine the age of organic materials, such as corn or wood, based on the radioactivity of their carbon content.

of a series of seven northward moving pairs of village sites, each of which exhibited increasing quantities of European goods, presumably as they became ever more accessible from the late 1500s through the late 1600s. Approximate dates for these village pairs were proposed by working backward in twenty-year intervals (thought to represent the average length of village occupations) from the known date of 1687, when two of the villages were attacked by French and Native allies. These dates underwent subsequent alterations based on arguments regarding Ontario glass-bead assemblages made by Ian Kenyon and William Fitzgerald (1986), revised estimates of the length of site occupations, and new analyses of other artifactual evidence (Wray et al. 1987, fig. intro-2; Wray et al. 1991, 410–11; Sempowski and Saunders 2001, fig. intro-3, 720–22). The site sequence as currently formulated, then, extends from the Adams and Culbertson sites, presently dated at ca. 1570–85, to the Ganondagan and Rochester Junction sites, dating to ca. 1670–87. More recently analyzed evidence suggests the probability of the extension of the Seneca sequence back in time to include a series of preceding sites to be discussed in this volume—the Harscher, Hilliard, Belcher, and Richmond Mills sites—whose occupations appear to encompass the period ca. 1520–25 to ca. 1570–75.

The most obvious sign of sameness across Iroquois League territory at the onset of the seventeenth century is seen in European-made glass beads (the polychrome or Dutch polychrome horizon) which, everywhere, increase dramatically in numbers (Sempowski and Saunders 2001, 682–83). At the Oneida Cameron site (ca. 1605–20), and the Seneca Dutch Hollow and Factory Hollow sites (ca. 1605–25), these artifacts appear suddenly in the archaeological record and in great volume. Thereafter, they afford the means to date archaeological sites with fair precision. Further, the Oneida dates from glass beads take into account the revised dating of Seneca sites (Bennett 1983; Pratt 1961a; Sempowski 2004a). And, of course, during the 1600s, historical tie-ins—such as that of the Oneida Thurston site with the van den Bogaert party of 1634–35 and the Oneida Sullivan site with its resident Jesuit priests about 1665–76—provide secure anchors of dating (Bennett and Wonderley forthcoming).

Finally, we note that several research projects are currently underway that may shed new or additional light on the dating of some of the Iroquoian sites under discussion here, as well as the chronologies of village relocation sequences in the areas we discuss (e.g., Birch 2015; Birch and Manning 2016; Sanft 2018). These studies aim to utilize radiocarbon dating along with statistical Bayesian modeling techniques that take account of other archaeological and contextual information to assess the probable accuracy of particular radiocarbon results versus others. The hope is to reach greater precision in the specific occupation dates assigned to the sites studied. We eagerly await publication of the results of this research, particularly as it pertains to the temporal underpinnings of the research that we present here. For the time however, we must confine ourselves to the best temporal estimates presently available for the eastern and western region sites that we include in our analyses.

Distinctive Nature of Archaeological Information from Eastern and Western Sites

It is also critical to highlight another potential source of discrepancy between the archaeological information relating to eastern and western Iroquoia. The former, including Mohawk, Oneida, Onondaga and Jefferson County sites, derives primarily from materials collected from site surveys, excavations, and surface collections of habitation areas. While not exclusively so, the majority of artifactual and contextual information cited for Seneca sites in western Iroquoia proceeds from mortuary contexts. As a result, the quantity and quality of artifacts and the fullness of contextual data from individual sites in western Iroquoia far exceeds that from the eastern sites, making it problematic to assume direct comparability.

Equally important, the nature of the available resources has dictated the focus of archaeological inquiry in the two areas. While questions surrounding settlement patterning have dominated investigations in the eastern sites, analyses and interpretations of mortuary behavior have taken precedence in studies of the western Seneca sites.

The latter provides the basis for the observation of two significant long-term archaeological trends in western Iroquoia—steadily intensifying mortuary ritual, manifested primarily in the use of valued materials, and increasing social complexity, as presented in chapter 6. By no means, however, should it be assumed that mortuary ritual played any less vital a role among the eastern groups. The data simply don't exist to make such determinations for eastern pre–Iroquois League sites.

1

The League Story over Time

Anthony Wonderley

The story of how the Iroquois League came about is still salient today. Indeed, it continues to resonate powerfully among contemporary Haudenosaunee (Iroquois) people. A summary of the foundation legend as commonly accepted today goes like this.

> Oral tradition holds that the Haudenosaunee were scattered and engaged in warfare with each other without restraint. A divine being from the Huron Nation, called the Peacemaker, or Deganawida, came to the Mohawk, Oneida, Onondaga, Cayuga, and Seneca people and converted them to the way of peace (health and order), power (unity and civil authority), and righteousness (a good mind and justice). Hiawatha and a powerful Iroquoian woman named Jikonsaseh assisted him in this difficult effort. Thadodaho, a very evil and powerful wizard of the Onondaga Nation, was so resistant to this message of peace that he used his magic to have Hiawatha's three daughters killed. Through the process of grieving, combined with divine events, Hiawatha discovered the funeral and mourning rituals that became the foundation of Haudenosaunee condolence ceremonies. It was supernaturally revealed to him that wampum is sacred and should be used at councils and funerals. Hiawatha forgave Thadodaho and personally combed the snakes out of his hair when he finally became converted. Thadadaho was then appointed by the Peacemaker to be the most noble and central of all chiefs. (Obamsawin 2005, 795)

Paul Wallace characterized this plot—the Deganawida epic—as the chronicle of a prophet divinely ordained to bring peace to a violent world (1986; see also John Mohawk in P. Wallace 1986, xv–xxiii). Other scholarly commentaries emphasize behavioral rather than ethical implications. Thus, Matthew Dennis thought the oral narrative shaped Iroquois actions during the seventeenth century (1993, 5–7, 77). Anthony Wallace argued that the Deganawida epic described a revitalization movement in which a prophet reformulated a body of belief to restore, among his followers, a meaningful sense of order (1958). Probably most academic researchers would agree that it is a narrative in which peaceful reaction to violent provocation is recommended. Allan Greer, for example, regarded the origin story as a charter myth for condolence rituals responding to bereavement in a socially constructive fashion (2005, 11–12). Similarly, Christopher Vecsey (1988) saw the account of the Iroquois League's founding as a political parable about achieving alliance not by force, but by offering consolation (condoling with wampum) to assuage grief and turn aside vengeance. For Jon Parmenter, the legend of the League of the Iroquois provided a rationale for mitigating the baleful effects of blood feud as well as the means to express an Iroquois penchant for mobility (2010, xlv–vi).

Archaeologists frequently make reference to the Deganawida epic to bolster or flesh out interpretations of the past, especially those concerning indications of violence in the archaeological record (Bradley 1987, 35; Funk and Kuhn 2003, 157; Snow 1994, 57–58, 230–32n10; Starna 2008, 308; Tuck 1978, 326). In addition to proposing general correlations of this sort, archaeologists are, not surprisingly, attracted to legendary details that might help date events in the past. The most specific chronological application of this kind is the claim that a solar eclipse mentioned in oral tradition can be used to date the founding of the League (Rossen 2015, 197–99; Snow 1991; Tuck 1978, 327).

Archaeologists drawing on this oral narrative material are applying a common-sense logic called the direct historical approach. It makes sense to work back in time drawing on what is known ethnographically and historically. This form of interpretation yields the best results when the terms of the comparison relate to the same social group at two moments in time that are not far apart (Steward 1942;

Strong 1942). Obviously, it is especially important to work within the same continuous tradition when investigating cultural phenomena and, just as obviously, these conditions are fulfilled among the Iroquois. Applying the recorded knowledge of the relatively recent to the more distant past has, in fact, long been a strength of Iroquois scholarship (Fenton 1940, 2002; Trigger 2001, 8–9).

However, when archaeologists project the Deganawida epic into the past, they are positing that the plot or details of the plot are true, that the epic faithfully or, in some important measure, documents something that took place long before. That assumption is really an unexamined assertion advanced without evidence. Better said, claims of this sort are not based on historical inquiry into the age, content, and development of the oral narrative.

That is the point of this chapter. The founding tradition of the Iroquois League is surveyed to better understand how the epic may be relevant to archaeologists trying to understand the past. Before elaborating on that, I think it important to explain in greater detail why I tackle the tale of the League's founding in historical, comparative, and socially functional terms.

Studying Oral Narrative

What intellectual orientation is appropriate to the job of examining the oral narrative relevant to archaeological thinking? Contemporary Native views are certainly worthy of respect. The problem with taking them at face value in this context is that we live in a world filled with people holding different views about most things—including the historical nature of the Deganawida epic. Scholars, accordingly, have long since developed a tried-and-true method for dialogue between and among people who have different opinions. It is what is pursued here.

The relevant framework for investigating the Deganawida epic from an archaeological point of view is a long-established intellectual field focusing on oral narrative—that part of traditional expressive culture comprising a people's verbal art or lore. For all humans, to think is to traffic in significant symbols (Geertz 1973, 45). For all humans, life is shared symbolic existence, a common social experience of abstraction and language. "People learn the perception of the world as it comes to them in the talk of people around them and is encapsulated in the categorization of reality and the presumptions about time, space, and causation in the world. The rich complexity of the narrative about reality that each of us gets sets the tone and character of our lives" (Goldschmidt 2000, 802; see also Eiseley 1957, 92–93). In a nonliterate setting, a culture's legends and myths are especially important mediums of oral narrative for conveying premises of belief and perception (Bruner 1991).

To specialists in oral narrative, the story of the Iroquois League happens to be both legend and myth—descriptive words used nonpejoratively. Legends describe human action "locally bound and historically rooted" (Grantham 2002, 3). They claim special and usually explicit credibility by alluding to what is regarded as historically true. But if legends are considered true, myths are truer because they are a people's most important stories. Myths tend to be regarded as older and more sacred and serious than legends. Myths typically explain how the world came to be ordered or how something significant came about. They tend to begin in primal time and often include cosmic activities. They feature supernatural beings, such as the Iroquois god Sky-Holder.

The important point is that legend and myth are aspects of traditional expressive culture comprising a people's verbal art or lore. Both can serve as signposts for people navigating together through the richly symbolic landscape that is the human condition. Some myths and legends are pressed into service to perform charter and existential functions by legitimating the present order and asserting its naturalness and rightness. Oral narratives of this sort "anchor the present generations in a meaningful, significant past, functioning as eternal and ideal models for human behavior and goals" (Vecsey 1988, 24; see also Cruikshank 1994, 407). They hammer out fundamental issues of identity and affirm self-worth during difficult times. They transform the experienced past and guide one's experience of history (Bricker 1981; Erickson 2003). In trying to make sense of the past, myths and legends not only talk about history, they also "attempt to reconcile a view of 'what really happened' with an understanding of 'what ought to have happened'" (Hill 1988, 10). Oral narrative, in other words, serves pragmatic ends in making the world seem a meaningful place (Klein 1997, 168).

All of this merely restates the key insight of anthropologist Bronislaw Malinowski (1984, 199), which is that myth fulfills "an indispensable function: it expresses, enhances, and codifies belief . . . it vouches for the efficiency of ritual and contains practical rules for the guidance of man." To the historically minded, Malinowski's finding is key to comparative and historical research. It means that some oral narrative is "not an idle rhapsody, not an aimless outpouring of vain imaginings, but a hard-working, extremely important cultural force" (1984, 196). Because it is significant to social existence, sense can be made of it in functional and social terms. That is the kind of understanding an archaeologist needs to have when looking to oral narrative for guidance about past social existence.

There is nothing new about approaching the story of the League's founding in this fashion. Scholars have long interpreted the epic in functional and social terms—but almost always with reference to recent versions of the story. The best-known versions of the League's origin were committed to writing on the Six Nations Reserve of present-day Canada around 1900 by Native scribes, including John Arthur Gibson and Seth Newhouse. Both Gibson and Newhouse compiled several versions of the founding between about 1885 and 1912. Both synthesized information relating to the Iroquois League—how that confederacy came about and how it was supposed to function (Fenton 1998, 80–97; Parker 1916; Scott 1912; Woodbury 1992).

The efforts of the two men sprang from a desire to record important knowledge for succeeding generations. They hoped to preserve culture by codifying custom and bringing order to tradition. Equally important, Gibson and Newhouse were responding to threats from the Canadian government to abolish the system of hereditary chiefs on the reservation. The chroniclers wanted "to justify traditional Iroquois government to the powers who might abolish it" (Fenton 1998, 5). Both Gibson and Newhouse sought to strengthen the concept of the Iroquois League by consecrating it with age and investing it with sacredness (Campbell 2004, 145–46; Fenton 1949; Fenton 1998, 39; Shimony 1994, xxxii; Weaver 1984). That means that accounts of the League from that time and place are at least partially understandable as rooted in the social reality of that setting. The story of the League's origins justified the traditional system of chiefs and, more generally, rationalized, in mythic terms, issues that were troubling people on the Grand River. "What is myth becomes the justification of the present," Fenton concluded (1949, 145).

The work of Gibson and Newhouse has been very influential. In fact, the interpretation mentioned at the outset implicitly reflects their writings, often by way of Paul Wallace's highly readable *White Roots of Peace* (1986; originally published in 1946), which synthesized some of the Gibson-Newhouse material. Accessibility and popularity aside, however, what an archaeologist should wonder in projecting Gibson-Newhouse into the past is, being products of human beings in specific circumstances, why one version offers better guidance than another and whether one version might be older than another.

In this chapter, I undertake to perform much the same kind of contextualizing as has been done with early twentieth-century material from the Grand River. I shall do so, however, more consistently and with even older material. I will examine the sociohistoric context of at least some versions trying to understand why a certain mythic creation appears suited to its setting and, ultimately, the applicability of the mythic creation to interpretations of archaeological data.

This survey of the Deganawida epic begins with the earliest documented account of the League's origins in the mid-eighteenth century and ends with early twentieth-century material. It is, therefore, a study based on documentary evidence, most of which derives from colonialist sources. That means there is bias, and that requires the researcher to be careful, honest, curious about bona fides, attuned to context, and self-critical—exactly as anyone dealing with any form of evidence should be. However, what is true specifically of written evidence is this maxim: The observations of historical phenomenon made by contemporary observers must normally be given greater weight than those of persons more distant in time unless substantial contrary evidence can be shown (Jennings 1984, 88). It is a precept central to the practice of any history, ethnohistory, and anthropology aspiring to objectivity. And, if one wants to learn what was said about the Deganawida epic in the past, this is a good reason to privilege historic sources over present-day tellings.

Another potential problem with written evidence is a dilemma characteristic of all historical research. Disciplines oriented retrospectively (e.g., anthropology, archaeology, and history) deal poorly with the absence of information. In the context of this archaeological book, all of us presumably understand that something written down at a certain point in the past means that that detail was known at that time. That certainly does not mean that other things were *not* known. Nothing, however, can be said on that score. In the absence of evidence, one cannot argue pro or con about hypothetical details. But— facts that do exist should be understood and taken into consideration.

Given the intellectual framework outlined here, how does one actually go about studying oral narrative? My answer is: Assemble and examine the evidence. Survey the data noting what is said across time and space. Line up the evidence chronologically to understand what was said, then compare that to what was said before and after. Note how content may differ from place to place. And, as the facts are laid out, look to the contexts of different versions trying to gauge how stories may seem appropriate to their settings and to archaeological applications (Wonderley 2004, 2009).

The evidence comprises many narrative accounts committed to paper over the course of a century and a half. Since the subject matter is complex and lengthy, the program of surveying it—particularly if done for the first time as is the case here—is complex and lengthy.[1] Content

---

1. As far as I know, no comparably substantive evaluation of the epic, one focusing on its content and change in content over time, has been performed. Vecsey (1988) compiled a useful list of sources. Clark (2004), Dennis (1993), Henige (1999), and Starna (2008) also reviewed aspects of a number of them. Easily the most impressive compilation and description of the numerous accounts of the beginning of the

matters and interpretations suggested on the basis of that evidence are—of course—tentative. They are advanced as the best fit, the best we can explain to others as accounting most parsimoniously for the most facts in culturally appropriate context of the time that they are written, as opposed to present-day concerns. The best, that is, until a better fit is demonstrated on the basis of the same or more or better evidence.

The payoff of researching in this fashion is that one learns new things. Facts come to light that archaeologists should be cognizant of. For example, applying the research program described here to the Iroquois story of creation, I discovered that the basic framework remained largely stable for many years. Then it changed drastically and suddenly in the context of altered social conditions (Wonderley 2001). Change is an important condition to establish, especially to archaeologists looking to oral narrative for interpretive help.

This survey begins, as I have said, with the earliest documented account of League origins, about 1750, and ends with versions recorded about 1900. That termination was chosen for two reasons. First, the chroniclers Gibson and Newhouse mark the moment at which the Deganawida epic definitively left the realm of oral tradition to become a physical presence belonging to the printed page. Second, Gibson and Newhouse are the sources most frequently cited by archaeologists. Their 1900 material—along with the survey of sources preceding them—accounts for nearly every source cited in archaeological interpretation.

A Mohawk Matter

No narrative about the League's inception is known before the mid-eighteenth century. What was enunciated in the historical record prior to that was a corpus of allegorical descriptions of Covenant Chain relationships—that is, ties of friendship established between the

---

League is that of Fenton (1998). The reader who looks at the citations will gain some appreciation of how much Fenton pulled together on the subject.

Iroquois and non-Native peoples. The accounts so offered, and duti-fully recorded in English between about 1677 and 1744, evolved as the years passed (Colden 1988, 87–89, 105, 153–56; Jennings 1984, 357–59). The names of Dutch individuals and events gave way, over time, to what Richter described as a "rehearsal of several distinct phases of alliance with the English, symbolized in their increasing strength, by a rope, an iron chain, and a silver or golden chain." This oral narrative, in other words, originated in certain social conditions and was altered because, as Richter concluded, "Iroquois interpretations of their past changed over time to meet current needs" (Richter 1992, 278).

Prior to 1677, figures of speech familiar from Covenant Chain usage certainly were employed by Iroquois speakers in contexts call-ing for the expression of alliance. Chief among them was the idea that brethren clasped arms in unbreakable friendship (Dennis 1993, 250; Jennings et al. 1985, 141, 149; Parmenter 2010, 88, 98, 108). Mary Druke has pointed out that interlocking arms were an image custom-arily employed by the Iroquois to symbolize alliance (Druke 1987, 39). A version of the Iroquois League's origin story told three cen-turies later featured Deganawida, informing the delegates assembled to consider confederation that they had now "taken one another by their hands and arms" (Hewitt 1892, 141). It seems likely, therefore, that whatever story (or stories) was then told about the League's origin incorporated this visual metaphor. However, we know nothing about the content of League histories told in the distant past.

Aside, then, from Covenant Chain rhetoric and familiar-sound-ing metaphors, not a whisper concerning the legend of the Iroquois League's commencement issues from an extensive documentary record of cultural interchange covering a century and a half. During that time, it is worth reiterating, not a single interested individual and not one knowledgeable chronicler—including several Jesuit mission-aries in the 1600s, Joseph François Lafitau and Cadwallader Colden in the early 1700s, and William Johnson in the mid-1700s—indicated knowing anything about the founding of the Iroquois League. "How is it," Fenton asked wonderingly, "that something so basic to Iroquois political philosophy escaped the notice of early writers on Iroquois manners and usages?" (1998, 51).[2] One of the greatest mysteries of Iroquois historiography, Fenton thought, is that nothing was documented about the legend of the League's founding until 1743.

The first recognizable account of the initiation of the League was written down in that year by the Moravian missionary John Christopher Pyrlaeus as he heard it from a Mohawk chief named Sganarady or David of Schoharie (Dennis 1993, 82–84; Fenton 1998, 53–54, Heckewelder 1991, 96–97). What Pyrlaeus was told, however, seems to refer to two events—the founding of the Iroquois League and a pact with the Dutch. The incidents are not clearly distinguished in the passage Pyrlaeus wrote about them.[3]

Pyrlaeus's Account

- A peace alliance of the Five Nations "was formed one man's life ago, before the white people built Albany, or rather, were first seen there in that area."
- The Mohawk were first to enter into the pact.
- The alliance was suggested by a Mohawk leader named Thannawage.
- Five "special chiefs who were the deputies of the nations that had formed the peace alliance" were the Mohawk Toganawita, the Oneida Otatschéchte, the Onondaga Tatotárho,

2. Why had no one mentioned it? Fenton's answer, as I understand it, was that non-Native people, overwhelmed as they were with practical concerns, were too busy to write it down (1998, 52).

3. Pyrlaeus's information about dating has usually been taken to mean that the Iroquois League was founded a generation before European contact (Fenton 1998, 69; Tooker 1978, 420). But, as recently translated by Corinna Dally-Starna (and quoted here), that is not the only thing Pyrlaeus said about dating in an ambiguous passage about two incidents. Starna argues that an Iroquois treaty with the Dutch, which Pyrlaeus seems to allude to, preceded the founding of the Iroquois League and was, in fact, "the starting point for the initiation and then expansion of alliances that eventually encompassed and involved all five Iroquois nations" (2008, 320–21).

the Cayuga Togaháyon, and the Seneca Ganniatarío and
Satagarúuyes.

• The united Iroquois called themselves "those who make up a
house, a family, the allies." (Starna 2008, 285–86)

Comments

This initial version of the Iroquois League's commencement introduces the name and character, often rendered today as Deganawida,
to the written record (Fenton 1998, 52). Here also may be the first
glimpse of Thadodaho as he steps onto the stage of history (Fenton
1998, 207, 714). One of the Seneca names mentioned here—Ganniatarío, or Handsome Lake—also is new to the documentary record.
Hiawatha, on the other hand, is not yet present, although a Hiawatha-
like character who proposes the alliance is named (Thannawage).

Yet, the name Hiawatha apparently was in use as that of an actual
Iroquois leader prior to 1743. We know that because William Fenton
combed the documentary record in search of Iroquois leaders bearing
the names of the fifty sachems on the official roster of Iroquois League
officials recorded in the mid-nineteenth century. Fenton found that a
headman named something like Hiawatha was first documented in the
late 1600s. Likewise, the Oneida, Cayuga, and the second Seneca names
mentioned by Pyrlaeus also have respectable antiquity as monikers first
recorded in the late seventeenth century (Fenton 1998, 531, table 6).

It seems a strange coincidence that the subject of the League's
genesis, referred to here for the first time, was taken up at almost
the same moment several miles to the west. In 1743 the interpreter
Conrad Weiser, attending a meeting of the Iroquois Confederacy at
Onondaga, reported hearing a public recitation of the founding of
the League. On that occasion, an Onondaga speaker "rehearsed the
beginning of the Union of the five Nations. Praised their Grandfa-
thers' Wisdom in establishing the Union or Alliance, by which they
became a formidable Body" (Beauchamp 1907, 428). Another orator
"added more in praise of their wise Fathers and of the happy union;
repeated all the Names of those Ancient Chiefs that established it"

(Starna 2008, 292–93). Weiser did not describe the founding story he heard, nor did he enumerate the individual names he heard spoken. He did, however, indicate that the Mohawk, "the first promoters of confederacy," were addressed in League council by a term said to mean "President, or Eldest" (Fenton 1998, 435–37).

Brant's Account

In 1801 Mohawk Joseph Brant elaborated a similar version of the formation of the Iroquois League:
- Two Mohawk brothers, one of good and the other of evil character, were the headman of two villages.
- Concerned about the cruel disposition of his younger sibling, Adergaghtha, Tekanawítagh "resolved to go westerly and look for people, and form an alliance with them."
- Tekanawítagh first met an Oneida, Odadseghte, whom he styled as his son.
- After some kind of delay (the Oneidas threw a tree across the path), contact was made with an Onondaga chief, Thadodarhoagh, who was offered equal status in the proposed union. After seeming to accept, the Onondaga leader had second thoughts. A member of the Mohawk-Oneida delegation who returned to retrieve a lost moccasin overheard Thadadahough grumbling about the arrangement.
- Further inducement being necessary, the Onondaga was placated by being awarded the location of the council meeting place along with the right to carry "their title." Four years later, the Cayugas (led by Shonónawendówane) and the Senecas (led by Chiefs Kanyadaríyoh and Shadekaroínyis) joined the union. (Boyce 1973, 288–89)

Comment

Five of the six names given for Oneida, Onondaga, Cayuga, and Seneca leaders are the same as those recorded on the list or Roll Call of the

Chiefs first documented in the mid-nineteenth century and acknowledged then, as in Brant's account, as founders of the Iroquois League.

To summarize, the first recorded account of the Iroquois League's
beginnings in 1743 seems to initiate a tradition documented over
some sixty years. Deganawida and, perhaps, Thadodaho are introduced
to the written record in this League tradition. Hiawatha is not mentioned. Two Mohawk who look as though they might play important
roles in the story, Thannawage and Adergaghtha, will never be documented again. On the other hand, some of the individuals named—
Oneida, Cayuga, Seneca—were identified as leaders during the 1600s
and will recur on the Roll Call of the Chiefs—the ritual enumeration
of the League's founders—which will be recorded in 1847.

There is little supernatural or folkloric embroidery in either Pyrlaeus's or Brant's account.[4] What we have seems like matter-of-fact
narrative purporting to recount what occurred in our world. What
appears to have happened involved several touchy men with easily bruised egos. It is a Mohawk story emphasizing the importance
of Mohawk action in the formation of the League. Why might such
a story be articulated and promoted at this moment in time? What
might the salience of such a story be?

By the 1740s, the once-mighty Mohawk tribe had diminished to
an insignificant level of four hundred to five hundred people. They
were virtual prisoners confined to two small villages surrounded by
a sea of perhaps ten thousand Euro-American people (Shannon 2000,
34, 236; Kelsay 1984, 46–47). Most whites, furthermore, were farmers
more interested in Mohawk land without Mohawks than in the occasional fur a Mohawk might bring to them.

A Mohawk's life tended to be short and precarious. These people
always seemed to be hungry. They were plagued by disease: smallpox

---

4. However, the two Mohawk brothers mentioned by Brant are reminiscent
of the twins in the Iroquois creation myth and the lost moccasin is a nice folkloric
touch.

in 1738 and 1743, and tuberculosis all the time. They seemed to drink a lot of rum while at the same time begging white authorities to keep it away from them (Kelsay 1984, 28–29, 40–41; Shannon 2008, 116).

A Mohawk's life did not foster high self-esteem. Indians could see that Euro-Americans had it better. Indians knew they were materially dependent on the other people and that, in the others' eyes, they lived in grinding poverty (Kelsay 1984, 24–25; Shannon 2000, 25–30). Having fallen to low estate, Mohawks knew perfectly well that many of their non-Indian neighbors and their Indian allies held them in contempt for it (Kelsay 1984, 152, 188; Shannon 2000, 48).

These were times to remind others of former Mohawk greatness. As the memory of the League's military victories faded, Iroquois chiefs generally were more and more inclined "to proclaim themselves a great imperial power," Isabel Thompson Kelsay observed. "But Mohawks, who kept the eastern door that directly faced the British, were particularly good at this bluster" (1984, 10).

Indeed, at precisely the moment the Mohawk League story appeared, Mohawks were trumpeting their importance in real life. About the time of King George's War (1744) and, as we have seen with Pyrlaeus and Weiser, the Mohawks aggressively reasserted their significance in treaty conferences at Albany, Montreal, and Boston. The burden of their song was that whites had to channel their communications to Indians through the Mohawks because the Mohawks were the traditional intermediaries sanctioned by custom (Shannon 2000, 30–36). Mohawks reforged the narrative story of their alliances to place themselves, rather than Onondagas, "at the head of Iroquois delegations" (Haan 1987, 56). Historical fact, the Mohawks further invited their hearers to imagine, included the central thesis of their League story: Mohawks originated the confederacy and, as eldest, they ranked highest. Beginning at the Albany Conference of 1754, Mohawks declared they were the head of the Five Nations (Jennings 1988, 98; Shannon 2008, 105).

For some years thereafter, Mohawks hammered the message home: Mohawks are eldest; Mohawks are the head of the League (Jennings

1984, 98; Fenton 1998, 473, 493, 504, 524–25, 527). The reason they emphasized that at this time was to make a symbolic and mythological point. As one Mohawk leader succinctly put it in 1768: "Altho' we be thought at present an inconsiderable People, we are the head of a confederacy that has Powerful Alliances" (Druke 1987, 32). Mohawks made their assertion of primacy stick. A few years after the Albany Conference, a spokesperson for the Onondagas acknowledged that, indeed, "the Mohawks are the head of our confederacy" (Fenton 1998, 486).

Agreement on this point implies that basic elements of the League account were accepted by all parties as incontrovertible fact. But, if the Onondagas had to concede the substance of the tale, they immediately counterattacked with politically loaded metaphor and symbol. In 1765 a delegation from the Onondaga tribe presented a list of nine Onondaga sachems for the approval of Sir William Johnson, royal superintendent of Indian affairs in the northern colonies. With the names came the assertion that Onondaga was "the proper Council fire for all the surrounding nations" (Fenton 1998, 530–32). The significance of this account, Fenton emphasized, is that, "the Onondagas were reasserting the tradition of league government in confederacy affairs."

What Sir William reviewed was the earliest known set of sachems with names that will appear on the later nineteenth-century Roll Call of the Chiefs. The 1765 list is headed by the sachem title Thadodaho, which, Fenton thought, was the first certain occurrence of that name in a historically attested setting. More remarkably, seven of the remaining names were documented here for the first time (Fenton 1998, 207, 530, 714, 721, table 6 at 531–33).

In effect, the Onondagas were announcing sachem titles they wished to have written down with the assurance that the Thadodaho, named in the Mohawk story, was prominently enshrined in an Onondaga context. This looks like symbolic pushback to the Mohawk story. One would think a better countermeasure would be to advance a legend about the League's formation emphasizing the Onondagas. As if on cue, that is what happens next.

Grand River Synthesis

Many of the Loyalist Iroquois gathered around the British fort at Niagara during the Revolutionary War. When hostilities ended, about one thousand of them joined Joseph Brant and fellow Mohawks along the Grand River of Ontario on a tract set aside for them by the British government. Almost immediately, about 1783–84, their leaders reestablished a new governing council, which, Fenton noted, "reinvented the league along traditional lines to govern what later became the Six Nations Reserve. The Grand River league kindled its fire at Middleport in the custody of Thadoda:ho? and the Onondaga firekeepers" (1998, 602). Very politically conscious, this new organization asserted its legitimacy and sovereign status by claiming that the newly created reservation government adhered strictly to traditional ways (Fenton 1998, 709; Surtees 1985, 79). This was fertile ground for mythmaking.

Norton's Account

Chief John Norton, an adopted Mohawk and formerly Brant's secretary, recorded the story of the Iroquois League's beginnings as it had developed in Canada by 1816.

- Long ago, a large village on New York's Salmon River broke up into emigrating groups, which became speakers of Algonquian and Iroquoian languages.
- The Iroquoian contingent traveled to a creek west of Oswego then separated. Some proceeded further west.
- Others, led by Chief Hayounwaghtengh, followed a creek upstream to an area where the salmon had ceased to run.
- Two men dispatched to investigate the phenomenon visited a village whose chief invited Hayounwaghtengh's folk to join his. Together, they ironed out the salmon problem.
- The two united groups then sent scouts ahead to Onondaga Lake. There they met another band—possibly the one that originally went west from Oswego—and the three effected

a juncture. The groups had clan names—the newest being
Bears; the followers of Hayounwaghtengh were Turtles.

• Having turned himself into an owl, a wizard named Oghsinou
bewitched one of Hayounwaghtengh's three granddaughters.
When the girl died, Hayounwaghtengh killed Oghsinou in
revenge.

• Attempting to join up with those already present, members of
the Wolf clan were crossing Onondaga Lake in their canoes
when they were dispersed by a storm conjured up by Thatotarho, chief of a village overlooking the lake.

• The Wolf clan somehow joined the others at a meeting held
secretly to avoid the enmity of Thatotarho.

• Thatotarho, however, attacked again by causing an eagle to fall
onto the crowd gathered below. A stampede of young warriors seeking feathers from the bird killed a second grand-
daughter of Hayounwaghtengh.

• Grief-stricken, Hayounwaghtengh departed, heading south to
the Susquehanna River. At one settlement, he accepted the
invitation of a village chief to stay and become co-ruler. But,
feeling he was not accorded proper respect, he continued
downstream.

• He arrived at another village, this one ruled by two brothers.
One of them intended to kill Hayounwaghtengh but the plot
was thwarted by the trick of sabotaging his bowstring. The
brothers then offered to share their governance of the village
with Hayounwaghtengh but, feeling ignored, he moved on
again.

• At a small lake near Windsor, New York, Hayounwaghtengh
saw geese shedding their feathers to take on anthropomorphic form. When challenged at their pretension to being
human, they flew off revealing, in their place, wampum in the
lake mud.

• Journeying further north into Mohawk country, Hayounwaghtengh walked into a longhouse and began reciting a speech
while holding strung wampum. This got the attention of

Chief Tekannawitagh, who promised the newcomer equal status in rulership. When Tekannawitagh asked why Hayounwaghtengh was wandering around in exile, the latter replied, "Thatotarho is angry."

• Tekannawitagh asked for volunteers to search out the abode of Thatotarho. Two respondents, turning themselves into cranes, flew to Seneca country, where they remained. This accounts for the Crane clan in that region.

• Two other volunteers became ravens who flew to Oneida, then on to Onondaga. There they found Thatotarho to be of terrifying aspect with snakes for hair. On their way home, the scouts paused in Oneida, New York, because the Oneidas had thrown a log in their path.

• Now knowing where to find Thatotarho, Tekannawitagh and Hayounwaghtengh prepared for the journey to Onondaga by laying out wampum as they named two chiefs. Those individuals, Tekarighhogea and Satekariwategh, then add their own wampum to the total. The new chiefly pair will henceforth bear sachem titles known today as Mohawk League titles 1 and 3.

• Setting off for Onondaga, Tekannawitagh encountered an Oneida who hailed him as "father." After naming the Oneida Odatsheghte, Tekannawitagh described his errand "to soothe the angry feelings Thatotarho; to reform his rugged appearance, and endeavor to make him like other men" (Klinck and Talman 1970, 103). The Oneida then detained Tekannawitagh by throwing another log across the path.

• Tekannawitagh assured Odatsheghte that, in spite of the latter's subordinate standing as son, they would be equals.

• Apparently mollified, Odatsheghte accompanied Tekannawitagh to Onondaga. There, with other chiefs, they spoke to Thatotarho while "delivering wampum until they had removed all his deformities" (Klinck and Talman 1970, 103). Supposing the mission accomplished, they returned home.

- However, a young man of their party, having forgotten his moccasins, returned to Onondaga, where he overheard Thatotarho grumbling in dissatisfaction.
- A year later, Tekannawitagh and Odatsheghte returned to Onondaga, apparently to finish rectifying Thatotarho's "concealed parts," and "to interest his heart in the welfare of the confederacy by inducing him to think, that his own interest and honor was linked to that of the public." Thatotarho was named firekeeper, given a pleasing wing fan, and named Roghscanakighte, or Title Bearer. His village was designated the meeting place for the confederacy. Soon after, the Cayugas and then the Senecas joined the alliance. (Klinck and Talman 1970, 98–105)

Comments

This account introduces the character of Hiawatha with a Hiawatha-like name and showcases him as the main character of a plot set in Onondaga. The Mohawk tale documented earlier has been grafted on to this Onondaga-centered plot by the narrative device of moving Hiawatha east to Mohawk country. As soon as he meets Deganawida, Hiawatha recedes into the background and Deganawida assumes prominence. Then comes the more familiar Mohawk sequence in which the Mohawk leader goes to Oneida, has logs thrown across his path, and so forth. Though Mohawk and Onondaga plots seem to have been spliced together, the two stories still remain sequentially distinct. While new to the historical record, the Onondaga storyline presumably is old enough to have seemed natural and true to Onondagas arriving in Canada after the American Revolution.

Uniting a Mohawk story with one identified as Onondaga seems a perfect mythic solution to the demands of new circumstances. At the Grand River, Mohawks welcomed representatives of the Iroquois League from other tribes, particularly those from the League's capital. An obvious mythic way to assert that the old League's authority resides in a new setting is to fuse a legend of Mohawk origins to a story of Onondaga commencement in this fashion.

The story told by Norton takes place in the timeless realm of folklore. Hiawatha starts out as a legendary figure directing a tribal migration. Then the telling assumes much of the character of an Iroquois hero tale filled with supernatural elements: transformation into birds; wizards who can magically kill, control storms, and cause giant birds to fall from the sky (Fenton and Moore 1974, 247–51; Randle 1953, 615; Wonderley 2004, 48–49). Gnarled in mind and correspondingly twisted in body, Thadodaho is now the quintessentially evil wizard of folkloric drama.

Norton's Iroquois League story describes Hiawatha's sorrow as resulting from the murder of loved ones by two evil wizards and how he deals with his grief. In the first instance, Hiawatha retaliates and kills the villain. A revenge killing, after all, is the proper ending to a duel between wizards in Iroquois folklore (Wonderley 2004, 94–95). In real life, however, the taking of vengeance was likely to provoke counter killing and that, in turn, could spiral easily into more revenge-motivated violence. In the second instance, Hiawatha does not retaliate but rather removes himself from the arena. Then he apparently forgives his enemy and works to heal that individual physically and spiritually. This, the story seems to say, is how to stop revenge killing, thereby avoiding the cycle of endless feud.

Given the association of wampum with League ritual, a narrative accounting for the League might also explain wampum and its League applications. Since Norton's story is the first to mention the substance, we should note that wampum is not explicitly identified here as wergild—an old Anglo-Saxon term used by anthropologists to mean blood money—or, more generally, blood payment. Nor is Norton's wampum described—again, explicitly—as something that condoles another's grief. Instead, wampum is something that accompanies the act of formal speaking and, perhaps, serves as a mnemonic. It is also linked to appointing sachems. The story suggests that wampum certifies and perhaps testifies to the truth of the word. Above all, Norton's wampum is a magical substance. Supernatural in origin, it is applied as a powerful medicine that somehow corrects Thadodaho's physical deformities and cures his twisted spirit.

Onondaga Lawgiver

Three accounts from the American side of the border date from the first half of the nineteenth century. While the stories vary widely, all showcase an Onondaga man who accomplishes unification of the Iroquois tribes. Furthermore, all are alike in failing to mention the Mohawk story of the League's establishment documented earlier. Mohawks, after all, were no longer present in the United States to promote their point of view.

Webster's Account

Ephraim Webster, a longtime resident and trader in Indian country, was the source of this version of 1815, a time when most Onondagas on the American side still lived at Buffalo Creek, where the council fire of the Iroquois League had been rekindled after the American Revolution. This account, however, came from the Onondagas' home territory, at that time (and still today) a reservation near Syracuse, New York.

- A low-ranking chief of the Onondagas named Oweko conceived the idea that the five Iroquois nations could repel attacks from western Indians if they united under one governing agency.
- When he proposed this to the Onondagas, Oweko encountered strong resistance from an unnamed principal chief who was a great warrior and a selfish man.
- Since Oweko "loved the welfare of others," he undertook secret journeys beyond Onondaga to convince others that confederating would be a good thing. He visited the Mohawks and Oneidas and, later, the Cayugas and Senecas.
- Having enlisted the other tribes in the cause, Oweko confronted his rival, who grudgingly consented, providing that he (the rival) be named principal chief and be credited with the plan's authorship.

- The former rival went on to gain the assent of others at a general meeting. He did so by demonstrating—the visual image supplied by Oweko—how several arrows bundled together are stronger than one. (Beauchamp 1895b, 215–16; Fenton 1998, 64)

Comments

Lacking references to supernatural events, the brief narrative seems straightforward in its manner of telling. It is purely an Onondaga story with an Onondaga setting and cast. The Mohawk plot with its Deganawida-like character is nonexistent. Even the notion of confederating, once credited to Mohawk Thannawage, is now attributed to an Onondaga. Mohawks have been reduced to being one of four places visited by Oweko on his recruitment tour.

The plot concerns two Onondagas, who play the roles of individuals later identified as Hiawatha and Thadodaho. The Hiawatha character, Oweko, is wise and statesman-like. He has to recruit the Thadodaho-like character by assuaging the latter's ego. Once mollified, that individual recommends the plan to confederate at a general meeting.

Cusick's Account

The first chronicle of the Iroquois League written by an Iroquois person was published, in English, by Tuscarora David Cusick in about 1827. Coming out of western New York, *Sketches of Ancient History of the Six Nations* is, in large measure, a compendium of oral narrative themes then current among the Iroquois of New York (Judkins 1987).

- The deity Tarenyawagon (Sky-Holder), traditional god of the Iroquois, conducted the Iroquois people out of a mountain near Oswego, New York, then had them occupy their familiar home territories.
- The god formed a confederacy and instructed the people in various ways. After preparing them for an afterlife involving the alternatives of heaven and hell, he departed.

• Tarenyawagon returned to deal with an invasion of monsters; among other things, Sky-Holder destroyed stone giants in a ravine near Onondaga. After instructing his people in the art of war, Sky-Holder departed a second time.

• "Perhaps 1,000 years before Columbus discovered the America," the five Iroquois tribes become independent and set to fighting one another. During these "unhappy differences":

Atotarho was the most hostile chief, resided at the fort Onondaga; his head and body was ornamented with black snakes; his dishes and spoons were made of skulls of the enemy; after a while he requested the people to change his dress, the people immediately drove away the snakes—a mass of wampum were collected and the chief was soon dressed in a large belt of wampum; he became a law giver, and renewed the chain of alliance of the Five Nations and framed their internal government, which took five years in accomplishing it.

At Onondaga a tree of peace was planted reached the clouds of Heaven; under the shade of this tree the Senators are invited to set and deliberate, and smoke the pipe of peace, as ratification of their proceedings; a great council fire was kindled under the majestic tree, having four branches, one pointed to the south, west, east, north; the neighboring nations were amazed at the powerful confederates; the Onondaga was considered a heart of the country; numerous belts and strings of wampum were left with the famous chief as record of alliances, etc., after he had accomplished the noble work he was immediately named Atotarho, King of the Five nations; and was governed by the Senate, chosen by the people annually; the successor of the kings to follow the woman's line. (Beauchamp 1892, 16–17; see 12–17 for references to the bulleted list)

Comments

The story begins in the realm of myth with the tribal god directing migrations. Sky-Holder then performs miracles to prepare the landscape, teach culture, and instruct in war. A mythological deity, therefore, is now connected to the tale. Indeed, the story moves even more strongly toward mythification by attributing the concept of unification to the god. Sky-Holder's league precedes the story of the Iroquois League, but both are part of the same narrative.

Snaky, cannibalistic Thadodaho is the evil wizard first described by Norton. After being cured, however, this Thadodaho becomes the mortal lawgiver of Webster's account. Cusick's version is essentially the Onondaga story of Webster but with Oweko and the rival chief fused into one character. Cusick's Iroquois League was founded to establish peace among the Iroquois tribes. Now, for the first time, Onondaga is celebrated as a seemingly holy place from which grows a great tree of peace.

Wampum is mentioned as a mnemonic; strings and belts of it being noted as the League's archives. This version hints at the magical properties of wampum by implying its connection with attaining a healthy physiognomy and outlook.

Clark's Account

This version was provided by the "head chiefs of the Onondagas," Abram La Fort and Captain Frost, in 1845. The latter individual, identified elsewhere as "Cold," was said to be the chief tradition-keeper of the American League at Buffalo Creek (Clark 1849, 31, 109, 124). Joshua Clark, an enthusiastic historian of his city (Syracuse) and county (Onondaga), probably collected this story at Buffalo Creek.[5]

- Ta-oun-ya-wat-ha, the deity presiding over fisheries and hunting grounds, was sent by the Great Spirit to benefit humankind by clearing stream channels, preparing good fishing places, and teaching humankind the use of maize.
- Arriving at Oswego in a white canoe, he met two Onondagas (unnamed). The trio set off on a journey around central New York, during the course of which Ta-oun-ya-wat-ha killed

5. Henry Schoolcraft's version of the Deganawida epic (1975, 270–83) was lifted from Clark's account (Henige 1999, 138; Tooker 1978, 423).

two huge water serpents, preventing the people from eel fishing. Then Ta-oun-ya-wat-ha opened a channel to Onondaga Lake, lowered the waters, and created useful salt springs.

- The trio arrived at a cabin in a chestnut grove that belonged to the witch Oh-cau-nee. She was killed by one of Ta-oun-ya-wat-ha's Onondaga companions, with the result that today chestnuts are freely available to all.
- Journeying on, the party encountered two red-feathered, long-necked monsters guarding the passage from Cross Lake to the Seneca River. Ta-oun-ya-wat-ha slew one, then pursued the other in an epic chase taking him through Oneida country. Eventually, the quarry was killed near Salina and from that spot came mosquitoes. Finally, the trio eliminated a pair of enormous eagles near the Cayuga marshes.
- Having set the landscape in order for people, Ta-oun-ya-wat-ha became a mortal named Hi-a-wat-ha.
- Fearing enemies to the north, Hi-a-wat-ha suggested the local tribes meet to discuss what measures should be taken.
- At the conference site, a giant white heron swooped down, killing Hi-a-wat-ha's daughter.
- A chief named Ho-see-noke was appointed to help Hi-a-wat-ha overcome his grief.
- Hi-a-wat-ha then convened a meeting to form a defensive pact against northern enemies. In the course of forming the confederacy, he explained to each Iroquois tribe its place in a united order. The Mohawks, for example, were to be the first nation because they are warlike and mighty. Thus was founded the Iroquois League.
- When this work was done, Hi-a-wat-ha ascended into heaven in his white canoe (Clark 1849, 20–31, 38–43).

Comments

A tribal god prepares the landscape of central New York for human life and performs various monster-slaying deeds. This is familiar folkloric material attributed to Sky-Holder as tribal deity and culture hero. The incident of the witch in the chestnut grove is also familiar folkloric material (Parker 1989, 128–32; Hewitt 1918, 147–51).

The Onondaga plot is now fully in the realm of myth. This is accomplished, first, by conflating the leader of Norton's tribal migration with Cusick's chronicle of Sky-Holder. Second, an Onondaga lawgiver, now named as Hiawatha, is described as an avatar of Sky-Holder. As he is deified, Hiawatha is deracinated and delocalized. He is no longer Onondaga in origin, having been brought to that place in a white canoe from the sky.

In mortal form and with different name, Clark's Hiawatha is Webster's lawgiver, he who was credited with creation of the Iroquois League as defensive alliance against outside foes. There is no Thadodaho-like character here and, lacking that rival, the incident of the big bird seems rather pointless. In the absence of the Mohawk tale requiring connection with the Onondaga story, Hiawatha's grief also seems irrelevant to Clark's plot.

That name Hiawatha—or something like it—appears here for the first time in an American context. Possibly it diffused from Canada, where it was documented earlier by Norton. The appearance of this name south of the border startled other researchers. William Beauchamp, for example, said the name was completely unknown until the mid-1800s (Fenton 1998, 65). Horatio Hale tried to explain the name away as a variant of Pyrlaeus's Hiawatha-like character, the Mohawk Thannawage (Hale 1969, 35). Daniel Brinton denounced Clark's mythic Hiawatha as "wholly spurious" (1974, 186). The apparent wonderment of these students suggests not only that they were unaware of Norton's earlier account, but that they were also ignorant of a distinctly different League tradition in existence decades earlier on the Canadian side.

Wampum is not mentioned in Clark's version. Was there less concern on the American side to provide a charter myth explaining the meaning and use of the substance? What can be said is that, overall, the American League narrative was essentially a one-man show in which the central figure was a lawgiver at Onondaga. Over time, tradition became increasingly myth-like as the protagonist became deified.

Introduced in the American versions is a narrative device that will become increasingly important in the future. Implied in Webster but made explicit in Clark is the idea that the Iroquois League is initiated when the lawgiver (an Onondaga named by Clark as Hiawatha) formally enumerates the constituent tribes at a general assembly of tribal representatives.

Morgan

Lewis Henry Morgan, the father of American anthropology, obtained the greater part of his information about the confederacy when he attended a meeting of the Iroquois League council on the Tonawanda Reservation in 1845 (Richter 1987, 13). There, he collected lists of sachem titles from a young Cayuga medical student, Peter Wilson, and a prominent Onondaga chief, Abram La Fort, who must have been talking to Joshua Clark about the same time (Fenton 1998, 191; Tooker 1994, 20). Perhaps Morgan was told something about the League's founding in Tonawanda, where he spent most of his subsequent (eleven) field sessions. However, he might have heard something on that subject at the Grand River Reservation in Canada in 1850. Certainly he gleaned a snippet or two on visits to Onondaga, New York, in 1845 (Fenton 1962, xl–xll; Fenton 1991, 76–77).

Morgan's Account

Morgan's chief interest in the Iroquois League was its organizational structure and how it worked, not in legends about its origin. A dismissive attitude toward the subject of oral tradition is implied by the fact that his longest passage about the League's founders is contained in a footnote. At any rate, what Morgan reported of the League story was this:

The nations were, at the time, separate and hostile bands . . . and were drawn together in council to deliberate upon the plan of a League, which a wise man of the Onondaga nation had projected, and under which, he undertook to assure them, the united nations would elevate themselves to a general supremacy. Tradition has preserved the name of Dä-ga-no-we'-dä as the founder of the League, and the first lawgiver of the Ho-dé-no-sau-nee. It likewise points to the northern shore of the Gä-nun'-ta-ah, or Onondaga lake, as the place where the first council-fire was kindled, around which the chiefs and wise men of the several nations were gathered, and where, after a debate of many days, its establishment was effected. (Morgan 1962, 61)

At the establishment of the League, an Onondaga by the name of To-do-dä'-ho had rendered himself a potent ruler, by the force of his military achievements. Tradition says that he had conquered the Cayugas and the Senecas. It represents his head as covered with tangled serpents, and his look, when angry, as so terrible, that who-ever looked upon him fell dead. It relates, that when the League was formed, the snakes were combed out of his hair by a Mohawk sachem, who was hence named Hä-yo-wen'-hä, "the man who combs." To-do-dä'-ho was reluctant to consent to the new order of things, as he would thereby be shorn of his absolute power, and be placed among a number of equals. (Morgan 1962, 67–68)

Dä-ga-no-we'-dä, the founder of the confederacy, and Hä-yo-wen'-hä, his speaker, through whom he laid his plans of government before the council which framed the League, were both "raised up" among the fifty original sachems, and in the Mohawk nation; but after their decease these two sachemships were left vacant, and have since continued so.

Dä-ga-no-we'-dä was an Onondaga, but was adopted by the Mohawks and raised up as first of their sachems. Having an impedi-ment in his speech, he chose Hä-yo-wen'-hä for his speaker. They were both unwilling to accept office, except upon the express condi-tion, that their sachemships should ever remain vacant after their decease. These are the two most illustrious names among the Iro-quois. (Morgan 1962, 101n1)

When the nations were enumerated, the Mohawks were placed first, but for what reason is not presently understood. (Morgan 1962, 97)

Finally, as Dä-ga-no-we'-dä announced the various regulations and rules of the League, he produced wampum strings "of his own arranging," which recorded the provisions. This was not "true wampum" in archaeological parlance. It was, supposedly, an ancient form made from the freshwater spiral shell called *Ote-ko-ä*, a name also applied to the more familiar wampum made from sea mollusks (Tooker 1994, 215).

Comments

Morgan reverses the identifications established in earlier versions. The Onondaga lawgiver, Hiawatha, is now Deganawida. The Deganawida of older versions has apparently become, with the addition of several biographical details, a new Hiawatha-like character. What were Morgan's sources for this new narrative? We know only that he did not hear this from his primary informant, the Seneca sachem Ely Parker. That individual later wrote an account of the League's birth at odds with Morgan's version but consistent with the plot given by Norton and other Canadian sources, which will be discussed later (Converse 1908, 187–90).

Could Morgan's attribution of Hiawatha as Mohawk relate to a Hiawatha-like name among the Mohawk sachem titles Morgan was recording at that time? Other details that Morgan apparently introduced certainly look as if they *could* be his interpretations of linguistic data. For example, Morgan was the first to write about Hiawatha combing the snakes from Thadodaho's hair—and Morgan had been told that Hiawatha means "man who combs."[6]

6. The name Hiawatha is an unsolvable problem linguistically because all we have is the work of English-writing scribes rendering sounds unknown to us in many different orthographies. That said, the whole business of pretending to translate Hiawatha is nonsense. In contrast to Morgan's "the man who combs" stands "Early

Morgan's popular *League of the Ho-dé-no-sau-nee, Iroquois* (1851) introduced the Iroquois Confederacy to an English-speaking audience. Influencing many who came after, the book also initiated a textually focused approach to the League story, one that often brought with it the assumption that what appeared on the printed page was superior to what one heard. William Fenton said, half-jokingly, that anthropologists invented the Iroquois League (1998, 713), partly in reference to the fact that certain features of the League narrative appear initially in Morgan's writings. Regardless of whether Morgan made things up, he was practicing a method of literary rationalization that would soon become increasingly popular.

Victorian Storytelling

The first sentence of Morgan's book declares that the author intends "to encourage a kinder feeling towards the Indian" (1962, ix). Both Morgan and fellow anthropologist Horatio Hale explicitly sought to place Indian culture in a favorable light, to demonstrate to their readers that Indians were respectable and intellectually legitimate topics (Hale 1969, iii). For both, the most important evidence clinching that argument was the League of the Iroquois. Both wrote their books to demonstrate that the League was a sophisticated political system "so intricately wrought, so profoundly based, so far-reaching, and so beneficently purposed" as to "put an end to war among all nations, and to bring universal peace" (Hale 1895, 45).

Researchers of the time worried that Indian oral narrative, accurately presented, would be unflattering to Indians because it was primitive and simple. It is difficult to see, Arthur Parker observed, "how

---

Riser," offered by the Native-speaking, traditionalist John Arthur Gibson (Fenton 1998, 193). The gifted linguist Horatio Hale rendered Hiawatha as "he who seeks the wampum belt" (1969, 21). Clark was told it meant "very wise man" (1849, 29). Other proposed translations include "the river-maker," "one who has lost his mind, and seeks it knowing where to find it," and "he was awake" (Beauchamp 1891, 295–96; Shimony 1994, 104).

any large body of rational men could hold as sacred truths such fictions as we may regard unworthy of serious consideration" (Converse 1908, 9). Sympathetic scribes, therefore, would want to improve the telling by raising the diction and narrating the plot in a style of writing then considered fashionable.

A common literary strategy was to dress the subject up in a toga, metaphorically speaking, then dilate on the subject's character and thoughts.[7] Thus, Hale's Hiawatha, famed for wisdom and benevolence, was pained by "the evils which afflicted not only his own nation, but all the other tribes about them, through the continual wars in which they were engaged, and the misgovernment and miseries at home which these wars produced. After much meditation, he had elaborated in his mind the scheme of a vast confederacy which would ensure universal peace." Thwarted by Thadadaho, Hiawatha "seated himself on the ground in sorrow. He enveloped his head in his mantle of skins, and remained for a long time bowed down in grief and thought. At length he arose and left the town, taking his course toward the southeast. He had formed a bold design. As the councils of his own nation were closed to him, he would have recourse to those of other tribes" (Hale 1969, 21, 23).

Stress on literary qualities encouraged respect for the printed word. More often than not, a chronicler preferred to take the information not from an informant but from a book. Writers of this time loved to copy from written sources.

Johnson's Account

The greatest copier of them all was Tuscarora writer Elias Johnson, whose Iroquois League story reprised the Onondaga lawgiver segment for a very good reason—he took most of it straight from Cusick and Clark, two of the printed sources describing the Onondaga lawgiver:

7. It was the Victorian historian Francis Parkman, who, in 1867, first dubbed the Iroquois the "Romans of the New World," according to Frank Speck (1955, 9).

- Tharonyawagon (Sky-Holder) taught the Iroquois tribes how to hunt and prepare the meat. He gave them corn, beans, and fruit and demonstrated how to plant and cook those foods. He taught the arts of war and of tribal governance. He cleared obstructions from the waterways.
- The god became a man named Hiawatha who took up residence at Cross Lake. He owned a magical white canoe. Hiawatha assumed leadership over the Onondagas by virtue of his great wisdom.
- Reacting to an invasion of enemies from the north, Hiawatha called "a general council of all the tribes from the east and west" (Johnson 1881, 47).
- As Hiawatha approached the site of the council in his canoe, a giant bird swooped out of the sky and carried off his daughter.
- When the council convened, Hiawatha's message was "We must unite ourselves into one band of brothers." Subsequently, "the union of the tribes into one confederacy was discussed and unanimously adopted" (Johnson 1881, 50–51).
- A great bird (presumably the one who took the girl) supplied the warriors with white feathers identifying them as soldiers of the confederacy.
- His task accomplished, Hiawatha ascended into the sky in his canoe.
- His place in the Iroquois League was taken by Ato-ta-rho, a leader considered second in wisdom only to Hiawatha. (Johnson 1881, 45–53)

As much as Victorian writers seemed to enjoy plagiarism, they were even more inclined to embroider content. Another authorial practice was to reinterpret the plot in order to preserve and even enhance the story's "natural beauty" (Parker in Fenton 1989, xvi). Many chroniclers of the time thought nothing of rewriting a tale to make it convey what they thought should have been said in the first place. Arthur Parker, who produced his fair share of imaginary retelling, explained it this way: "The transcriber attempts to assimilate the ideas of the myth tale as he hears it, seeks to become imbued with the spirit of the characters, and, shutting out from his mind all thought of his own culture, and momentarily transforming himself into the culture of the myth teller, records his impressions as he recalls the story" (Converse 1908, 12).

The result of such reconfiguration was, of course, fabrication, which Parker decried in writers other than himself.

> Many have employed this method of entirely recasting primitive ideas in their own thought molds, eliminating all the original idioms and picturesque eccentricities of expression and presenting the folk tale in all the verbiage of contemporary literature. The plot and motive of the original relation is warped and modified to fit modern requirements, the original elements are lost and the story becomes simply a modern one built upon the shattered skeleton of the old. The use of this method has produced a mass of florid, ocherous, recast and garbled folklore, which nevertheless is presented as genuine. (Converse 1908, 12)

A good example of how things could get garbled by indulging this approach is furnished by Hale, who said that his friend Chief John Buck, a traditionalist of the Six Nations Reserve, related this in 1882:

> Another legend, of which I have not before heard, professed to give the origin both of the abnormal ferocity and of the preterhuman powers of Atotarho. He was already noted as a chief and a warrior, when he had the misfortune to kill a peculiar bird, resembling a sea-gull, which is reputed to possess poisonous qualities of a singular virulence. By his contact with the dead bird his mind was affected. He became morose and cruel, and at the same time obtained the power of destroying men and other creatures at a distance. Three sons of Hiawatha were among his victims. He attended the Councils which were held, and made confusion in them, and brought all the people into disturbance and terror. His bodily appearance was changed at the same time, and his aspect became so terrible that the story spread, and was believed, that his head was encircled by living snakes. (Hale 1969, 86–87)

Chief Buck probably got this anecdote from Harriet Converse, the most inventive of all the Victorian parlor-genre writers. Converse wrote, among other fictions, about a seagull-like supernatural being ("Ji-Jo-gweh, the Witch Water Gull"; Converse 1908, 87), which she then linked to Thadodaho's formative years.

> The legend runs that in his [Ot-to-tar-ho's] youth he was gentle and mild, fond of innocent amusements and the chase, and was beloved by his people who looked forward to the time when he would be chosen their chief and become their counselor. But one day when hunting in the mountains he chanced to kill a strange bird which, though beautiful in plumage, was virulently poisonous. Unaware of its deadly nature Ot-to-tar-ho, delighted with his prize, plucked its bright feathers to decorate his head and while handling them inhaled their poison which entering his brain maddened him and upon his return to the village in insane rage, he sought to kill those whom he met. Amazed at the strange transformation the people were in great consternation and fled from him in fear. No more the gentle Ot-to-tar-ho; no more did he care for their games; no more did he care for the chase; but was sullen and morose and shunned all companionship with his people who also avoided him for he had developed a mania for killing human beings. (Converse 1908, 117)

This strange tale of toxic poisoning is given, as is typical, without attribution ("the legend runs"). Chief Buck may have read it in manuscript (possibly it was written in the early 1880s). He may have heard about it from Converse or from a reader of Converse, or perhaps Buck and Converse both got it from yet another source. In any event, Buck took it seriously enough to share it, and everyone—both non-Native and Native—seems to have been happy passing material of this sort back and forth.

Another example of adding to content was furnished by Elias Johnson in a section separate from the one summarized earlier. It was he who first introduced a peace queen into the narrative of the Iroquois League (Fenton 1998, 51–65; Hewitt 1917, 437; Wonderley 2009,

14–42). He did so by recurring to Cusick who, in *his* history, provided a long account of a Seneca war with a tribe called the Kahkwas.
A major character of the war was Yagowanea. Called the mother of
nations, she supervised a "Peace House" supposed to be secure from
violence at a place called Kienuka.

Johnson claimed that that woman was present when the Iroquois
League was created. Further, her presence had been institutionalized
as a female sachemship, the office of peace queen. The Iroquois, however, did not reappoint a successor to the original titleholder because
the first behaved egregiously and confirmed the sachems' suspicions
that women were unsuited to political office. The title of peace queen,
however, had recently been revived in the person of a Seneca woman
who married a prominent Tuscarora man. About the year 1878:

> There was a virgin selected from among the Tonawanda band of the
> Seneca nation by the name of Caroline Parker . . . who was ordained
> to the high office of queen, or Ge-keah-sau-sa. She is now the wife of
> a noted sachem of the Tuscarora nation, Mr. John Mount Pleasant,
> of no common wealth. She is located about two miles southwest of
> the antique fort Gah-Strau-yea, or Kienuka, on the Tuscarora res-
> ervation, where she ever held open her hospitable house, not only to
> the Iroquois, but of every nation, including the pale faces. Allegori-
> cal [*sic*] speaking, she has ever had a kettle of hominy hanging over
> her fire-place, ready to appease the hunger of those who trod her
> threshold. (Johnson 1881, 184–85)

Yet another way to upgrade the Indian material was to downplay
magical content that might imply the Indians were credulous and
superstitious. Consequently, the narratives of this era contained fewer
miracles and less magic. Non-Native authors did this, of course, but
so did Native sources. When asked about the snakish hair and supernatural characteristics of Thadodaho, for example, Hale said that "the
grave Counsellors of the Canadian Reserve, who recite his history as
they have heard it from their fathers at every installation of a high
chief, do not repeat these inventions of marvel-loving gossips, and

only smile with good-humored derision when they are referred to it" (1969, 21). One could accomplish this by leaving out details smacking of the marvelous. The magical properties of wampum, for example, are mentioned infrequently at this time. Or, one could deemphasize the supernatural by handling it in a seemingly rational fashion.

The Victorian era, then, witnessed transformations in the preferences and methods of storytelling with an overarching emphasis on textual authority. This trend culminated in the work of John Arthur Gibson, a sachem on the council of chiefs at Six Nations Reserve. Though blinded in 1880 at the age of thirty-one, Gibson clearly knew about Iroquois League writings accumulating around him. That is evident from the fact that he pulled together what he regarded as traditional material to reinterpret the story of the Iroquois League in 1899, 1900, and again in 1912 (Fenton 1998, 85–92; Scott 1912; Woodbury 1992). Of Gibson's three versions, the most historically influential was that of 1900.

Chiefs' Account

In 1900 the ruling Council of Chiefs at the Six Nations Reserve commissioned a telling of the League legend, which would refute a version recently authored by Seth Newhouse. In place of that narrative said to be "faulty in arrangement and erroneous or spurious in many of its statements," the council equipped itself with a committee-written version whose principal author was John Arthur Gibson, commonly regarded as the most knowledgeable authority on Iroquois ritual at the turn of the twentieth century (Campbell 2004, 196; Hewitt 1917, 430; Woodbury 1992, xiv). The resulting text was not only endorsed, it stands as the sole version of the narrative officially certified as authoritative by a Native government.

- It is stated, prefatory to the narrative, that the formation of the League occurred about the year 1390 (Scott 1912, 196).
- De-ka-nah-wi-deh was born of a virgin on the northern shore of Lake Ontario near the Bay of Quinte. His grandmother was informed in a dream that the Great Spirit had sent this child

with the mission to bring peace and life "to people on earth and in heaven" (Scott 1912, 198). The earth, we will come to learn, is a place of cannibalism and murder.

- When he grew to manhood, De-ka-nah-wi-deh built a stone canoe and indicated that a certain tree would bleed if he died in the course of his travels.
- De-ka-nah-wi-deh traveled across the lake. Encountering a party of hunters, he instructed them to return to their home with his tidings of peace.
- De-ka-nah-wi-deh went on to the dwelling of a cannibal named Tha-do-dah-ho and climbed to the roof so he could peer down through the smoke hole. Seeing De-ka-nah-wi-deh's face reflected in the pot boiling on the fire, Tha-do-dah-ho supposed he gazed upon his own better nature. This caused him to empty the pot of its human remains. De-ka-nah-wi-deh told Tha-do-dah-ho that he (Tha-do-dah-ho) had now repented of his evil and should go home to preach peace and friendship.
- De-ka-nah-wi-deh next visited the woman Ji-kon-sah-seh to upbraid her for feeding the violent men passing by her home. Hereafter, she "shall be the custodian of the good tidings of Peace and Power, so that the human race may live in peace in the future" (Scott 1912, 202).
- De-ka-nah-wi-deh was welcomed at a village whose leader he christened Hah-yonh-wa-tha because he got no sleep awaiting the coming of De-ka-nah-wi-deh.
- De-ka-nah-wi-deh announced the good tidings of peace and power to Hah-yonh-wa-tha's town. One skeptical listener suggested De-ka-nah-wi-deh could demonstrate the truth of the message by submitting to a deadly ordeal. Accordingly, De-ka-nah-wi-deh climbed a tree, which was chopped down to fall into a precipice. He overcame death, however, and was sighted the next day. After appointing two Mohawk sachems, De-ka-nah-wi-deh continued on his way.
- Back in the Mohawk town, two of Hah-yonh-wa-tha's daughters died mysteriously. To divert the father, warriors staged

a lacrosse match but ended up chasing a beautiful, low-flying bird. The stampeding contestants accidentally trampled Hah-yonh-wa-tha's third and last daughter. Hah-yonh-wa-tha wandered off grief-stricken.

- As Hah-yonh-wa-tha neared a foreign settlement, De-ka-nah-wi-deh suddenly appeared to advise that a man guarding a corn field should be approached without being seen. Further, Hah-yonh-wa-tha should fashion beads from elderberry twigs and string them. "Do not react to the people of this town," De-ka-nah-wi-deh counseled, "unless they respond appropriately with similar strings."

- After they did that, Hah-yonh-wa-tha accepted their invitation to deliver his message of good tidings of peace and power. The reply he received was that it sounded good but the people of the town would do nothing until another arrived.

- Hah-yonh-wa-tha was secretly visited that night by De-ka-nah-wi-deh, who said they must visit someone De-ka-nah-wi-deh had already met, the one (it is now revealed) who continually intoned in Hah-yonh-wa-tha's ear: "It is not yet."

- De-ka-nah-wi-deh and Hah-yonh-wa-tha encountered that person, apparently Tha-do-dah-ho, on a hill by a lake. The two visitors stated the tidings of peace and power will be promulgated in council. The "It-is-not-yet" man replied that he would await the council's coming.

- De-ka-nah-wi-deh and Hah-yonh-wa-tha repaired to the most recently mentioned village, which now accepted their message. De-ka-nah-wi-deh now conferred the first three Oneida sachem titles, beginning with the name Oh-dah-tshe-de, given to the man who had been guarding the corn field.

- At that time or earlier, De-ka-nah-wi-deh had been among the Cayugas and Senecas securing acceptance of the glad tidings of peace and power. Two messengers who became crows were dispatched from Oneida to summon those tribes to the lake of the "It-is-not-yet" man, Tha-do-dah-ho.

- As De-ka-nah-wi-deh led the Cayugas and Senecas east, Hah-yonh-wa-tha conducted his Mohawk folk to Oh-dah-tshe-de (lying like a log across the path), then led both peoples on toward Tha-do-dah-ho.
- De-ka-nah-wi-deh and Hah-yonh-wa-tha and other chiefs crossed the (Onondaga) lake to reach Tha-do-dah-ho. Cruising in De-ka-nah-wi-deh's white stone canoe, they survived storms summoned up by Tha-do-dah-ho to sink them.
- De-ka-nah-wi-deh and Hah-yonh-wa-tha and other chiefs demanded to know whether Tha-do-dah-ho accepted the good tidings of peace and power, but Tha-do-dah-ho remained silent. The stone canoe was sent back to fetch Ji-kon-sah-seh and, in her presence, Tha-do-dah-ho was importuned again.
- "Then the twisting and contortionate movements of the fingers and the snake-like movements of the hair of Tha-do-dah-ho ceased." All the visiting lords participated in finishing off the transformation "by rubbing him down, and taking the snake-like hair off him and circumcising him" (Scott 1912, 219).
- De-ka-nah-wi-deh then announced the titles, protocols, and rituals of the Iroquois League to the assembled representatives of the five tribes. This section of bylaws comprises over half the total text.
- After prophesying hard times ahead, De-ka-nah-wi-deh departed.

Comments

Neither Mohawk nor Onondaga, the Christ-like Deganawida is a divine sent from above to reform the violent world by bringing it, as formulaically repeated throughout, the good tidings of peace and power—a political formation, a tribal confederacy. Hiawatha, a Mohawk and a reformed cannibal, is a relatively minor character charged with furthering Deganawida's program. Hiawatha's grief is treated as the device to get him moving west from Mohawk country to perform his ministry in Oneida and Onondaga. Thadodaho is characterized as an evil wizard but his wickedness has been greatly toned down. He functions mainly as the personification of the fifth and final tribe needed to complete the confederation. His transformation is accomplished by having others rub him down.

Wampum in this version originated from beads made from elderberry twigs. The explanation is relatively unimportant, however, because the substance is quickly assumed to be true wampum. Its use is carefully specified, particularly as paraphernalia in the condolence ceremony to raise up a new sachem. This text is not so much a mythic charter as a set of instructions.

The narrative is a charter myth for the Iroquois League—or, more accurately—the League's actual charter. While the storyline establishes the existence of the League, that plot is secondary in length to a description of Deganawida defining the League's rules and regulations, its symbols and metaphors, its office titles and the rite (Condolence Council) for maintaining those titles (Woodbury 1992, xi, xxxiii). In effect, the presentation is an instruction manual on how things must be done. The exegesis is proclaimed in a strongly authoritative, literary voice. Further, as is so often the case in Victorian times, the content draws on other published sources. At least one major section ("The Ceremony Called 'at the Wood's Edge'"; in Scott 1912, 237–45), for example, was copied verbatim from Hale (1969, 117–39).

The authoritative tenor of plot and protocol derive in no small measure from the underlying assertion that what is said is divine truth. Clark's account, it will be recalled, identified the lawgiver with the old tribal god. Here, in contrast, the lawgiver's father, the Great Spirit, caused a human virgin to conceive a son destined to bring peace to the world. Gibson's version, in other words, strengthens the implication of divine authority by presenting a lawgiver not only linked to a high god but also identified as a savior in terms comprehensible to any God-fearing Christian.

The whole thrust of the story is similar to the Hiawatha tale of the American side except that, now, Deganawida takes Hiawatha's place as both Onondaga lawgiver and leading actor throughout. In telling things this way, Gibson advocates the interpretation first written out by Morgan. In addition, Gibson incorporates the character of Ji-kon-sah-she, the woman textually introduced by Elias Johnson.

Recounting the story in this fashion, however, means departing from the earlier documented traditions. That, in turn, alters the narrative logic advanced in preceding versions and causes some logical difficulties. Gibson tries to resolve such problems by experimenting with alternative solutions in his three versions of the League's founding. For example, if one regards Deganawida as the prime mover while retaining the full cast of characters, the roles and motivations of the other characters have to be reconsidered. One can sense Gibson thinking this through as he wonders who Deganawida's reformed cannibal should be: Hiawatha, Thadodaho, or a person left unidentified? And, in borrowing Johnson's peace queen as a character involved in the formation of the Iroquois League, Gibson has to figure out where she should go and why. Trying to solve that, he experiments with placing her at different points in the narrative and offering different explanations of her meaning.[8]

8. About the cannibal: In the 1899 account, the cannibal transformed in the smoke-hole incident is Hiawatha (Fenton 1998, 88–92). In the 1900 account, the cannibal is Thadodaho. The cannibal remains unnamed in the 1912 account (Woodbury 1992, 78–88).

About the peace queen: In Gibson's earliest version (1899), Deganawida first— that is, after crossing Lake Ontario—visits a woman named Djigonhsahsen, called the Mother of Nations (Johnson's peace queen). After establishing a mother-son relationship with her, Deganawida explains the Great Law, indicating that, from that time on, maternally based families will be at the heart of the system. "At that time," Fenton remarks, "the Mother of Nations apparently understood the proposition and accepted it. It was then, in this traditional historical precedent, that Deganawida laid down the proposition that women should possess the title to chiefship, inasmuch as the Mother of Nations first accepted the principles of righteousness and peace. Deganawida was then prepared to deal with the cannibal" (1998, 88).

In the 1900 and 1912 versions, Deganawida visits the woman Ji-kon-sah-seh after the incident of the cannibal glimpsed through the smoke hole. The woman, who seems not to be Deganawida's mother, is upbraided for feeding the violent men

The Persistence of Tradition

Late in the nineteenth century, Horatio Hale unwittingly confirmed that the Iroquois League tradition of Norton still existed in Canada. Before documenting that, Hale summarized the part of the League narrative he heard from chiefs on the Onondaga Reservation near Syracuse, New York, in 1875.

Hale's Account

- War was being waged against the Cayugas and Senecas by the Onondagas, led by Atotarho, who had, it was said, snakes for hair. "He was a man of great force of character and of formidable qualities—haughty, ambitious, crafty and bold—a determined and resourceful warrior" as well as a "stern and remorseless tyrant" (Hale 1969, 20).
- Hiawatha, another Onondaga chief, dreamed of a government that would bring peace.
- Atotarho thwarted every attempt by Hiawatha to call the Onondagas together to explain his vision. Finally, Hiawatha decided to leave Onondaga in order to pitch the plan elsewhere.

To this point, Hale's narrative does not differ greatly from earlier versions concerned with the plot of the Onondaga lawgiver. The next part of the story, however, specifically attributed to Canadian chiefs, is similar to the narrative Norton reported some sixty years earlier.

- Hiawatha plunged into the forest. A lake he crossed "had shores abounding in small white shells" (Hale 1969, 23–24). Thus wampum was discovered.

---

passing her home. Hereafter, she "shall be the custodian of the good tidings of Peace and Power, so that the human race may live in Peace in the future" (Scott 1912, 202; Woodbury 1992, 91–93). Overall, there is less explicit rationalization being offered in Gibson's later versions about establishing the matriarchal principle in the Iroquois League.

- Floating down the Mohawk River, he met two leaders one of whom, Tekarihoken, was first chief by hereditary right. Hiawatha preferred the other, Dekanawidah, respected for personal achievements. "They found in each other, kindred spirits. The sagacity of the Canienga [Mohawk] chief grasped at once the advantages of the proposed plan, and the two worked together in perfecting it, and in commending the people to it" (Hale 1969, 25).
- The idea of a confederacy was explained to the neighboring Oneidas. After delaying a year, their chief, Odatsehte, accepted it.
- Dekanawidah and Odatsehte went on to Onondaga to importune Atotarho. After the latter rejected their proposal, they proceeded on to Cayuga to enlist the leader at that place, Akahenyonk.
- Dekanawidah, Odatsehte, and Akahenyonk then convinced Atotarho to join them.
- Now enthusiastic for the plan, Atotarho helped to recruit the Senecas and their two leading chiefs, Kanyadariyo and Shadekaronyes.
- Advised by Hiawatha, an assembly of chiefs from all the tribes meets at Onondaga "to settle the terms and rules of their confederacy" (Hale 1969, 29).

As of about 1875, then, Canadian Iroquois could speak about Hiawatha of Onondaga, who went to Mohawk country to join up with Deganawida. Thereafter, Deganawida became the main actor in events that won over Thadodaho to the plan of tribal union. This was the story told by the Onondaga sachem and firekeeper at the Six Nations Reserve, John Skanawati Buck—he who shared the Thadodaho–poisonous bird anecdote—in 1888.

Buck's Account

- The "notorious and unscrupulous wizard and tyrant," Tha-do-dá-hó, made things hard at Onondaga. The people tried to meet secretly to decide what to do about him. Crossing the lake in canoes to attend that concourse, some were drowned in a storm caused by the magician.

- A second meeting was arranged around the person of a great chief named Hai-yo^n-hwat-há. Tha-do-dá-hó disrupted this gathering by causing a beautiful winged creature to fall from the sky. The people, rushing to see it, trampled and killed Hai-yo^n-hwat-há's pregnant daughter.
- Inconsolable, Hai-yo^n-hwat-há traveled south, where he discovered wampum on a lake bottom after ducks flew up taking the water with them.
- Hai-yo^n-hwat-há visited, in turn, two bark lodges, but continued to move on.
- At a third, he told his host, De-ka-na-wida, that he was wandering around because Tha-do-dá-hó killed his three children.
- De-ka-na-wida took the matter to his council. There, it was decided that Tha-do-dá-hó would be dealt with but, to do that, they would need wampum.
- After Hai-yo^n-hwat-há gave them wampum, two sachems were appointed.
- In search of Tha-do-dá-hó, two messengers turned into crows. They got as far as Oneida, where a chief said he would place himself in De-ka-na-wida's way like a log. That way, the chief pointed out, De-ka-na-wida would have to take the Oneida with him.
- Proceeding on to Onondaga, the messengers were shocked at Tha-do-dá-hó's appearance: "a thing—a shape—that was not human but rather supernatural and deformed; for the hair of Tha-do-dá-hó was composed of writhing, hissing serpents, his hands were like unto the claws of a turtle, and his feet like unto bear's claws in size and were awry like those of a tortoise, and his body was cinctured with many folds of his *membrum virile*—truly a misshapen monster" (Hewitt 1892, 136).
- After stopping by Oneida again, the messengers returned home to report what they had learned about Tha-do-dá-hó.

- De-ka-na-wida then led a procession of Mohawks and Oneidas, including Chief O-'tatc-heq-te', to Onondaga.
- At Tha-do-dá-hó's longhouse, De-ka-na-wida racked up a set of wampum strings then rubbed the wizard down. A string was held up for each body part as De-ka-na-wida named and healed it.
- De-ka-na-wida and Hai-yo^n-hwat-há proclaimed that all must now work for the common welfare, peace and tranquility.
- Roughly half the text describes De-ka-na-wida's announce-ment of laws, procedures, rituals, and symbols of the League, which now, without explanation, includes the Cayugas and the Senecas.
- With that task completed, De-ka-na-wida died and was buried.

Comments

In Buck's account, Deganawida holds up thirteen strings of wampum, one at a time, for each of Thadodaho's body parts as he heals them. This is precisely analogous to the ceremony for appointing Iroquois League chiefs: In that rite, thirteen strings are employed to raise up a new sachem in the requickening address of the condolence ceremony.[9] Hence, reference is being made, apparently for the first time, to wam-pum as the condoling substance for League ceremonialism.

Overall, the description of ritual consumes a considerable portion of Buck's narrative. Furthermore, this is the first version of the epic in which the "bylaw" content—the announcing of League procedure and symbolism—looms large and seems at least as important as the storyline about how the League came about.

While many new or unfamiliar details are proposed here, the core substance of Buck's account is recognizably the same as that of Hale

---

9. As described ethnographically, fifteen—not thirteen—strings or "matters" are frequently attributed to the requickening address (Tooker 1978, 438–39). But, because of duplication and the questionable relevance of the last one, "the proper elements of condolence reduce to thirteen" (Fenton 1998, 181; see also Fenton 1946, 120).

and Norton's versions. Beauchamp discerned it as the Canadian plot of the story of the Iroquois League (1891, 305). It is the storyline Seth Newhouse believed to be genuine.

Newhouse's Account

Of Onondaga-Mohawk parentage, Newhouse had long been questioning the old people on the Grand River about their memories of the Iroquois League's origins. He wrote at least two accounts of the League's foundation, the earlier of which is dated 1885 (Woodbury 1992, lvi; Fenton 1998, 80–83). It, or something like it, was rejected by the council of traditional chiefs, the body then governing the Six Nations Reserve, as being insufficiently authentic by their lights (Campbell 2004, 184–86). Sometime after 1899, Newhouse added a passage to this manuscript stating that Deganawida was divinely conceived, born of a virgin, and vested with the mission of bringing peace to the world (Fenton 1949, 152). Clearly derived from Gibson's version, these details presumably were added to please the chiefs' council. As it stands, that plot segment is neither relevant nor obviously related to the story Newhouse presents in the balance of the manuscript.

The narrative summarized here was said to have been collected by Arthur Parker on the Six Nations Reserve in 1910. The original manuscript apparently is lost but its contents, as published by Parker in 1916, had been revised to an unknown extent by another Native scribe, then extensively reworked by Parker himself (Fenton 1968, 38–39; Parker 1916, 12). Even so, the revisionist schizophrenia of the earlier manuscript is still in evidence here. A preface states that Deknanwidah, born of a virgin mother on the north shore of Lake Ontario, had been sent by the Great Creator to establish the Great Peace. When grown, Deknanwidah crossed the water to reach Mohawk country. This introductory passage differs, again, in content from what follows and, again, seems unrelated to it. What is more clearly Newhouse's story of the Iroquois League is as follows:

- Fighting and violence were everywhere.
- Adadarho, an evil wizard ruling at Onondaga, had snakes for hair.

• A person named Hayontawatha called a council to deal with
Adadarho. However, the latter caused a storm, which sank the
canoes of many on their way to the meeting.

• People going to conciliate Adadarho were buzzed by a bird summoned by the wizard. The bird, Hagoks, created panic when
people rushed to grab its feathers.[10]

• An unnamed fellow dreamed that Hayontawatha would travel
to Mohawk country to meet someone who will prevail. In the
reality of the story, however, Hayontawatha loves his seven
daughters too much to leave. Therefore, the Onondagas,
convinced of the dreamer's prophecy and wanting it to come
true, hired a shaman, Osinoh, to bring it about.

• Osinoh, in the form of an owl, bewitched and killed all the
daughters. Though wounded by an arrow, Osinoh apparently
recovered and moved out of the story.

• Hayontawatha wandered off in sadness.

• From "round, jointed rushes," Hayontawatha made three strings
and announced he would use these to remove the grief of
others. He then saw ducks fly up from a lake lifting the water
with them. Walking on the lake bed, Hayontawatha discovered snail shells; some white, some black.

• When Hayontawatha came to a settlement, he declared his
desire to condole with his strung shells. He was taken to the
town council but, not having been asked to participate, he left.

• At another settlement, he was again invited to council but,
again, not asked to contribute. A messenger said that Hayontawatha would meet a Mohawk with whom he will establish
the Great Peace.

• Journeying on to a Mohawk town, Hayontawatha met Dekanawida. After preparing more strings of shells, the latter

10. Fenton identifies Hagoks as the Onondaga-Cayuga term for the Dew Eagle,
mystical patron of the Eagle Society and Dance, and mythical protagonist in the
"Roc" stories of Iroquois folklore (1991, 75, 88–95).

utilized them to condole Hayontawatha. This is how such
strings will be used in the future, Dekanawida stated.
Dekanawida then suggested that they compose and practice a
peace song to be performed for Adadarho.

• Dekanawida and Hayontawatha proposed a plan for peace to the
Mohawk council. The council recommended that the idea
be passed on to the Oneidas. A year later, the Oneida chief
Odatshedeh agreed to the proposition.

• Dekanawida and Hayontawatha sent the plan on to the Onondagas, Cayugas, and the Senecas. All agreed there should be
a gathering to consider the proposal. Dekanawida then told
the Mohawks, after five years, we have the consent of all five
tribes but Adadarho's concurrence will still be needed.

• Volunteers were called for to find Adadarho. Those capable of
transforming themselves into cranes, herons, hummingbirds,
crows, and deer presented themselves. The deer people were
chosen.

• Dekanawida and Hayontawatha announced the rules for establishing the Great Peace. Then, based on information from
their messengers, all the tribes proceeded to Onondaga sing-
ing their League songs.

• Dekanawida, the one who sang the songs correctly, rubbed
Adadarho. This action healed the wizard in body and mind.

• Then, in a section comprising about three quarters of the total
text, Dekanawida proclaimed the laws of the confederacy.
This rendering of the "constitution" is an extensive rewrite of
rules and procedures originally given in the chiefs'—that is,
Gibson's—version of 1900 (Fenton 1998, 80–83).

Comments

Newhouse, as noted earlier, was familiar with Gibson's version defining Deganawida as divinely appointed to bring peace to the south
shore of Lake Ontario. Obviously, however, he was uncomfortable
with that approach because it was not the story he thought was right.

The tradition of the Iroquois League's founding Newhouse set forth as true resembled, at least in broad outline, what Norton, Hale, and Buck had documented.

The narrative initially focused on an Onondaga would-be lawgiver, who linked up with the Mohawk Deganawida. Together, the two promoted confederacy by going back to Onondaga to overcome the hostility of the Onondaga Thadodaho. In Norton, Hale, and Buck, and still in Newhouse, the tale consists of two recognizably separate plot segments stitched together by the movement, motivated by grief, of Hiawatha from Onondaga to Mohawk country. The early nineteenth-century League story in Canada was still broadly intact late in the century.

Newhouse, to be sure, advocated some new or, at least, unfamiliar points. Even so, there is nothing in his account to rival the amount of innovation Gibson introduced by, for example, describing Deganawida in New Testament terms, codifying a new character, or reversing fundamental characteristics of previously known actors. This finding is at variance with a perception that Gibson was the truer historian, that his versions are, as Fenton described them, "as close to the traditional record as we can hope to approach" (1998, 83; Goldenweiser 1916, 436; Hewitt 1920, 538; Campbell 2004). On the contrary, of the two great *annalistes* and synthesizers on the Grand River about 1900, it was Newhouse who was closer to documented tradition.

The Eclipse

Some may find it puzzling that a topic of temporal importance introduced at the outset—a solar eclipse dating the time of the Iroquois League's founding—has not been further mentioned. Now, however, the attentive reader can see why. The episode was not recorded in any of the League accounts examined here. In this instance, therefore, the documentary net has to be recast beyond the 1750–1900 parameters in order to pick up whatever source(s) archaeologists draw upon in citing an eclipse incident.

The earliest archaeological allusion to an eclipse may be that of James Tuck remarking: "It is interesting that there is mention of

Deganawida blotting out the sun as part of the traditional account of the founding of the Iroquois league. A solar eclipse was visible to central New York in the year 1451" (1978, 327). Although Tuck cited no source for this, he clearly was acknowledging Elisabeth Tooker's comments on an eclipse in the same volume of *Handbook of North American Indians*:

> Although not a part of the long versions of the epic recounting the founding of the League, one Iroquois tradition suggests a mid-fifteenth-century date. One version of this tradition states that at the time the Senecas were considering whether or not to join the League, there was a total eclipse of the sun ("the sun went out and for a little while it was complete darkness") and that this eclipse took place when the grass was knee high or when the corn was getting ripe (P.A.W. Wallace 1948, 399). Another version states that a total eclipse occurred when the Mohawks, angered at the Senecas for having taken some Mohawks captive, were about to attack a Seneca village. This eclipse, which took place when the corn was receiving its last tilling, was taken as a sign that the war should end and the Seneca should join the Confederacy (Canfield 1902, 23, 40, 197–98). Some examination of the dates on which total eclipses occurred in this region suggests that the one referred in these accounts occurred June 28, 1451. (Tooker 1978, 420)

Of Tooker's two sources for an eclipse incident, one was an article by Paul Wallace quoting a brief text by Ray Fadden, a colorful raconteur living among the St. Regis Mohawks. Wallace introduced the passage with the comment: "There has recently been drawn to my attention . . . a curious piece of evidence which I think worth presenting, though I do so without making any claim for its infallibility" (1948, 399). Fadden's note, attributed to one Paul Nash of the Six Nations Reserve, read:

> When the peace messenger of Deganawidah went on to the Seneca Nation he was not at first welcomed, that is, he was not welcomed by one section of the Senecas, that section who dwelt further to the west. As they were thinking it over, there occurred a strange event.

The sun went out and for a little while it was complete darkness. This decided those Senecas who were in doubt. They thought this a sign that they should join the Confederacy. This happened when the grass was knee high, I think, or when the corn was getting ripe. (P. Wallace 1948, 399)

Fadden was sharing a version of the League's origins that he thought should be added to what Wallace had just summarized in *The White Roots of Peace* (1986, originally published 1946). That book, synthesizing what Gibson and Newhouse knew of League tradition as of about 1900, did not mention an eclipse.

Tooker's other source was William Canfield, a non-Native newspaperman in Utica, New York, who, in 1902, published a book of Iroquois lore titled *The Legends of the Iroquois, Told by "The Cornplanter."* Its contents, Canfield claimed, derived from the eighteenth-century Seneca chief Cornplanter as well as from Governor Blacksnake. Written down by an unnamed scribe in about 1800, Cornplanter's words had, in some fashion, come into Canfield's possession. *The Legends of the Iroquois* specified that the Seneca-Mohawk incident described earlier took place, as Tooker reported, "when the corn was receiving its last tillage" (Canfield 1902, 206).

The next archaeologist interested in the eclipse was Dean Snow, whose sources ("several ethnohistorical accounts") turned out to be the same as Tooker's: Wallace (1948) and Canfield (1902). Analyzing a range of eclipse dates, Snow concluded that the two dates most appropriate for the founding of the Iroquois League would be 1451 and 1536 (1991, 141). Subsequently, Snow became increasingly dubious about the report of an eclipse (1994, 60), a skepticism shared by other archaeologists (Sempowski and Saunders 2001, 710).

Inclined to date the inception of the Iroquois League as early as possible, the archaeologist Jack Rossen recently proposed that event coincided with an eclipse occurring in 909. "Ethnohistorians," he averred, "have matched aspects of oral history to astronomical events such as eclipses, specifically the black sun that appeared as the Seneca debated in council on joining the confederacy in some versions of the Peacemaker epic" (2015, 197). Rossen's primary ethnohistorical sources were, yet again, Wallace (1948) and Canfield (1902). His "black sun," in particular, probably derives from Canfield's account:

> Then the voice of one of the young Mohawk girls rose in a cry that fastened the attention of the warriors of both parties. Her gaze was directed toward the sun, and from her lips came words that carried fear and consternation to all their hearts.
>
> "See, see, my Brothers! The Great Spirit hides his smiling face and will not look upon the battle of the red man. He will go away and leave them in darkness if they burn the villages and with their poisoned arrows send the hunters and the women and the children on their long journey before they have been called. Look thou, my brothers, he has seen the Mohawk maidens happy in the lodges of the Senecas, and he will not look upon them in misery and death. He hides his face, my brothers! He hides his face!"
>
> A moan of terrible fear went up from the warriors—men who could meet death on the chase or in the battle with a smile were unnerved by that awful spectacle. They saw a black disc moving forward over the face of an unclouded sun. (Canfield 1902, 36–37)

In the archaeological literature of the eclipse, then, the same two sources are repeatedly acknowledged but with little concern as to whether they derive from a stock of orally transmitted knowledge. Nothing further, for example, has been ascertained about the pedigree of the Fadden material, except to note that it may be derivative. That is to say, Fadden's eclipse could well have been inspired by the only other written reference to such a phenomenon. "Inasmuch as Canfield's book had been published for a half-century, and copies of such works inevitably reach Iroquois readers," Fenton observed, "quite possibly Canfield was the source" of the passage Fadden relayed to Wallace (1998, 71). Since no one has ever seen or heard of the manuscript material Canfield said he drew on, scholars have rated Canfield as a problematic voice of authentic tradition (Henige 1999; Vecsey 1988, 96).

What prevents Canfield from seeming traditional to me is the recognition that he was a practitioner of the genre of Victorian parlor literature described earlier. Recall that several writers of the time successfully pedaled anthologies of stories claimed to be Native American to a Euro-American audience. Their works typically combined authorial embroidery and fabrication to such an extent that, if there was any actual Native content, it has been rendered worthless for application in archaeological interpretation.

Canfield was of this ilk, and he actually informed his readers of imaginary content. The subtitle defines the stories as being "From Authoritative Notes and Studies"—by the author. Canfield admitted to writing a creative work, although his statement to that effect resists easy reading. "The perusal and study of these stories will, it is believed, give as much pleasure to the reader," Canfield explained, "as the study of the Indian character made necessary in order to clothe their almost forgotten legends with something like their original embellishment, has given the author" (1902, 11).

In sum, both sources of the eclipse incident are repeated in the archaeological literature without critical examination. Both seem murky as regards their traditional character. Recurring to the content of this chapter, let us recall that no one recounting any aspect of the Deganawida epic for 150 years—from Pyrlaeus to Gibson and Newhouse—referred to an eclipse. When added up, it becomes reasonable to observe that no one mentioned an eclipse because no one had heard of it. The eclipse incident is not appropriately applied archaeologically as authentic evidence from oral narrative.

The eclipse incident does, however, illustrate the difficulty of disentangling published material from what is presented—even if only implicitly—as orally transmitted knowledge. That is another reason why this chapter's survey of oral narrative traditions ends with Gibson and Newhouse around the turn of the twentieth century—that is, at the point the epic enters, for everyone, the realm of print.

Summary and Conclusions

There has always been a story about how the Iroquois League started, many say, a story furthermore that is substantially as known today

(Abler 2004, 481–82; Fenton 1998, 494; Richter 1987, 16; Tooker 1978, 422). While that may well be so, the assertion is not grounded in historical evidence. Prior to the mid-eighteenth century, no one mentioned anything about a narrative explaining the origin of the Iroquois League. That seems incredible and it presents, as Fenton noted, a major intellectual problem in Iroquoian studies (1998, 5). My approach to the problem has been, first, to take stock of what the facts are of the oral narrative and, second, to try to understand the facts better by relating mythic content to social context. Such research is potentially worthwhile because the Iroquois, like all human beings, adapted myth and tradition to fit living circumstances (Fenton 1998, 512).

The first plot of the League's inception to be documented indicated that the confederacy resulted from the efforts of a Mohawk leader named Deganawida. Told by Mohawks, the story seems appropriate to a setting in which Mohawks were loudly asserting their importance. Granting, of course, that the data are incomplete, the evidence that we do have suggests the League story could have been articulated at a time not far distant from the moment it attracted the attention of people who were curious and literate.

Late in the eighteenth century, the fire of the League was reignited in Canada by Onondaga guests of Mohawk hosts. Forging a legendary basis for the new League required that those two interests be expressed and reconciled. What resulted, as recorded by John Norton, was a plot that looks like two originally separate storylines—one Onondaga, the other Mohawk—were stitched together. The Onondaga tale introduces Hiawatha as an Onondaga chief who tries to promote union. After contesting the initiative with another Onondaga leader, the evil Thadodaho, a grief-stricken Hiawatha exits the Onondaga scene. His journey to the east narratively connects his story to the one known earlier, which featured the Mohawk Deganawida. The Mohawk plot was documented in New York in 1743. The Onondaga plot presumably traveled with Onondagas from New York to Canada in the late 1700s.

On the American side of the border during the early 1800s, we get a lawgiver at Onondaga—the original League hearth in New

York—who is variously named. Though highly diverse in three versions, the overarching plot was essentially Norton's Hiawatha story shorn of the Mohawk loop. By mid-century, the lawgiver was identified as the Hiawatha known earlier in Canada. Further, the story moved from legend to myth as the protagonist was deified. In the United States, Hiawatha was identified with the tribal god Sky-Holder.

The written description supplied by pioneer ethnologist Lewis Henry Morgan nullified the traditional descriptions of Deganawida and Hiawatha by altering their characteristics. Most importantly, Morgan reversed the main protagonists by assigning the characteristics of the Onondaga lawgiver, Hiawatha, to Deganawida.

Morgan's popular *League of the Ho-dé-no-sau-nee, Iroquois* introduced the Iroquois Confederacy to an English-speaking audience. Influencing many who came after, the book also initiated a textually focused approach to the League story, which often brought with it the assumption that what appeared on the printed page was truer than what one heard.

Non-Native and Native researchers alike privileged the written word and thought nothing of embroidering their texts with authorial invention. These tendencies culminated in three versions of the League story by the Grand River chronicler John Arthur Gibson.

All of Gibson's versions advocated the interpretation first set out in Morgan in which Deganawida replaced Hiawatha as both Onondaga lawgiver and leading actor throughout. Further, Gibson consistently highlighted the importance of a peace queen who had been introduced into the printed record a short time before. In addition, he emphasized the Christ-like character of his main actor. Gibson's 1900 version is especially important for understanding the history of the League story because this one was not only published—it was certified as true by the reservation's governing council.

Contemporary with Gibson, another Grand River chronicler was tapping into an older vein of League tradition. Seth Newhouse told the Norton story about Hiawatha, an Onondaga would-be lawgiver, who linked up with the Mohawk Deganawida. The two then went to Onondaga, New York, to promote confederacy by overcoming the hostility of the Onondaga Thadodaho. After many years, this tale still retained the quality of being two plots connected by the act of Hiawatha leaving Onondaga to go to Mohawk country.

If one reviews the reasons given in oral tradition for confederation, the idea is sometimes put forward that the Iroquois League was founded for survival, to unite as a defensive pact in the face of foreign threat (as in Webster, Clark, and Johnson). When, in Norton, an Onondaga story is added to the Mohawk tale, its message, at least implicitly, is: Do not avenge the murder of one of your own by killing another. In Brant, the reason for the League seems to be that a good brother seeks allies who will help him combat his evil sibling. In Cusick and Morgan, the League apparently responds to the problem of Iroquois tribes fighting one another. In later Canadian versions of the Norton tradition (Hale, Buck, Newhouse), the Iroquois League comes about to counter the tyranny of Thadodaho. Gibson, in contrast, proposes that a high god sends his son, conceived in a human virgin, to bring peace to a violent world in which individual warriors run amok murdering, scalping, and cannibalizing. Whatever the ethical or rhetorical merits of such a view may be, it stands without precedent in the recorded tellings of the tradition prior to about 1900. Historically, it is original.

The actual act of forming the Iroquois League, according to Pyrlaeus, came out of a meeting of delegates representing all five Iroquois tribes. In subsequent versions by Webster, Clark, and Hale, the League was instituted by an Onondaga lawgiver addressing an assembly of all the tribes (or their representatives) at Onondaga. Clark and Hale name the influential orator as Hiawatha. While Morgan changed Hiawatha to Deganawida, he also pictured the protagonist proposing union to a gathering of all at Onondaga. The later Grand River sources—Buck, Gibson, and Newhouse—all apparently followed Morgan in picturing Deganawida as the influential speaker laying down League principles to a convocation that included members of all the tribes.

However, in the hands of the late-period tellers, the incident of intertribal alliance was transformed into what is essentially an instruction manual for Iroquois League ritual. The recounting of legend in

Buck's version of 1888, in Gibson's of 1900, and in Newhouse's of about 1910 comprises only a quarter to a half of the total presentation. In all cases, what seems to more important than storyline is a "constitution," or set of bylaws. Emulating Euro-American written laws, each is a description of League protocol, which includes ceremonial instruction, transcribed speeches and songs, appropriate metaphors and symbols, and proper roles and rules of order. These later materials, Fenton found, "suffer from presentism, a tendency to project recent phenomena such as familiar ritual practice into the past, and it must be understood that these narratives were composed during periods of tension and social change. They are rationalizations for maintaining the system of life chiefs to confront movements for elected councilors of the Six Nations Reserve" (1998, 123, see also 81, 83, 98; see also Fenton 1949, 145). The purpose of recording League-related matters was to systematize and preserve them, yes, but also, when cast as the words of an ancient prophet, to invest them with the aura of traditional age and sacred authority. It is worth emphasizing that what was recorded in about 1900 and claimed then as ancient, does not, solely by virtue of that claim, constitute evidence for great age.

That is true, as well, of apparent founding dates for the Iroquois League provided in two of the accounts. One—that of Pyrlaeus, seems historical—the League "was formed one man's life ago, before the white people built Albany, or rather, were first seen there in that area" (Starna 2008, 285). Assuming, however, that a "lifetime ago" is estimated with reference to an individual living in 1743, then two times (a lifetime since and prior to Albany) are referenced in a passage otherwise known to be conflating two events. Choosing one date over the other as testimony for the time of the League's formation requires evidence from historical sources and, perhaps, a little special pleading for excluding the other. The second apparent dating of the League's establishment is that of Cusick: one thousand years before Columbus's arrival in the Americas in 1492. Obviously mythological or rhetorical in character, the estimate is a good reminder that legendary estimates of age are not objective statements of chronology. They should not be taken as historical fact without outside corroboration.

This chapter has been chiefly concerned with understanding the nature of the Deganawida epic. The epic, it turns out, is many different versions setting forth different details and emphases, not a few of which are mutually contradictory. The simple fact of multiple versions raises serious problems for the archaeologist wishing to apply the material to an archaeological context. "On what grounds," Ronald Mason asks, "does one choose to accept as factual one item in an oral tradition but reject another without falling into the trap of arbitrary selectivity?" (2006, 142).

My answer is to consider the age of the various accounts. The oldest documented strain of Iroquois League tradition describes an Onondaga lawgiver traveling east to pair up with a Mohawk leader. Together, they overcome an evil Onondaga shaman and, thereafter, initiate tribal union. Archaeologists projecting oral narrative into the past should favor the older material as being closer in time to the phenomena being interpreted. In what follows, we will recur to apparent historicity and veracity in the oral narrative with respect to the archaeological record.

2

An Interaction Sphere
of Pipes in Eastern Iroquoia,
Late 1400s to Early 1500s

Anthony Wonderley

Settlement pattern has afforded, to date, the best archaeological evidence for tribal formation. Populations seem to consolidate and fuse into a large village or village cluster to form, as we suppose, a tribe. In Ontario, further settlement consolidation hints at the coming together of tribes uniting to form a confederacy (Birch 2012; Dermarkar et al. 2016, 87; Snow 2001, 22; Tuck 1978, 329). In New York, on the other hand, apparent tribal clusters form, then remain roughly fifty miles apart (Engelbrecht 1985, 164–67; Trigger 1981, 14). Since multitribal alliances among those entities seem not to register spatially, we cannot argue for the existence of the League of the Iroquois from the drawing together of residential remains attributed to the Mohawks, Oneidas, Onondagas, Cayugas, and Senecas.

What about the Iroquois League's formation might register materially and survive in the archaeological record? "The most robust evidence for interaction is invariably examined in the ritual sphere," Susan Jamieson reminds us, because "ritual is used to symbolize, simplify, and enhance political messages"—to build political organizations and to create political legitimacy (1999, 177). One material correlate of political activity in the more distant past might therefore be smoking pipes: ritualistic artifacts of imperishable material, some of which were

embellished with material symbols pertaining to intergroup cooperation (Drooker 1997, 57).

The distribution of such pipes broadly reflects members of different communities interacting politically and socially, a milieu of
peaceful communication and diplomacy. Archaeologically, it is an
"interaction sphere" in which the sharing among several communities of distinctive material culture is thought to result from episodes
of a particular kind of behavior (Caldwell 1964; Hall 1997, 155). Since
recurrent, pipe-smoking diplomacy may amount to alliance-forming,
this could be the evidence for political union ancestral or antecedent
to the Iroquois League—in effect, the earliest stage of the League.

Before developing that interpretation, I describe the Iroquois'
world of confederacies, what those social formations were designed
to do, why they came about at a particular juncture in time and place,
and how all of that might relate to pipe smoking.

Contentious Confederacies

European newcomers encountered ethnic confederacies of Native
peoples throughout much of the present-day eastern United States
and Canada. "Villages, bands, and tribes speaking similar languages,
holding similar customs, and sharing a tradition of common origin
usually combined into a loose union that at least minimized warfare
among themselves," Anthony Wallace observed. "The Illinois Confederacy, the 'Three Fires' of the Chippewa, Ottawa, and Potawatomi,
the Wapenaki Confederacy, the Powhatan Confederates, the tripartite
Miami—all the neighbors of the Iroquois were members of some confederation or other" (1972, 42).

The best-known of these confederacies was, of course, the League
of the Iroquois (or Haudenosaunee), with a population of perhaps
twenty thousand. In the early 1600s, it shared its stage with other ethnic coalitions of Iroquoian-speaking tribes, the largest and best documented being the Huron (or Wendat) and Neutral Confederacies (see
map 1). Situated on the eastern shore of Lake Huron's Georgian Bay,
the Huron comprised four or five tribes with roughly twenty thousand

people living in twenty-five villages. The Neutrals, located in south-western Ontario west of the Niagara River, were a coalition of at least six tribes and perhaps ten thousand people in forty villages (Fenton 1998, 21; Finlayson 1998, 26; Trigger 2000, 31–32, 94–96; Warrick 2008, 208).

Very likely there were other tribal coalitions, among them the Petun or Tobacco Nation (Tionontaté), possibly an alliance of two groups living southwest of the Hurons (Garrad 2014, 16, 26; Garrad and Heidenreich 1978; Warrick 2008, 11), and the Eries, probably a coalition of two or more tribes in western New York (Trigger 2000, 96; White 1978a, 412). The Susquehannocks of the Susquehanna River drainage in Pennsylvania may have been a tribal alliance, and the Monongahela people of southwest Pennsylvania could have been another Iroquoian-speaking union of several tribes (Grumet 1995, 306; Tremblay 2006, 16; Johnson 2001, 82). Hence, the landscape of the Iroquois League was composed of a number of intertribal coalitions, mostly formed by fellow Iroquoian speakers.

Historically, these confederacies often fought one another, partly for cultural reasons. War, for the Iroquois, Father Joseph François Lafitau observed, is their most indispensable custom and outstanding passion. Their elders, he added, are "very glad to see their young people exercising and enjoying themselves in the warlike spirit" (Fenton and Moore 1977, 98–99, 101). The other side of the coin was, as Louis Hennepin put it, that "those amongst the *Iroquoise* who are not given to war, are held in great contempt, and pass for lazy and effeminate people" (quoted in Richter 1992, 36). Young men were ambitious to begin fighting because war defined and validated manhood. War offered the clearest path to glory, honor, and prestige (Trigger 2000, 51, 105, 143; A. Wallace 1972, 30–33). To the individual Iroquois male, war was the central fact of life, which "locked the participant in a career from which the exits were capture, torture, and death or graduation to the status of old men, the ancients" (Fenton 1998, 220). Since men were expected to fight, warfare was an ineluctable feature of Iroquois life throughout the seventeenth and eighteenth centuries.

The justification for fighting most frequently given was, as the Huron affirmed, to avenge injustices done to them (Trigger 2000, 68). Similarly, the Iroquois fought "to revenge the affronts they had at anytime received from their neighbors" (Colden 1988, 20–21). The Iroquois felt, according to one observer, "the absolute necessity of avenging themselves upon those by whom they believe themselves to have been offended" (Brandão 2003, 67). The attitude is vividly illustrated by Seneca reaction, in 1647, to having one of their numbers killed by members of the Petun Nation in a village of the Neutral Confederacy (Garrad 2014, 249). Holding the Neutrals to blame, the reported Seneca response was to destroy the place where the crime had occurred:

> These Aondironnons are a tribe of the Neutral Nation who are nearest to our Hurons. Not being at war with the [Senecas], they had received them in their villages as friends, and had prepared food for them in all their cabins, among which the [Senecas] purposely divided themselves, the more easily to strike their blow. Their stratagem was successful, for they massacred or seized all who might have resisted, before the latter could perceive their evil design, because they all commenced the massacre at the same moment. (Thwaites 1896–1901, 33:81–83)

The Iroquois fought to right a wrong done them, to punish a perceived slight, or to repay an insult—anything, in fact, interpretable as a challenge to their sense of honor. The ideal Iroquois man was "a stern and ruthless warrior" bent on "avenging any wrong done to those under his care" (A. Wallace 1972, 30–31). Acting on such values made low-level warfare an endemic feature of life (Trigger 2000, 416).

This cultural logic dictated the necessity of punishing those regarded as guilty and dispatching one's young men to commit violence against the offenders. That, in turn, caused continuous intergroup feuding in which the participants sought to redress a current injury or to avenge an earlier loss by killing or capturing a person from an enemy group. The result was chronic hostility. In these conditions communities were forced to cooperate for mutual defense by developing alliances (Trigger 2000, 244, 416). Once established, a defensive coalition necessarily channeled the energies of its aggressive males outward (A. Wallace 1972, 46). That meant, according to Bruce Trigger, that "a successful coalition left neighboring communities at a disadvantage, unless they too merged to consolidate themselves into larger groupings" (2000, 158). Confederacies, therefore, were contemporaneous rivals who competitively challenged each other into existence. They were not born alone, suddenly, or in isolation. Since they did not happen one at a time, the origin and development of any one of them is likely to be bound up in the context of a rapidly developing whole.

Formulated most persuasively by Trigger (2000, 158–65), the analytic focus on competing leagues has been employed in several scenarios attempting to clarify how the League of the Iroquois came into being (Bradley 1987, 104–6; Engelbrecht 2003, 144; Graymont 1988, 45–46; Sempowski and Saunders 2001, 709; Snow 2001, 22–23; Tuck 1971b, 222). As a model, the idea of contentious and contemporaneous confederacies is simple and crude in its avoidance of demographic, economic, and environmental variables. Obviously, the construct is not meant to tackle deeper causal factors such as exogenous influence or resource competition (Hasenstab 1987; Gramly 1977). Instead, the notion of contentious confederacies assigns cause to culturally mandated behavior, which, admittedly, is subject to charges of ethnocentric bias. In its defense, the model is historically informed. In our defense, we try to be self-critical enough to keep evidence from the past separate from moralistic judgment and presentist projection.

More positively, the paradigm encourages interpretive thinking on a level of process higher than the single example and, in doing so, directs our attention to confederation as a regional phenomenon with important temporal implications. Where we find one confederation, we are likely to find another at about the same time and then, shortly after, more. Trigger proposed that the Huron Confederacy originated in the union of two tribes in the mid-fifteenth century (2000, 163; see also Birch and Hart 2017, 17–18; Finlayson 1998, 8; Warrick 2008, 11, 192). Suspecting something similar in the New York case would give us a general time frame to look for corresponding alliance behavior.

In fact, a search for beginnings has been expedited by a rounding up of the usual suspects. "It is probable that the Onondaga, Oneida, and Mohawk concluded an early alliance," according to William Engelbrecht. "From both an archaeological and linguistic perspective there are many similarities between the Onondaga, Oneida, and Mohawk on the one hand and the Cayuga and Seneca on the other" (2003, 130). The first Iroquois reference to what I would call League history occurred in 1689 when League spokesmen stated that, many years before, the Mohawks, Oneidas, and Onondagas had welcomed the Dutch and, apparently later, drew the Senecas and Cayugas "into the General Covenant" (O'Callaghan 1853–87, 1:79–80; Parmenter 2010, 23–24).

Peace Pipes

Iroquoian smoking habits first came to European attention in the person of Jacques Cartier who, in the 1530s, noted wonderingly:

> They have a plant, of which a large supply is collected in summer for the winter's consumption. They hold it in high esteem, though the men alone make use of it in the following manner. After drying it in the sun, they carry it about their necks in a small skin pouch in lieu of a bag, together with a hollow bit of stone or wood. Then at frequent intervals they crumble this plant into powder, which they place in one of the openings of the hollow instrument, and laying a live coal on top, suck at the other end to such an extent that they fill their bodies so full of smoke that it streams out of their mouths and nostrils as from a chimney. They say it keeps them warm and in good health, and never go about without these things. (Tremblay 2006, 67)

Later documentary evidence from Iroquoian peoples reinforces the impression that men were the primary owners and users of smoking pipes (Biggar 1993, 69; Kuhn 1985, 58–67). Over and over again, men are described smoking pipes as a leisure or recreational activity, passing the time puffing away "through pleasure and habit" (Fenton and Moore 1977, 86). This form of relaxation was so pervasive that reference to it served as metaphor for the good life. "We should have nothing to do," one Oneida said wistfully. "but sit in our doors and smoke our pipes in peace" (Cantine and DeWitt ca. 1793, 123–24).

What is probably Native testimony on the subject of smoking concerns effigy pipes—that is, pipes bearing naturalistic images of apparent humans, birds, mammals, reptiles, and other subjects. Such representations were created on the bowl facing the smoker to provide food for thought. Thus, Hurons were said to render pictures of various subjects on their pipes because they enjoyed looking at them (Wrong 1939, 98). "They say good thoughts come whilst smoking," René-Robert Cavelier de La Salle observed in 1669 (Beauchamp 1907, 427). It appears that smoking—presumably and especially with an effigy pipe—was regarded as "a mental device used by the smoker to concentrate his thoughts" (Brasser 1980, 96).

Gregory Vincent Braun (2015) proposed that unembellished pipes precipitated memories pertaining to cosmology, identity, and ritual. If so, those offering imagery (effigies) surely expedited ratiocination, and many have wondered what smokers of such pictorial implements were thinking about. Effigy pipes, it has been suggested, may have commemorated historical incidents worth pondering, offered realistic portraiture for viewing pleasure, or alluded to life-crisis events worth recalling (Kapches 2003; Kearsley 1997, 115–25). Pipes bearing likenesses of human faces possibly represented masks covering faces (Ritchie and Funk 1973, 367). Those showing animals may have called seasonality to mind or reminded the smoker of clan affiliations (Kinsey 1989; Noble 1979). It seems likely that some effigy pipes reflected ideas about the supernatural or shamanistic practices that could have included healing and divination (Brasser 1980, 100; Garrad 2014, 326; Hamell 1998, 272; Mathews 1976; Sempowski 2004b; von Gernet 1992). The documentary record, however, is silent on the subject of specific ratiocination.

What the written evidence indicates is that pipe smoking was a persistent theme of Iroquoian political life. Smoking was what one did to receive foreign visitors and to assure them of peaceful intent. When Hurons "wished to entertain someone and demonstrate their friendship for him, they presented him with a lighted pipe after having smoked it themselves" (Tooker 1991, 57). Visitors to an Iroquois village were met by an elderly "word-bearer" who, "after lighting his pipe . . . tells them very eloquently that they are very welcome" (Fenton and Moore 1977, 174). Smoking was a prominent feature of receiving ambassadors at the rite of welcoming at the wood's edge. When a foreign embassy arrived near an Iroquois League village during the 1670s, "a fire is lighted, as a sign of peace, at the spot where the elders of the village are going to wait for them; and, after smoking for some time and receiving the savage compliments that they pay one another, they are led to the cabin set apart for them" (Thwaites 1896–1901, 58:187–89).

Smoking was what one did while discussing political matters. "They [Hurons, 1636] never attend a council without a pipe or calumet in their mouths. The smoke, they say, gives them intelligence, and enables them to see clearly through the most intricate matters" (Thwaites 1896–1901, 10:219). Iroquois men entering the council setting (1669) would "seat themselves . . . and at once get some fire to light their pipes, which do not leave their mouths during the whole time of the council" (Fenton 1998, 22). When a man rose to speak at a League meeting, "all the rest sat in profound silence, smoking their pipes" (Beauchamp 1907, 429). The basic Iroquois council was defined, about 1720, as a group of men, all of whom have pipes in their mouths (Fenton and Moore 1974, 296). "From earliest times Iroquois chiefs have affected the pipe, and 'to smoke together' is almost synonymous with 'holding council'" (Fenton 1991, 155).

More generally, smoking together was a figure of speech connoting peaceful interchange. Leaders of the Five Nations assured potential enemies (1645) that "Iroquois chiefs only smoke [meaning, hold council] in their country, that their calumets [pipes] are always in their mouths" (Fenton 1985, 130). "We will take your pipe" the Iroquois told Catawba ambassadors in 1751, and "sit and smoke, and think of you and not fight" (Druke 1981, 213). "We meet to smoke our pipes together"; "we bring our pipes together to enter into conversation"; "we come together with our pipes in peace"—such phrases were the staple of Iroquois diplomatic language (Hough 1861, 102, 106, 196, 235).

Accompanying the exchange of words was an exchange of objects, including pipes. For example, Cherokee peace delegates presented a pipe to the Iroquois League in 1759 saying, "Light the pipe whenever you meet upon public affairs, and don't let any people that carry false and trifling reports smoke out of it" (Fenton 1991, 169). East Coast Indians requesting Oneida help in 1774 gave the Oneidas a pipe, "so at your assemblings ye might look on it; and smoke out of it, and remember us" (McCallum 1932, 165). In 1784 negotiations with the state of New York, Oneidas said as "testimony of our approbation of your rekindling this council fire, we present you with this pipe of peace, there to remain as a token of peace from us, agreeable to the custom of our ancestors" (Hough 1861, 53).

Hence, some pipes are material correlates of male political action and diplomatic protocol. Certain pipes—presumably the most distinctive ones—surely functioned "in ritual contexts involving men, perhaps in the negotiation or mediation of power relationships" (Ramsden 1990b, 94). Distributed interregionally, such pipes probably signal peaceful sociopolitical relations (Finlayson 1998, 410; Kuhn 1985, 106–7; see also Drooker 2004, 73).

As male objects of diplomacy, pipes furnish what may be the best evidence for dating the Five Nations Confederacy. That union, from an archaeological perspective, can be regarded as an alliance grounded in collective, ceremonial pipe smoking and in the exchange of pipes as gifts (Kuhn and Sempowski 2001). Therefore, the appearance of Mohawk pipes in the Seneca region in about 1600, concurrent with a substantial increase in Seneca use of pipes, probably indicates the entry of the Senecas into the Iroquois League (see chapter 6; see also Engelbrecht 2003, 133; Sempowski and Saunders 2001, 700).

Pipe Types

The dominant form of pipe throughout the Northeast during the 1400s–1500s was an elbow-shaped object (about six inches long) of fired clay (Rafferty and Mann 2004, xii). Its conical or trumpet-shaped bowl held a small amount of tobacco (*Nicotiana rustica*) more powerful than the kind familiar today. The pipes were small. They look as though they were used individually, not as calumets or peace pipes, meant to be passed around and shared. What is seen archaeologically is confirmed in the documentary record. "There are few instances of circuitous pipe passing in Iroquois rituals," William Fenton found. "The early sources speak of individual chiefs sitting in council, each smoking his own pipe incessantly." Iroquois pipe smoking has always been individualistic (1991, 111, 176–77). In archaeological collections, a minority (less than 25 percent) carried effigies.

The focus here is on three types of effigy pipe of an especially notable character that were present in the regions historically identifiable with the Mohawk, Oneida, and Onondaga tribes. However, they were even more present—if one may say such a thing—in an archaeological region north of the eastern Iroquois. Village remains of those called by archaeologists St. Lawrence Iroquoians extend eastward from the Lake Ontario shores of New York along the St. Lawrence River to well beyond the city of Québec (map 2).

Material remains of the St. Lawrence Iroquoians comprise an archaeological culture area with its own characteristics that set it apart from other Iroquoian societies in New York and Ontario. At least some St. Lawrence Iroquoians spoke Iroquoian languages (Lounsbury 1978). Archaeologists recognize as many as nine more-or-less distinct subregions within the St. Lawrence Iroquoian region (Engelbrecht and Jamieson 2016a, 82; Jamieson 1990a; Pendergast 1991b; Tremblay 2006, 112–13).

Present-day Jefferson County was, archaeologically, the westernmost subregion of the St. Lawrence Iroquoian zone. Containing the remains of at least fifty-five villages, it boasts one of the densest concentrations of sites anywhere in Iroquoia (Engelbrecht 1995, 37). It is also the subregion best known for its effigy pipes. Nowhere else, in Alanson Skinner's estimation, did "effigy pipes attain such a high degree of development" (1921, 118; see also Ritchie 1980, 320).

All three of the pipes examined here—figure-in-arch, figure-in-crescent, and Dougherty—share the highly distinctive feature of anthropomorphic imagery incised on what looks like a signboard

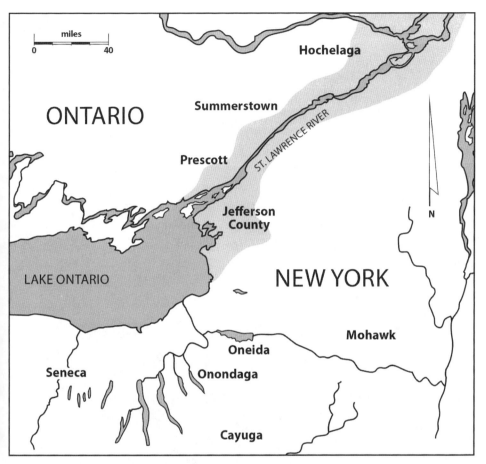

Map 2. Region of the League of the Iroquois and of the St. Lawrence Iroquoians (Wonderley 2009, map 3).

facing the smoker. All appear to have been in contemporaneous use during the late fifteenth century.[1]

The design of the first pipe comprises a human-like face or figure within an arch (fig. 1). Typically, two or more incised lines radiate

1. In addition to the estimates of age given in the text, an example of the figure-in-crescent, is known from Roebuck, just northeast of Jefferson County (Grenville, Ontario) in the St. Lawrence Iroquoian Prescott cluster of sites dated to approximately 1450 (Tremblay 2006, 71; Canadian Museum of Civilization 1998).

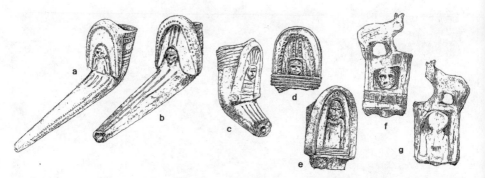

1. Figure-in-arch ceramic pipes (a–e) and object of carved bone (f–g), front and back views (Wonderley 2009, fig. 1). The artifacts are from the Mohawk (a), Oneida (b–c, f–g), and Onondaga (d) areas, and from Jefferson County (c).

outward and upward from the head to the interior apex of the arch. Provenience information exists for nineteen examples of the figure-in-arch (Wonderley 2005a). Eight derive from Jefferson County, four are from the Mohawk Valley, three from Oneida country, and two from the Onondaga area. Two other pipes were found in widely separated locations elsewhere in upstate New York.

The design of the second pipe features a moon-like image that may be unembellished, notched with incised decoration, or equipped with horseshoe-like markings (fig. 2). A human-like face appears within the crescent although multiple faces and one quadruped are also known. Usually the face is shown not so much on the flat surface enclosed by the crescent as on the edge of the signboard-like plane where the crescent is open. I will return to this point. Of thirteen figure-in-crescent pipes from known provenience, nine are from Jefferson County, one is from the Mohawk area, two are from the Onondaga region, and the last is from a St. Lawrence Iroquoian context north of Jefferson County.

The complicated design of the third type of pipe, the Dougherty (fig. 3), comprises four registers: (1) At the top is a row of three to four human-like faces with ray- or fanlike elements flaring up and outward; (2) The heads rest on a platform, whose ends rise to frame the heads on each side. It looks like a bracket or a squarish letter *c* on its back; (3) Below that are two circular depressions, usually relatively large and

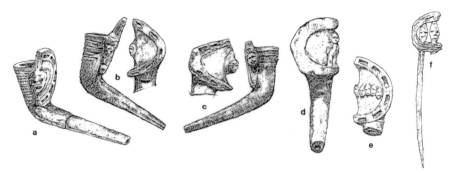

2. Figure-in-crescent ceramic pipes (a–e) and carved antler comb (f) (Wonderley 2009, fig. 2). These are from Jefferson County and the greater St. Lawrence Iroquoian area (a–e) and the Mohawk Valley (f).

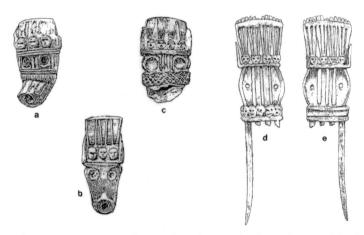

3. Dougherty pipes (a–c) and carved antler comb (d–e), front and back views (Wonderley 2004, fig. 20). Pictured are objects from northern Pennsylvania, carved from stone (a), the Mohawk Valley (d–e), and the Oneida (c) and Onondaga (b) areas.

separated by vertical lines or strips; (4) Finally there is a zone of geometric incision of simple lines or cross-hatching which, in the case of the comb, includes another row of heads lacking the ray-like element noted earlier. Not all the registers need be present—a phenomenon reminiscent of the metaphorical process called synecdoche, a figure of speech in which a part makes reference to the whole. However,

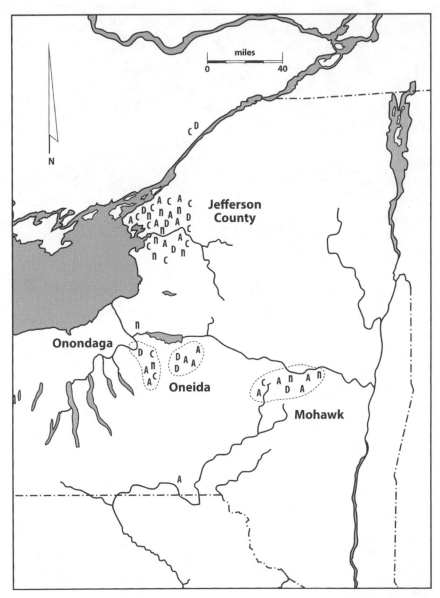

Map 3. Composite distribution of effigy pipes in eastern New York and adjacent Canada. *A* = figure-in-arch (*n* = version in stone); *C* = figure-in-crescent; *D* = Dougherty (Wonderley 2009, map 4).

whatever registers are present must, apparently, adhere to that relative order, implying that the overall sequence is essential to the meaning.

Of the nine known ceramic examples of the Dougherty pipe, four derive from Jefferson County, two from Oneida sites, one each from the Mohawk and Onondaga areas, and one other St. Lawrence Iroquoian location not in Jefferson County.

All three pipe forms, then, cluster in Jefferson County (twenty-one examples) but also show up in the lands of the Mohawk (six), Oneida (five), and Onondaga (five) tribes of the Iroquois as historically known (map 3). I find the designs on all of them haunting. Clearly, they are material symbols—that is, "tangible formulations of notions, abstractions from experience fixed in perceptible form" (Geertz 1973, 91).

Pipe Meaning

These three effigy types present an unusually rich corpus of representational imagery. They rank among the most complex material symbols in Northeast archaeology and, in the Dougherty, include the single most elaborate Iroquoian visual composition I have seen. All feature images of symbolic import presumably understood in each of their settings. What did they mean?

Long intrigued by these artifacts, archaeologists have offered a creative range of interpretations to account for at least the first two pipe types. The figure-in-arch design, it has been speculated, might depict the niche of a saint, a boat, a longhouse, or the Sky Dome motif (Beauchamp 1898, 124; Hamell 1979, fig. 7; Mathews 1982, 47–48). Dean Snow referred to the composition as "hooded human" (1995b, 155). Richard Hosbach (1992) suggested it was an eastern Iroquois image representing a scene of birth, one possibly connected to the formation of the Iroquois Confederacy. In the case of the figure-in-crescent, the arc-like element has been identified as a headdress—or, more commonly, a crescent moon (Beauchamp 1898, 134; Mathews 1982, 48; Parker 1920, 1:152).

My inquiry into meaning is the poor person's iconography, a commonsense formal analysis based on the similarity of, especially, the first two pipe types. In both the figure-in-arch and the figure-in-crescent a human-like face or figure is at least partially enclosed by a framing device, the whole being presented to the eye on a specially constructed surface. If the pipes resemble one another, they may have been fashioned to convey something similar. A promising entrée into an otherwise closed system of meaning is that face within the crescent shown as leaving the surface of the composition. This unusual convention requires the viewer to take notice of a head exiting the composition (fig. 2a–c). The head appears to be coming out; it is emerging into our world.

Depictions of coming out may illustrate an old Iroquoian belief about human origins—people emerged from the earth. Prior to the early 1800s, the Iroquois did not attribute the appearance of humans to a divinity's creative act (Wonderley 2001). On the contrary, "when asked concerning their origin, they regularly answer, that they came up out of the ground, in the regions where they now live" (Dwight 1822, 203; see also Klinck and Talman 1970, 85, 110). Thus, Hurons and Wyandots long remembered that their forefathers "first came out of the ground" near Québec (Hale 1894, 6; see also Garrad 2014, 118–21). Mohawks said that after dwelling in the earth, they "concluded it best for them all to come out" (Heckewelder 1991, 251; Andrews 1716, 243). The Onondagas believed they emerged from the hills of Onondaga, New York, or came out of the ground on the banks of the Oswego River (Bradley 2001, 30; Morgan 1962, 7). The corresponding Seneca tradition of the late 1700s was that "they broke out of the earth from a large mountain" near Canandaigua (Seaver 1990, 142). An Oneida creation account of the late 1700s states those people "came up out of the ground in human form" and "used to show the precise spot of ground, a small hollow, where they said their ancestors came up" (Lounsbury and Gick 2000, 161).

That is why an Iroquois speaker at the Lancaster Treaty in 1744 said: "You came out of the ground in a country that lies beyond the seas; there you may have a just claim, but here you must allow us to be your elder brethren, and the land to belong to us" (Jennings 1984, 357). This, Bronislaw Malinowski observed (1948, 116), is the literal claim of being autochthonous and owning the land for that reason. The myth of emergence is fairly common in North America (Rooth 1957; Wheeler-Vogelin and Moore 1957), especially among horticulturalists staking claim to their territory (Bernouw 1977, 57, 92; Lankford 1987, 136–39). Coming out of the earth is an origin myth telling how some things started and came to be as they are now. It ranks among a culture's key narratives for it accounts for and, at the same time, is an important expression of community identity (see Urton 1990, 39).

If coming out of the ground is what the figure-in-crescent illustrates, the figure-in-arch may show the same thing from a different perspective. What looks like a carved bone version of the figure-in-arch (fig. 1f) makes this seem likely because its figure appears to be inside a cave or hill. I am not aware that the depiction of the same subject from different angles has been reported as a feature of Iroquoian representationalism, but it would not be surprising. The convention was employed elsewhere in native North American art (Lankford 2007, 10, 29).

The Dougherty Pipe

Is the more elaborate Dougherty pipe interpretable in the same frame of reference as a theme of emergence? Perhaps. The composition of the Dougherty is a complex rendering suggestive of an *imago mundi*, or mythic cosmogony. Its ordered sequence of imagery calls to mind the developmental, linear syntax necessary to narrative. Because the incidents of a story are temporally related—one preceding and being the precondition of the next—a tale has to be presented in a certain sequence, not unlike this composition. It would not be surprising if this pipe imagery had a narrative referent, perhaps relating to a story performed, told, or contemplated. This looks like a myth of substantial ideological/religious importance, a story lost to us today.

I know of no surviving myth offering a simple register-by-register reading of this visual object. But I can suggest a partial and speculative reading on the assumption that the hierarchically arranged space of the composition relates, at least in part, to a depiction of space on a vertical axis. This pipe reminds me of a famous Iroquois folktale in which a monster swallows a village.

The first documented Seneca account of emergence (cited earlier) was told in conjunction with a story about a huge snake. "They originated and lived on a well-known hill . . . where they were put in eminent peril of utter destruction by a monstrous serpent, which circled itself about the fort and lay with its mouth open at the gate" (Schoolcraft 1975, 60). Confounded by its noxious breath, the villagers fled to their doom through the gate and into the serpent's open maw. Finally slain by a young survivor with a magical weapon, the snake rolled downhill, discharging human heads as it tumbled into a lake. The conclusion to this curious tale is that the Indians gathered at this "sacred place, to mourn the loss of their friends, and to celebrate some rites that are peculiar to themselves" (Seaver 1990, 143; see chapter 3).

There seem to be two separate stories here: emerging-from-the-earth and the snake-that-swallowed-a-village. Though they are linked in the telling, their only apparent connection is that they occurred in the same place. Yet one would suspect a closer relationship in content on the basis of comparative mythology. Elsewhere, snakes play a prominent role in accounting for ancestral and tribal beginnings; so much so that "it is impossible to overstate the importance of the association of the serpent with human origins" (Drummond 1981, 658).

Recorded mostly in Seneca country but also known on the Six Nations Reserve in Canada, the snake-that-swallowed-a-village story was one of the most popular Iroquois narratives on any subject during the nineteenth and early twentieth centuries (Beauchamp 1892, 20–21; Hewitt 1918, 106, 420–21; Waugh n.d.; E. Cook 202n24). The story also is notable for the attention it has drawn from non-Native analysts, who see in it an allegory about the formation of the Seneca tribe (see chapter 3) or of the League of the Iroquois (Hamell 1979, fig. 17; Schoolcraft 1975, 61).

For Marius Barbeau (1951, 85; 1952, 116), the act of entering the serpent's mouth as described in the narrative signifies dying and being buried in the ground. Hence, the snake is the earth. On the basis of ethnographic testimony, Barbeau claimed that the snake-that-swallowed-a-village story was the origin myth of the Ohgi:we ceremony—an annual or semiannual feast held to placate spirits of a community's dead. While that specific assertion has never been confirmed, other ethnographers concede that Ohgi:we implies some invocation of chthonic powers and seems to be of great antiquity (Fenton and Kurath 1951). The dance patterns of Ohgi:we, suggestive of coiling and uncoiling, "may echo a half-forgotten myth about an all-devouring earth-serpent" (Kurath 1952, 129).

Attributable to the late 1700s, the snake-that-swallowed-a-village tale also happens to be one of the oldest stories documented. Indeed, its presence among the Oklahoma Wyandots (Barbeau 1915, 146–48), descendants of Huron and Petun people, implies an age at least a century and a half older. The reasoning here is homologous to identifying languages that are genetically related. Wyandot and Iroquois folklore similarities are so detailed and pervasive that they are unlikely to be related to chance, independent development, or recent borrowing from each other. In all probability, they are cognate beliefs derived from a stock of oral tradition held in common by early seventeenth-century ancestors of Iroquois and Wyandots (Wonderley 2004, 104–7).

Because it is a story of such extraordinary age and interest, we should consider the possibility that the snake-that-swallowed-a-village is referenced on the Dougherty pipe. By this reading, the two prominent circles of the third register would be the serpent's eyes, with the lowest register corresponding to a body filled with the skulls of swallowed people, as shown on the comb example in figure 2d–e. This seems plausible to me because *snake*, *death*, and *beneath the surface* are documented as conceptually related terms among early seventeenth-century Iroquoians. The Hurons believed "there is a kind of monstrous serpent which they call *Angont*, which brings with it disease, death and almost every misfortune in the world. They say that that monster lives in subterranean places, in caverns, under a rock, in the woods, or in the mountains, but generally in the lakes and rivers" (Thwaites 1896–1901, 33:217).

On the Dougherty pipe, the theme of emergence presumably occurs on the top register in the form of several human faces resting on the square-shaped bracket element. In the aforementioned early versions of the Iroquois League tradition, the chief personified the settlement/tribe in such a way that leader and people were metaphorically synonymous. Each head may stand for a community or a community's mythological beginning. This depiction of emergence then, would link the three to four communities together by ascribing to them a common origin.

By the same reasoning, the Dougherty pipe provides visual evidence that the emergence-from-the-earth and the snake-that-swallowed-a-village tales were closely related as components of the same story. Now the theme of emergence becomes a more encompassing narrative alluding to death as well as birth. The Dougherty pipe seems to combine the narrative strands we know vaguely as being about earth/emergence/birth with serpent/burial/death.

Tribal Context

All three pipe forms, in sum, cluster in Jefferson County but also show up in the lands of the Mohawk, Oneida, and Onondaga tribes of the Iroquois as historically known. All feature images of symbolic import very possibly referring to ideas of emergence and beginning.

Most of these pipes are assigned nothing but the most general provenience in museum records. Here I look more closely at the few pipes attributable to specific sites in order to place the subject into better temporal and sociological context. It turns out that the earliest known occurrences tend to fall at the beginning of a regional sequence, or at that part of an area's prehistory hypothesized as being the place and time of tribal formation.

Researchers have resolved the welter of Jefferson County sites into four clusters, each believed to represent a discrete community moving to different locations over the course of many years (Abel 2001). What appears to be the earliest is Rutland Hollow, characterized by a high frequency of effigy pipes with escutcheon designs (Abel 2002,

168–69). *Escutcheon* usually means an image incised on a signboard facing the smoker. In the case of the Rutland Hollow cluster, two kinds of escutcheon with anthropomorphic depictions are associated with specific sites. A figure-in-arch pipe comes from Camp Drum no. 1 estimated as dating between the mid-1400s and early 1500s (Abel 2016, 73; Kuhn 1994, 78). Examples of the Dougherty type are known from the Putnam and Stewart sites (Wonderley 2005a).

South of Jefferson County, a continuous sequence of sites attributable to the historically known Oneidas begins with Nichols Pond, a three-acre, palisaded site south of present-day Canastota, New York. Its date (ca. 1450–75) is an informed estimate from the dean of Oneida archaeology, Peter Pratt (1976, 107, 148; Pratt and Pratt 1986, 12; Weiskotten 1995). What came before? The mystery of Oneida beginnings is that, unlike the situation documented among the Mohawks to the east and the Onondagas to the west, no horticultural villages are known with certainty in the Oneida residential heartland prior to Nichols Pond (Wonderley 2006, 1–2). By virtue of absence, Nichols Pond and its approximate contemporary, the Dougherty site, are the only candidates one can nominate for the honor of birthplace of the Oneida tribe. Attributable to Nichols Pond and Dougherty are the Dougherty pipe (fig. 3c), and the figure-in-arch composition on a pipe (Dougherty, fig. 1c) and carved in bone (Nichols Pond, fig. 1f).

In the east, "a clear Mohawk nationality emerged," according to Snow, as previously independent communities began to merge in new, defendable locations during the fifteenth century. The outstanding example of the process was the hilltop site of Otstungo, 1.9 acres in extent and protected by both palisade and earthworks (1995b, 91, 115). A figure-in-arch pipe and the figure-in-crescent design on a bone artifact came from that late fifteenth- to early sixteenth-century site (1995b, 119–20).[2]

2. Snow believes that Otstungo was occupied at about 1450 and abandoned around 1525 (1995, 115). Kuhn's dating estimate of the site is 1500–1525 (2004, 150). Here I emphasize Snow's placement of Otstungo as squarely within Snow's Chance phase (1400–1525).

In the west, Onondaga as a tribe or nation came into being when two previously separate communities located themselves next to one another in about 1400–1450 according to James Tuck (1978, 326–27). In the Burke and Schoff archaeological sites, "a symbolic alliance between two communities was probably consummated for reasons of mutual defense," Tuck thought. "This can be interpreted as the founding of the Onondaga Nation" (1971b, 215).[3] James Bradley thought the process was less clearly indicated in the archaeological record. Nevertheless, he agreed with Tuck that tribal coalescence was a fact at the end of the Chance phase, which Bradley dated to the late fifteenth century. That would mean, in Bradley's site sequence, Burke again, a palisaded site, two to four acres in extent. From Burke, the last and largest of the Chance phase villages, came a figure-in-crescent pipe (1987, 26, 34, 45; 2001, 27–28, 30, 211n22).

These data strengthen the ballpark notion of late fifteenth- to very early sixteenth-century dating for the pipes in question. In southern Ontario, where settlement pattern has been intensively studied, the late fifteenth century witnessed, probably as a result of violence, the amalgamation of a number of small villages into a few large, palisaded settlements (Birch 2012). We would suspect that to be the archaeological footprint of tribal crystallization (see the introduction). Comparatively speaking, however, the New York evidence for the phenomenon is not as good. Of the four locations associated with the pipes, two have been interpreted as the birth and capital locations for historically known tribes. All four might have been—plausibly could have been—the locations of emergent tribes.

---

3. Tuck saw the process of village amalgamation and increasing propinquity as leading ineluctably to a state of increased peaceful communication and, therefore, after tribal formation to the intertribal alliance of the Iroquois League. Originally, he guessed that occurred during the Garoga phase, presumably meaning the 1500s (1971, 140). Later, Tuck implied that the League-beginning event was remembered as "Deganawida blotting out the sun as part of the traditional account of the founding of the Iroquois league"—that is, the solar eclipse of 1451 (1978, 326–27; see also chapter 1).

Tribes have to be in existence before alliances between and among tribes are possible (Sempowski and Saunders 2001, 711). The development of tribal units may, however, have been immediately succeeded by the fashioning of larger social units. At that point, our "model" of confederacies alerts us to the fact that tribal alliances called one another into being and must, therefore, begin about the same time. The Huron Confederacy may have started around the mid-fifteenth century. Our pipes imply that some kind of intertribal partnership—an interaction sphere, a proto-League—formed among eastern Iroquois and St. Lawrence Iroquoian partners about the time of the earliest Huron alliance.

League Beginnings

In sum, effigy pipes bearing humanoid imagery cluster in Jefferson County but also show up among the Mohawks, Oneidas, and Onondagas during the late 1400s to early 1500s. The pictorial theme, emergence, may relate to tribalization, the process of individual nations or tribes coming into conscious being. However, the overall distribution is suggestive of an interaction sphere centered in New York's St. Lawrence region. Later historic evidence in the same cultural tradition indicates some pipes were employed in male councils involving deliberation and diplomacy. The pipes discussed here probably were so used, their symbolically prominent compositions of emergence being congruent with display in a political context. The interaction sphere reflects peaceful interchange among pipe-smoking representatives of several communities, probably over a period of time. That suggests, in turn, that we have, in the pipes, the earliest evidence for alliance activity in upstate New York and, very plausibly, an important clue to the formative condition of the Iroquois League.[4]

4. There is, however, little if any evidence for trade accompanying the hypothesized diplomatic relations. For example, Jefferson County folk evidently were not receiving or gaining access to the Onondaga chert available to the eastern Iroquois groups (Engelbrecht and Jamieson 2016a).

Scholars have long suspected that the Iroquois League emerged gradually from a series of widening alliances, culminating in the admission of the Senecas (Engelbrecht 1985; Fenton 1998, 72–73). The logical precursor, the most obvious proto-League would consist, as Robert Funk and Robert Kuhn hypothesized, of some cooperative arrangement among the easternmost tribes.

> It seems highly likely that the eastern Iroquois (Mohawk, Oneida, Onondaga) maintained a relationship, alliance, or even a confeder-acy of sorts that existed before the Five Nations Confederacy. These tribes derive from a common population and cultural origin. They were located close in space and shared similarities in most aspects of their culture. An intertribal relationship marked by peace, coopera-tion, and shared rituals may have existed between these three tribes for a long time. Later, this relationship probably became the basis for the Five Nations Confederacy. (Funk and Kuhn 2003, 157)

Pipes are the best evidence we currently have for the beginning of the Iroquois alliance, a precontact proto-League (Parmenter 2010, 16). With pipes, we look generally and vaguely to the second half of the fifteenth century and the opening of the sixteenth century as the probable time of first intertribal partnership. There must have been a fair passage of time involved to go from three to four—or the other way around—participants as suggested by the heads featured on the Dougherty compositions.

Activities implied by the pipes evidently occurred in a pre-Columbian time frame, which suggests, of course, that confederacies, including the Iroquois League, were brought into being or "caused" by non-European circumstances. The climate of peace implied by the pipes and their symbolism relates the three eastern Iroquois locations to one another and to a fourth locality. The most surprising conclu-sion of this study is that the diplomatic activity included the Rutland Hollow cluster of Jefferson County and may even have originated and centered there. But, perhaps similarly, a recent study of ceramic decora-tion highlights the centrality of Jefferson County in a "ceramic social signaling system" with the eastern Iroquois from about 1450 to 1550 (Dermarkar et al. 2016:96–97; see also Hart and Engelbrecht 2017).

Iroquois oral narrative provides little testimony bearing on this archaeologically constructed scenario of eastern alliance. With the qualification—in some instances—that one tribe initiated the process, the majority of origin legends accord equal status to all five tribes in the creation of the Iroquois League (Pyrlaeus, Webster, Cusick, Clark, Morgan, Johnson). Several Canadian accounts (Gibson, Hale, Newhouse) mention characters and locales that are Mohawk, Onondaga, and Oneida prior to mentioning characters and locales that are Cayuga and Seneca. Yet, in all, all five tribes are described as participants in the founding of the League. Three versions—those of Norton, Brant, and Buck—clearly indicate cooperation among the eastern tribes as preceding the formation of a five-nation confederacy. None of the latter, on the other hand, posits an early eastern Iroquois alliance with Jefferson County.

The earliest Iroquois mythic history (1827) does speak of a northern confederation in existence after the creation but before the time of the Iroquois League. According to Tuscarora David Cusick, a body of *Ukwehu:wé* (the Iroquois term for "themselves," in Oneida) were once encamped on the St. Lawrence. Beset by various difficulties, including an invasion of giants from the north, "a convention were held by the chieftains in order to take some measures to defend their country." Later, "the [same] northern nations formed a confederacy and seated a great council fire on river St. Lawrence" (Beauchamp 1892, 5). So while Cusick documented an early nineteenth-century Iroquois belief in a northern confederacy antedating the League of the Iroquois, the tradition he reported made no provision for Mohawk, Oneida, or Onondaga participants.

What purpose was served by these specific pipes? As Iroquois men smoked from these implements, they contemplated origin accounts reified in objects made of a freely available material. The clay of the pipes required no specialized knowledge or skill to work. Yet, being a substance easy to manipulate and durable when fired, it was an ideal medium for expressing cultural meaning in an egalitarian setting.

Such meaning is often "fixed" in ritualistic contexts (Hodder 1986, 151). Further, new social circumstances may require materialization of new symbols identifying, authorizing, and reinforcing those conditions (Earle 2004). In this case, the establishment of alliance through political ritual is the altered social state expressed materially. As Iroquois men employed these pipes in diplomatic settings to foster a climate of peace, they also were creating a common political culture surely expressed in the idiom of close kinship and shared origin (e.g., Ray 1987). The latter found mythic expression agreed on and, perhaps, codified in compositions rendered on those pipes: "Visible to all, material symbols are used to define moments of social change and to make those moments permanent through the life of the symbols" (Earle 2004, 123).

The iconographic approach pursued here complements a study of Mohawk pipes, which posited that smoking implements, as male artifacts, "provide a superior measure of interaction patterns related to sociopolitical relationships between tribal groups" (Kuhn 2004, 158). Testing clay composition to determine whether pipes were locally made, Kuhn found that, of a handful of exotic examples thought to derive from Iroquoians to the north, three dated to the 1400s, one to the early 1500s. The apparent disappearance of foreign-made pipes, Kuhn suspected, signaled the cessation of peaceful interaction between Mohawks and northern Iroquoian groups "as reflected by the decline in the trade and exchange of symbolically, socially, and politically important ceramic smoking pipes that may reflect the end of peaceful relations between their groups and the onset of conflict" (2004, 158). Conflict will be the topic of chapter 4, when consideration of the easternmost Iroquois is resumed.

3

Smoking Pipes and Alliance-Building in Western Iroquoia

Martha L. Sempowski

Introduction

While the timing of the formation of the League of the Iroquois has long been debated, there is general agreement that it was a protracted process, occurring gradually over many decades, rather than as a singular event (Engelbrecht 1985, 177; Fenton 1998, 72, 85, 95; introduction by Fenton to Hale 1963 [1883], xxi; Snow 1991, 139; Trigger 2000, 163). It seems clear, then, that a fuller inquiry into how that process unfolded in particular areas of the League's development—the factors that precipitated it in each region and those that may have facilitated it—will enrich our general understanding of the confederacies that dominated Native political and military dynamics in northeastern North America during the seventeenth century.

In chapter 2 Wonderley proposed that small-scale, fifteenth-century alliances in eastern Iroquoia presaged the development of the Five Nations League by more than a century. In this chapter we turn to western Iroquoia, specifically the western Finger Lakes region of present-day New York State, the traditional homeland of the historic Seneca Iroquois (see map 4). Here we find evidence for alliance-building processes that look surprisingly similar to those in eastern Iroquoia even though they appear to have taken place several decades later than those in the east. If temporally accurate, the population consolidations and accompanying political alliances that are thought

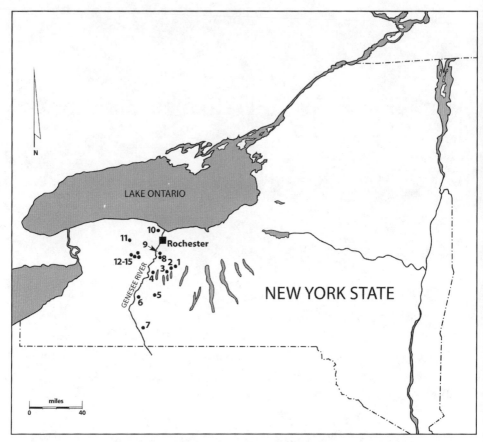

Map 4. Late prehistoric era sites with distinctive human effigy smoking pipes discussed in this chapter. Site key: 1. Harscher; 2. Belcher; 3. Richmond Mills; 4. Long Point; 5. Dansville Flats; 6. Portageville Fort; 7. Belmont/Saunders; 8. Burgett/Peter Burgett; 9. Stull; 10. Schultz; 11. Flanigan's Island; 12–15. (West to east) Fort Hill LeRoy, MacArthur/McCann, William Buzzie, L. J. Frisbie (precise locations of last two uncertain). Map adapted from Sempowski and Saunders 2001, fig. Intro-1.

to have occurred in western Iroquoia during the early to mid-1500s underpinned the emergence of the Seneca as a tribal entity later in the century, and its subsequent incorporation into the classic Five Nations League, by the turn of the seventeenth century (Kuhn and Sempowski 2001; see chapter 6).

Late fifteenth- and early sixteenth-century Iroquoia was characterized by a climate of chronic warfare brought on by the need for blood vengeance to redress past wrongs in a never-ending reciprocal cycle among neighboring groups (see chapter 4 for a detailed discussion of this issue in eastern Iroquoia). Within this tumultuous environment of attacks and counterattacks, tribes coalesced and alliances among them were formed for mutual defense and greater aggressive potential. The larger groups had a competitive advantage over smaller unallied neighbors, such that these early alliances "challenged one another into existence," as Wonderley suggested in chapter 2.

During the late 1400s and early 1500s, in western Iroquoia, the small populations scattered across the western Finger Lakes region were surrounded by neighboring Iroquoian groups—ancestors of Cayugas to the east, those of Wenros, Neutrals, and Eries to the west, and those of Petuns and Hurons to the north. At least some of these neighboring groups were becoming larger and more powerful during this period. It is presumed that all ascribed to a similar code of blood revenge, and thus must have been experiencing very similar pressures to compete with one another.

Of interest here is that sometime in the mid-1500s, a highly distinctive kind of human effigy smoking pipe (type I head-bowl in fig. 4 and type II body-bowl in fig. 5) began to show up in the western Finger Lakes region. Interestingly, similar, and in some cases, nearly identical examples also occurred in sites along the Genesee River, as well as just west of the river, and beyond, in territory identified by Marian White as ancestral Wenro (1978b, 407–11).

It is proposed that the distribution of these stylized human effigy smoking pipes across the Genesee Valley, or at least of the symbolic concepts influencing their manufacture, reflects direct diplomatic or political interactions among males, as early sixteenth-century alliances were being negotiated. Daniel Richter (1992, 111) has noted that incipient alliances between Iroquoian groups sometimes involved the exchange of adult males as temporary "hostages" while agreements were being established. In any event, the stylistically similar smoking pipes found in disparate areas of western Iroquoia during the early to

4. Type I head-bowl human effigy pipe: RMSC/RF 10005/14, Burgett site. Approximate width of face = 3.5 cm. Object on loan to the Rochester Museum & Science Center, Rochester, New York, courtesy of the Rock Foundation Inc. Image used with permission of the Rock Foundation Inc. and artist Gene Mackay.

mid-sixteenth century appear to indicate a period of incipient alliance-building, much as Wonderley has argued for a slightly earlier period in eastern Iroquoia.

Many other lines of archaeological evidence from sites across the entire western Finger Lakes and Genesee River Valley also lend support to the probability of population consolidations and alliance-building

5. Type II body-bowl human effigy pipe: NYSM 34840, Richmond Mills site.
Approximate height = 6 cm. Object courtesy of the New York State Museum,
Albany, New York. Image used with permission of the Rock Foundation Inc.
and artist Gene Mackay.

in the region during this period: ceramic analyses indicating potential relationships among groups; demographic anomalies in some of the burial populations; evidence of violence or trauma on a number of sites; increased occurrence of exotic marine shell; and an intensification of mortuary ritual behavior, as indicated by increasing use of material grave goods. It is contended that throughout the sixteenth century, widely recognized beliefs regarding kinship, mortuary ritual, and the symbolic nature and function of marine shell (see chapter 5) helped bind these disparate groups together in ways that simulated familiar kin relationships (see chapter 6).

The Sites

Mary Ann Palmer Niemczycki (1984, 122–26) provides an outline of the chronology of late prehistoric sites in the region, approximated as AD 1450–1550, by means of ceramic analysis and seriation. More recently, this proposed time interval has been adjusted upward to approximately AD 1525–70 to reflect revisions in the chronology of historic Seneca sites (Sempowski and Saunders 2001, 3–5, 720–22). Thus, the most recent of these late prehistoric sites, Richmond Mills, may have been occupied up to as late as AD 1570, immediately preceding the earliest recognized sites in the dual historic sequences of the Seneca, the Adams, and the Culbertson sites (Wray and Schoff 1953; Wray 1973). (See the introduction to this volume regarding the relative imprecision of archaeological site dating.)

Table 1 shows six late prehistoric sites located in the western Finger Lakes area of Ontario and Livingston Counties; these sites provide the central focus of this inquiry (see map 4). While it is impossible to date these sites with certitude, the Harscher, Hilliard, Belcher, and Richmond Mills sites seem likely to represent a temporal sequence of village movements from northeast to southwest within the watersheds of Mud Creek and Honeoye Creek. The Harscher and Hilliard sites are located on low and seemingly unfortifiable knolls on minor streams, while the Richmond Mills and Belcher sites are situated on high terraces surrounded by deep ravines of the Honeoye Outlet and

Table 1
Focal late prehistoric sites (ca. AD 1525–1570) located in the western Finger Lakes area

SITE NAME	SITE NUMBER	NO. OF PIPES
Harscher	Can 038	1
Hilliard*	Can 003	—
Belcher	Hne 008	4
Richmond Mills	Hne 005	23(+1?)
Long Point	Hne 004	1
California Ranch*	Hne 022	—

* Late prehistoric sites lacking effigy pipes under study here. See chapter 3, note 1.

the Honeoye Creek, respectively. It is conceivable that the latter two sites—Belcher and Richmond Mills—were occupied simultaneously, as proposed by Charles Wray (1973, 8), but it seems more likely, given the nature of the associated artifactual materials presently known for the two sites, that Belcher preceded Richmond Mills, as is suggested here. More intensive analysis of existing collections is needed to distinguish between these two chronological hypotheses. The last two sites—Long Point and California Ranch—do not appear to be full-time, year-round occupation sites. Located in a very different physical setting, close to the shores of the Conesus and Honeoye Lakes, they seem to represent specialized seasonal fishing encampments.

Later in the sixteenth century, the western Finger Lakes area was home to the well-known sequences of historic Seneca Iroquois village sites (Wray and Schoff 1953; Wray 1973, Wray et al. 1987, 1991; Sempowski and Saunders 2001). Intriguingly, it is also the locale identified in Seneca oral traditions as the birthplace of the Seneca Iroquois (Beauchamp 1905; Converse 1908, 112–14; Houghton 1922; Parker 1989).

All but two of these sites produced one or more of the stylized human effigy pipes distinguished here.[1] These two sites were included

1. Note that two of these sites, Hilliard and California Ranch, did not contain examples of the distinctive human effigy smoking pipes highlighted here. Similarly,

Table 2
Late prehistoric sites (ca. AD 1525–1570) in areas on periphery of the western Finger Lakes

SITE NAME	SITE NUMBER	NO. OF PIPES
Genesee River–East		
Stull	Hne 021	2
Peter Burgett	Hne 123/Hne 124	1
Burgett	Hne 123/Hne 124	1
Genesee River/Canaseraga Creek–South		
Belmont/Saunders	Blt 001	1
Dansville Flats	Wld 010	2
Portageville Fort	Ptg 001	1
West of Genesee River		
Fort Hill Leroy	Bgn 001	1
MacArthur/McCann	No Site #	2
William Buzzie	No Site #	1
L. J. Frisbie	No Site #	1
Schultz's Woods	Roc 013	1
Flanigan's Island	Abn 003	1
Alhart*	Bgn 015	—

* Late prehistoric sites lacking effigy pipes under study here. See chapter 3, note 1.

because of their proximity temporally and geographically to the late prehistoric sites in the Western Finger Lakes region. This group of focal sites, then, gives us a starting place for consideration of several archaeological dimensions identified here as possible material correlates of alliance-building among northeastern Iroquoian peoples: ceramic smoking pipes; shell (both marine and freshwater); demography of the burial population; evidence of violence; and elaboration of

---

the Alhart site was also included in the group from west of the Genesee River because of its potential relevance even though it did not contain one of the pipes discussed here.

mortuary practices, as indicated by the proportion of graves containing surviving material goods.

Table 2 indicates sites outside of the focal area, which were selected because they, with the exception of Alhart, yielded examples of these distinctive human effigy smoking pipes. All are located within a fifty- to sixty-mile radius of the western Finger Lakes region (see map 4). One group of sites clusters along the Genesee River almost due west of the focal area, close to present-day Avon, New York. The second grouping is located to the south, either on the Genesee River or the Canaseraga Creek. The third group includes sites located west of the Genesee River, several at some distance from the western Finger Lakes region.

Human Effigy Smoking Pipes

One cannot help but be struck by the unprecedented appearance and relative abundance of human effigy smoking pipes occurring in the western Finger Lakes region during the early to mid-sixteenth century (see figs. 4–5). Of further interest is their nearly simultaneous occurrence within a wider circle of neighboring sites within a fifty- to sixty-mile radius of the western Finger Lakes region. While other pipe types occur within this time frame, such as the classic trumpet and coronet styles, it is the sculpted human effigy pipes—commonly referred to as "helmeted" pipes—that stand out in terms of their distinctiveness and frequency (Sempowski 2004b).

These pipes take one of two major forms, head-bowl and body-bowl, although several key diagnostic characteristics allow one to recognize them as similar in conception, style, and potential meaning:

1. Depiction of a human face, which, after initial molding of the basic form, has been completed by pre-fire sculpting and carving of the facial features (perhaps when the pipe is leather dry).
2. The human face appears to be emerging from, or enshrouded in a sort of hood, which extends above the eyes and often around the face and under the chin.

3. Some sort of simple linear design on the hood, such as diago-
nally incised lines, spade-shaped impressions, gouges, or
circular punctates.
4. Features of the face, particularly those of the eyes, which give
the impression of vacancy or lifelessness.
5. Prominent rectangular slots at the ears, on the top of the head,
or on a chest plaque.

Type I Head-Bowl Pipes

The common feature typifying the head-bowl pipes is that the face
effigy constitutes the front of the pipe bowl itself (figs. 6 and 7). See
table 3 for locations of sites where this type of pipe occurs. The head-
bowl pipes are characterized by faces that range from distinctly triangular in shape (fig. 7a), to rounded (fig. 7b), to almost square-shaped
(fig. 7c). Rectangular-shaped slots are another very common feature,
most often located on both sides of the head, either angling upward
toward the back of the head or in vertical fashion alongside the face.
The eyes consist of narrow, slanted, oval slots, in some cases puffed
around the outer edges. The noses are generally somewhat pug, with
shallow, gashed nostrils often expressed. Mouths consist of oval openings, again often puffed around the edges, and in most cases, with teeth
clearly indicated (fig. 8a, front view). The band, or "headgear," above
the face varies considerably in width and in the style of markings. It
is most frequently adorned by a series of incised diagonal lines, less
often by spade-shaped gouges or impressions, and in two cases by pro-
nounced punctates. These lines of markings vary from a single row to
two or three rows, or in a couple of cases, to covering the entire headgear. Often the headgear, with its rows of markings, sweeps around and
slightly upward to the back of the head, culminating in a narrow "tail"
at the rear (fig. 8b, side view). Two pipes are characterized as "Janus
type," with one face oriented to the smoker on the front, and the other
away from the smoker on the back. Two others exhibit signs of a long-
bodied animal crawling up the back of the bowl, along with straight,
low-relief limbs along the sides of the head and the pipe stem (fig. 9).

6. Type I head-bowl human effigy pipe: RMSC/RF 1/101, Richmond Mills site. Approximate height = 4.5 cm. Object on loan to the Rochester Museum & Science Center, Rochester, New York, courtesy of the Rock Foundation Inc. Image used with permission of the Rock Foundation Inc. and artist Gene Mackay.

Table 3
Pipes by catalogue number, pipe type, site, and present location*

Western Finger Lakes area

CATALOGUE NO.	PIPE TYPE	SITE	PRESENT LOCATION
RMSC/RF 1/101	Head-bowl	Richmond Mills (Hne 005)	RMSC
RMSC/RF 61/101	Head-bowl	Richmond Mills (Hne 005	RMSC
RMSC/RF 62/101	Head-bowl	Richmond Mills (Hne 005)	RMSC
RMSC/RF 63/101	Head-bowl	Richmond Mills (Hne 005)	RMSC
RMSC/RF 6020/101	Head-bowl	Richmond Mills (Hne 005)	RMSC
RMSC/RF 6441/101	Head-bowl	Richmond Mills (Hne 005)	RMSC
RMSC/RF 6442/101	Head-bowl	Richmond Mills (Hne 005)	RMSC
RMSC/RF 6443/101	Head-bowl	Richmond Mills (Hne 005	RMSC
RMSC/RF 6444/101	Head-bowl	Richmond Mills (Hne 005)	RMSC
RMSC AR19215	Head-bowl	Richmond Mills (Hne 005)	RMSC
RMSC AR19216	Head-bowl	Richmond Mills (Hne 005)	RMSC
RMSC AR19238	Head-bowl	Richmond Mills (Hne 005)	RMSC
RMSC AR37738	Head-bowl	Richmond Mills (Hne 005)	RMSC
RMSC AR39026.4	Head-bowl	Richmond Mills (Hne 005)	RMSC
RMSC AR39026.5	Head-bowl	Richmond Mills (Hne 005)	RMSC
NYSM 15070	Head-bowl	Richmond Mills (Hne 005)	NYSM
NYSM 15308	Head-bowl	Richmond Mills (Hne 005)	NYSM
NYSM 34760	Head-bowl	Richmond Mills (Hne 005)	NYSM
NYSM 35955	Head-bowl	Richmond Mills (Hne 005)	NYSM
AMAI 3/9229	Head-bowl	Richmond Mills (Hne 005)	AMAI
MHS 884-11	Head-bowl	Richmond Mills (Hne 005)	MHS
OCHS I-26	Head-bowl	Likely Richmond Mills (Hne 005)?	OCHS
RMSC 78.14.625	Head-bowl	Belcher (Hne 008)	RMSC
RMSC 78.14.637	Head-bowl	Belcher (Hne 008)	RMSC
RMSC/RF 15000/200	Head-bowl	Belcher (Hne 008)	RMSC
RMSC/RF 85/17	Head-bowl	Long Point (Hne 004)	RMSC
RMSC AR1371	Body-bowl	Richmond Mills (Hne 005)	RMSC
NYSM 34840	Body-bowl	Richmond Mills (Hne 005)	NYSM
RMSC/RF 9/179	Body-bowl	Harscher (Can 038)	RMSC
RMSC AR 28757	Body-bowl	Belcher (Hne 008)	RMSC

Table 3 *(continued)*
Pipes by catalogue number, pipe type, site, and present location*

Genesee River: East Side

CATALOGUE NO.	PIPE TYPE	SITE	PRESENT LOCATION
NYSM 15310	Head-bowl	Stull (Hne 021)	NYSM
NYSM 15308	Head-bowl	Stull (Hne 021)	NYSM
RMSC/RF 10005/14	Head-bowl	Peter Burgett (Hne 123/124)	NYSM
RMSC/RF 194/O	Head-bowl	Burgett (Hne 123/124)	RMSC

Genesee River: South

CATALOGUE NO.	PIPE TYPE	SITE	PRESENT LOCATION
NYSM cat. no. ?	Head-bowl	Belmont/Saunders (Blt 001)	NYSM
RMSC/RF 6168/188	Body-bowl	Portageville Fort (Ptg 001)	RMSC
RMSC/RF 7480/206	Body-bowl	Dansville Flats (Wld 010)	RMSC
RMSC/RF 7481/206	Body-bowl	Dansville Flats (Wld 010)	RMSC

Genesee River: West Side

CATALOGUE NO.	PIPE TYPE	SITE	PRESENT LOCATION
RMSC/RF 6002/177	Head-bowl	L. J. Frisbie (Genesee City?)	RMSC
NYSM 567	Head-bowl	MacArthur/McCann (NYSM #2661)	NYSM
NYSM 747	Body-bowl	MacArthur/McCann (NYSM #2661)	NYSM
NYSM 35526	Body-bowl	Fort Hill Leroy (Bgn 001)	NYSM
RMSC AR10389	Body-bowl	Schultz (Roc 013)	RMSC
RMSC Unknown cat. no.	Body-bowl	William Buzzie (Genesee City)	RMSC
PC F-I	Body-bowl	Flanigan's Island (Abn 003)	Private collection

* Key to catalogue abbreviations:
   RMSC/RF: Rock Foundation Collection on loan to Rochester Museum & Science Center
   RMSC: Rochester Museum & Science Center Collection
   NYSM: New York State Museum Collection
   NMAI: National Museum of the American Indian Collection
   MHS: Mendon Historical Society Museum Collection
   OCHS: Ontario County Historical Society Museum Collection
   LCHS: Livingston County Historical Society Museum Collection
   PC: Private collection

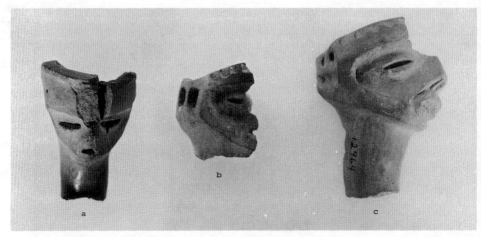

7. Type I head-bowl human effigy pipes. (a) RMSC/RF 85/17, Long Point site; (b) RMSC AR 39026, Richmond Mills site; (c) RMSC/RF 6441/101, Richmond Mills site. Approximate height of (a) = 4.3 cm. Items (a) and (c) on loan to the Rochester Museum & Science Center, Rochester, New York, courtesy of the Rock Foundation Inc.; (b) courtesy of the Rochester Museum & Science Center.

8. Type I head-bowl human effigy pipe, RMSC AR 19238. (a) front view; (b) side view, Richmond Mills site. Approximate height of pipe = 6.2 cm. Courtesy of the Rochester Museum & Science Center, Rochester, New York.

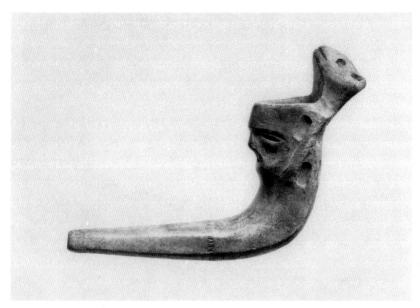

9. Type I head-bowl human effigy pipe, NYSM 567, MacArthur/McCann site. Approximate length = 10.3 cm. Object courtesy of the New York State Museum, Albany, New York. Image used with permission of the Rock Foundation Inc. and artist Gene Mackay.

Type I Head-Bowl Pipes: Geographic Distribution

About 79 percent of the pipes identified in this category were found at late prehistoric sites in the heart of the western Finger Lakes region (map 4): twenty-one at the Richmond Mills site; three at Belcher; one at Long Point; and one at an unidentified site in the region, most likely Richmond Mills (see table 3 for a full listing of pipes).

Pertinent to this study, of course, is the occurrence of very similar pipes in sites located to the south and west within a fifty- to sixty-mile radius of the focal western Finger Lakes region. Among sites identified as probable late prehistoric sites, the remaining seven pipes appear in the following sites (table 3 and map 4):

• Due west, along the Genesee River: the Burgett sites (RMSC/RF194/0; RMSC/RF10005/14) and the Stull site (NYSM 15310; NYSM unknown cat. no.) in Livingston County.

- South along the Genesee River, at the Belmont/Saunders site (NYSM unknown cat. no.) in Allegany County.
- West of the Genesee River at the MacArthur/McCann (NYSM 567) and the L. J. Frisbie (RMSC/RF 6002/177) sites in Genesee County.[2]

While there is a range of variation in the characteristics of these type I head-bowl pipes, it is interesting that those from the westerly sites located along and west of the Genesee River bear a striking resemblance to those from the Seneca heartland in the western Finger Lakes region, in terms of the defining characteristics as identified earlier. Compare for example, figure 7a from Long Point and figure 4 from Burgett; compare also figure 7c from Richmond Mills and the face on figure 9 from the MacArthur/McCann site. The latter also exhibits the long-bodied animal crawling up the back of the bowl as does one noted earlier from the western Finger Lakes region (OCHS I-26). Similarly, although quite different in execution, double-faced Janus pipes are found at both the Belmont/Saunders site (NYSM unknown cat. no.) and at the Richmond Mills site (NYSM 34760).

Type II Body-Bowl Pipes

In this subgroup of human effigy pipes, type II body-bowl, the body of the figure, not the head, forms the actual bowl of the pipe, while the head (or heads) projects off the rim of the pipe bowl. The most intact of these pipes (NYSM 34840; fig. 5) from the Richmond Mills site illustrates both the characteristic treatment of the body of the pipe bowl with flexed limb, and the projecting head. Another (NYSM 35526) from the Fort Hill Leroy site appears to have been intact when it was illustrated in Beauchamp (1898, 427, fig. 209), although the double projecting heads (probably NYSM 35526) have now become separated

2. It should also be noted that similar pipes have been found at the Shelby Fort site in Orleans County, at the Newton-Hopper site in Erie County, and at the Ripley site in Chautauqua County.

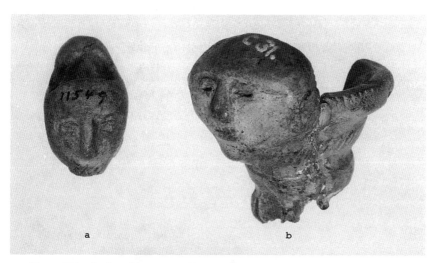

10. Type II body-bowl human effigy pipes. (a) RMSC/RF 6168/188, Portageville site; (b) RMSC AR 10389, Schultz site. Approximate height of (a) =
2.9 cm. Item (a) on loan to the Rochester Museum & Science Center, Rochester, New York, courtesy of the Rock Foundation Inc.; (b) courtesy of the
Rochester Museum & Science Center.

from the body of the pipe. Two additional pipes of this type (RMSC/
AR 1371 from Richmond Mills and F-I from the Flanigan's Island site
in a private collection) are also reasonably intact. The remaining six
examples show traces of the main effigy, while in several cases, little
more than the fragmentary head exists for study (e.g., fig. 10a from the
Portageville site, and fig. 10b from the Schultz site).

Like the human effigies on the type I head-bowl pipes, these heads,
which range from triangular to almost square-jawed in shape, show the
same type of well-sculpted features: oval slits (sometimes puffed around
the edges) for the eyes, pug nose, oval-shaped mouth, and generally
lifeless-looking appearance. The faces again appear to be enshrouded
in or emerging from some sort of headgear that encircles the entire
face. The rows of incised decoration are not as apparent on the headgear of these individuals as they are in the type I effigies. One from the
Richmond Mills site (fig. 5) does exhibit what appear to be animal ears
on the back of the individual's head and a distinct row of rectangular

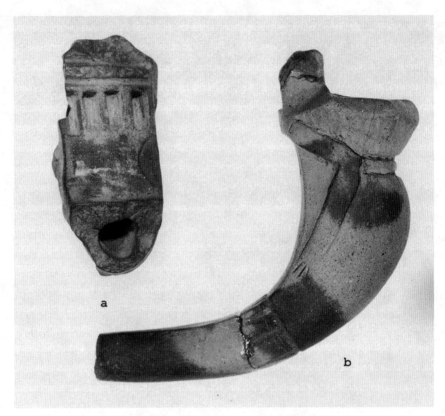

11. Type II body-bowl human effigy pipes. (a) RMSC RF 7480/206, Dansville Flats site; (b) RMSC/RF 9/179, Harscher site. Approximate height of (a) = 6.7 cm. Objects on loan to the Rochester Museum & Science Center, Rochester, New York, courtesy of the Rock Foundation Inc.

slots across the top of the head. Four of the pipes—RMSC/RF 9/179 (see fig. 11b), RMSC/AR 1371, cat. no. F-1 from a private collection, and NYSM 35526 (Beauchamp 1898, 427, fig. 209)—appear to have twin heads projecting from the front of the pipe bowl, both oriented in the same direction toward the smoker, although in some cases, this is indicated only by the double-breakage pattern.

In those cases in which the body of the bowl has survived sufficiently for description, these pipes exhibit a chest plaque with three to four rectangular slots similar in dimensions to those around the faces of the type I pipes and on the top of the head of one mentioned earlier (fig. 5). The row of vertical slots on the chest plaques are surmounted by a series of inverted triangles or gashed markings, and in some cases an additional row of incised markings further down the stem (fig. 11a, Dansville Flats site; fig. 11b, Harscher site). The other distinguishing feature found on almost all of the pipes intact enough for examination is a well-modeled basket or pottery vessel on the back of the individual, thus constituting the back of the pipe bowl. Low-relief, bent limbs are sometimes evident along the sides of the bowl and down the stem (e.g., figs. 5 and 11b).

Type II Body-Bowl Pipes: Geographical Distribution

The body-bowl pipes numbered twelve in the late prehistoric sites studied in the region. In the reverse of the pattern noted for distribution of the head-bowl type, only four, or 33 percent of the total, proceeded from sites in the western Finger Lakes region. Two are from the Richmond Mills site, including a double-headed example (RMSC/AR 1371) and the intact pipe with the apparent animal headdress (fig. 5), one from the Belcher site and one fragmentary, but seemingly two-headed example from the Harscher site (fig. 11b).

Again focusing on an area within a fifty- to sixty-mile radius of the western Finger Lakes, the remaining eight examples of these body-bowl pipes occur in the following sites:

• Five pipes proceeded from sites some miles to the west of the Genesee River. Three of these occurred in sites located close together in Genesee County, about twenty miles west of the river: the Fort Hill Leroy site (NYSM 35526), the MacArthur/McCann site (NYSM 747), and the William Buzzie Farm (unknown cat. no.), located in close proximity; one from Flanigan's Island (cat. no. F-I), some twenty to twenty-five miles to the northwest in Orleans County; and one from the Schultz site (RMSC/AR 10389) located north, about six miles west of the river, in Monroe County near Lake Ontario.

• The other three pipes were found to the south: one at the Portageville Fort site (fig. 10a RMSC/RF 6168/188), and the others
at the Dansville Flats site (King Site area) (fig. 11a RMSC/
RF 7480/206; RMSC/RF 7481/206) along the Canaseraga
Creek at the southern edge of Livingston County.[3]

The distribution of both types of pipes in sites in the western Finger Lakes region and areas to the west, northwest, and south of it
in the Genesee Valley revealed some interesting findings regarding
the contemporaneity of the two types. While most of the referenced
neighboring sites have also been classified as late prehistoric in age (ca.
AD 1450–1550) (Niemczycki 1984, 123–25), later occupation dates (ca.
AD 1525–70) have been extrapolated from dates proposed for Seneca sites (Sempowski and Saunders 2001, 3–5). Thus, precise dating
of many of these sites is quite tentative (see the introduction to this
volume regarding the relative imprecision of archaeological site dating
for this period), raising the troubling issue of potential contemporaneity. It may be worth noting that both major pipe types, head-bowl and
body-bowl, occasionally occurred in the same sites, suggesting that
time was not a major factor in their distribution.

In sum, then, the distribution of this unusual body of artifacts
suggests that pipes were largely circulating during the mid-1500s (ca.
AD 1525–70), within a region encompassing the Bristol Hills area of
the western Finger Lakes, the area along or adjacent to the Genesee
River, and a region to the west of the Genesee River. The question
remains as to whether the pipes reflect a sphere of male political interactions involving pipe smoking, which indicates the building of small-
scale alliances and related population consolidations drawing from the
wider region. And if so, do these same processes continue to be at play
in later developments in the western Finger Lakes region, involving

3. It is interesting that a fragment of a pipe similar to this type (RMSC/AR
18286) was located at the Seneca Factory Hollow site, occupied some fifty years later.
At this time, it is the only known example from a later site in the area. Another pipe
(RMSC/RF 6209/205) occurred at the Genoa Fort site in Cayuga territory, and a
third at the Schmidka site (two-headed RMSC/RF 11016/235) in the Onondaga area.

the historic Senecas? A number of other lines of archaeological and traditional information seem relevant to these questions.

Relevant Archaeological Evidence

Ceramic Analysis

Niemczycki's (1984) ceramic studies compare decorative techniques from several earlier sites in the western Finger Lakes region. She concludes that until the late fifteenth century, small sites in the Bristol Hills (e.g., the Footer, Fletcher, and Andrews sites) appear ceramically distinct from those of the late prehistoric sites in the area, such as the Richmond Mills, Belcher, and California Ranch sites (Niemczycki 1984, 77). Niemczycki finds that around this time, a population originating in Cayuga territory—or more likely from an area between Seneca Lake and Canandaigua Lake—migrated into the region and merged with these local groups at the Richmond Mills and California Ranch sites (1984, 77; 1995, 45; Engelbrecht 2003, 115). Niemczycki also points to a probable source of population from the Genesee River area (1984, 98), and while the precise dates are not clear, she does suggest that populations from that area had withdrawn "further south and east and palisaded villages appear in the southern Genesee and western Finger Lakes soon after" (1987, 36). While Niemczycki does not specifically confirm the input of Ontario-style ceramics from west of the Genesee River on early sixteenth-century sites in the western Finger Lakes region, analyses of data from subsequent Seneca sites in the region do suggest such incorporation (Wray et al. 1987, 243–45; Sempowski et al. 1988, 101–2; Wray et al. 1991, appendix D).

Evidence of Violence/Trauma/Warfare

Archaeological data from regional sites studied here confirm a pattern of violence and trauma during this period. Among the sites in the Genesee River area, the Dansville Flats site (see map 4) yielded evidence of the "arrow sacrifice" of a young adult male, first noted and pointed out by Engelbrecht (2003, 40, fig. 13), as well as the presence of a large fire pit at the site (RMSC Site Records). Several other sites in the area, which did not contain the pipes in question, and were probably occupied slightly earlier, also yielded potentially relevant data. The Wadsworth Fort site showed a surface concentration of burned human bone and the Markham site, a number of disarticulated skulls, discovered in Rochester Museum & Science Center excavations (RMSC Site Records). West of the river, of course, we have the widely known example of a massacre at the Alhart site discovered in excavations by Hamell in 1976 (RMSC Site Records) and analyzed by Saunders (1976) in which fifteen adult male skulls had been disarticulated and burned in a large pit while still fleshed (Sempowski et al. 1988, 104–5).

Within the western Finger Lakes area itself, two sites showed evidence of violence—the Richmond Mills and Belcher sites. According to Parker (1918, 13), a deep layer of ash and charcoal at underlying levels at the Richmond Mill site indicated that the site might have been burned at some point. Parker said further that human skulls and burned human bone in refuse suggested signs of possible attack on the site. At the Belcher site, a decapitated individual was discovered in archaeological investigations (GRVCAP 2001).

James Wright has suggested that among the Ontario Iroquois, "Warfare, including cannibalism and headhunting increased, reaching its apogee in the A.D. 1500–1550 period" (1966, 91), and Bruce Trigger maintains that it declined after that period (2000, 162). Susan Jamieson proposes that the introduction of these practices reflects the influence of a southern religious ideology—the "Mississippification" of southern Ontario Iroquois, involving, among other practices, chronic warfare and cannibalism (1992, 75, 77). According to Jamieson, these cultural influences moved northward, along with marine shell from southern sources, by way of the upper Ohio River drainage. It may be that similar effects were being felt in the area under study here.

Demographic Anomalies

A survey of the demographics represented in burial data relating to the sites under study revealed a strikingly disproportionate number of adult females, two-thirds or more in the burial populations of four of the six late prehistoric sites located in the western Finger Lakes area (see table 4). This demographic pattern is not apparent at the Harscher site—the earliest in the proposed sequence of villages set forth here—nor is that pattern noted for any earlier sites in the region. These data suggest a temporal trend reflecting heightened numbers of females in the burial populations of sites in the western Finger Lakes area—beginning with the Hilliard site, followed by Belcher, and then Richmond Mills, as well as at the seasonally occupied California Ranch site.

Atypical numbers of female burials were not identified in late pre-historic sites in the other three areas studied. It is noteworthy, how-ever, that at the subsequent, large, early historic Adams site, located in the focal western Finger Lakes area, demographic analysis indicated three times as many adult female burials as those of adult males in two of the three cemeteries that were investigated (Sempowski et al. 1988, 103–4). Interestingly, one of these two cemeteries with a large number of females also showed the greatest degree of osteological divergence in terms of discrete skeletal traits (Saunders 1986; Sempowski et al. 1988, 103–4). Anomalous demographic patterns such as these are gen-erally interpreted as the result of the incorporation of female captives

Table 4
Proportions of adult females to adult males in the burial populations of late prehistoric sites (ca. AD 1525–1570) in the western Finger Lakes region*

SITE NAME	%FEMALES TO %MALES	N
Harscher	42.9–57.1	n = 34
Hilliard*	70.0–30.0	n = 10
Belcher	66.7–33.3	n = 48
Richmond Mills	75.0–25.0	n = 67
California Ranch**	85.7–14.3	n = 13
Long Point	Insufficient data	

* Adapted from Sempowski, mortuary data 1975–83.
** See chapter 3, note 1, regarding the California Ranch and Hilliard sites.

or refugees in the local site population, the result of warfare—either with one another (i.e., as captives), or with a third party (i.e., as refugees) (Sempowski et al. 1988, 104–6).

Intensification of Mortuary Ritual

Mortuary data from four sites located in the western Finger Lakes area show initial evidence of an intensification of funerary treatment—namely, increasing inclusion of material goods in graves—as compared with earlier sites in the region: Harscher (15.2 percent of graves, n = 33); Belcher (10.4 percent of graves, n = 48); Richmond Mills (17.9 percent of graves, n = 67) and California Ranch (30.8 percent of graves, n = 13).[4] One of the sites located on the Genesee River also showed a relatively high percentage of graves with inclusions of durable material goods: Burgett (40 percent of graves, n = 16).[5] Unfortunately, comparable data were not available for the other sites studied here (Sempowski 1975–83). While these percentages do not approach the 50–71 percent of graves with material inclusions indicated for six subsequent sites in the region—Adams, Culbertson, Tram, Cameron, Dutch Hollow and Factory Hollow (see Sempowski et al. 2001, table C-3)—they certainly seem to point to a trend that continued into early historic era Seneca sites. Again, Jamieson (1992, 75, 77) attributes changing forms of mortuary behavior among Ontario Iroquoian groups to the influence of "Mississippian" polities to the south. Needless to say, during the early sixteenth century, some of these groups (at the terminus of a likely Ohio River–Allegheny River–Genesee River exchange route) were located within the Genesee River Valley interaction area under study here, making it conceivable that they were sources of both population and funerary innovations for groups in the western Finger Lakes area.

4. Very small sample size at the California Ranch site.
5. Very small sample size at the Burgett site.

Increasing Availability of Marine Shell

Regional access to and use of marine shell and other exotic items constitutes yet another line of evidence bearing on the etiology of this sphere of interactions among the people of western Iroquoia. Given the highly symbolic and desirable nature of exotic marine shell, it may have served, paradoxically, as both a motivating factor for attacks on other groups who had access to this valued material, as well as the "coinage" of peace protocols, as discussed by my co-author in chapter 5.

No evidence of marine shell is recorded for late fifteenth-century sites (e.g., Footer, Fletcher and Andrews) in the western Finger Lakes area (RMSC Site Records),[6] making its seemingly abrupt appearance at the Harscher, Belcher, and Long Point sites together with its relative abundance at the Richmond Mills, and California Ranch sites worthy of note. Shell assemblages from Richmond Mills were especially rich and diverse, including beads and pendants produced from the marine bivalve species *Mercenaria mercenaria*, as well as several species of dextrally whorled univalves, *Busycon carica/canaliculatum*, and two possible examples of sinistrally whorled *Busycon perversum/strombus* spp., also identified in 107 beads from the California Ranch and Long Point sites (Ceci 1986, 17–20).

Interestingly, several of the late prehistoric sites located along the Genesee River—Dansville Flats, Portageville Fort, Stull, and Peter Burgett—in this study also yielded evidence of exotic marine shell, as did two others of about the same time period, the Dansville Fort and Farrell sites (Ceci 1986; RMSC Digital Artifact Catalogue). Further west, at the Alhart site, a probable ancestral Wenro site, an impressive number of marine shell artifacts were recovered, considering the limited excavations that were undertaken there. They included twenty-one proto wampum beads (*Busycon carica/canaliculatum*), three larger beads and one pendant (*Strombus* spp.), and nineteen marginella beads

6. One whole freshwater shell was found at the Fletcher site.

(*Prunum guttatum*) (Ceci 1986, 18; RMSC Digital Artifact catalogue; RMSC Site Records).

It may be instructive that no examples of *Busycon perversum* or *Strombus* spp. were identified in analyses of shell assemblages from the later sixteenth- and early seventeenth-century Seneca sites studied, a distinction first commented on by James Pendergast in the late 1980s (1989, 102–3; Wray et al. 1991a, 394–95; Sempowski and Saunders 2001, 687). Pendergast found such "left-handed" or sinistrally whorled marine shells to be common in Ontario sites of the same period (1989, 102; 1991a) and was intrigued by its lack in contemporary Seneca sites. This distinction is significant because sinistrally whorled shell species are not available on the Atlantic coast north of the Chesapeake Bay area, while the dextrally whorled varieties can be recovered from a much broader Atlantic coastal range, thus shedding light on the potential sources and distribution routes of marine shell accessible to the people of the northeast during different periods.

It may be of interest that *Prunum guttatum*, a marine gastropod identified by Lynn Ceci at the Alhart site, is also sinistrally whorled and found only in more southerly waters. Laura Kozuch found a preference for the sinistrally whorled "spiral" shells in Mississippian sites that she studied (Kozuch 1998, viii), but there is no evidence that there was necessarily a cultural preference in the Genesee Valley. We suggest that it may be merely a case of availability of different sources of marine shell at this particular time. This evidence, however slim, may be consistent with Jamieson's explanations regarding the movement of southerly marine shell along with ideas and ceremonial practices northward along the Ohio River drainage to Ontario Iroquois groups in western New York and southern Ontario at this time (1992, 75, 77).

It may also be worthy of note that a number of spiral-shaped freshwater gastropod shells, many "perforated for stringing," were identified from sites in three of the western Iroquoia regions. Ceci identified the following species: *Pleuracera acuta*, *Goniobasis livescens*, and *Campeloma decisum* at some of the sites under study here (1986, 15–20). Given their use alongside marine shell, in some cases, occasionally in mortuary contexts, it seems possible they may have similar symbolic significance relative to the questions under discussion here.

Several other "exotics" discovered at the Richmond Mills site may also indicate access to new sources of trade available in the region: a rare catlinite platform pipe, a fragmentary copper alloy spiral or ring, and tubular beads composed of both native copper and copper alloy (Bradley 1987, 221n12),[7] (see Bradley forthcoming, chapter 3, n57, for fuller details on analyses of these materials). A small piece of iron was also found in the Richmond Mills site collections, as reported by Charles Wray (Bradley, personal communication, May 6, 2019). Whether access to these various exotic commodities was due to direct exchange, or to raids on sites or enemy-trading parties is of course uncertain.

Seneca Oral Tradition and an Interpretation of Pipe Symbolism

In an earlier publication (Sempowski 2004b), it was proposed that these distinctive human effigy pipes portrayed human shamans in an ecstatic trance, a state of transformation into another life-form—an interpretation that may still bear consideration at some level of meaning. Nevertheless, in light of the complex social processes evident during this period, as summarized archaeologically earlier, the limited temporal duration of this particular type of pipe, and especially to an oral tradition regarding Seneca origins on Bare Hill located near the south end of Canandaigua Lake in the western Finger Lakes area, I now offer an alternative interpretation.

Senecas, traditionally known as the "Great Hill People," or O-non-dowa-gah (Seneca Nation of Indians), subscribe to a legend regarding their origins near the head of Canandaigua Lake in the western Finger Lakes area (Converse 1908, 112–14; Houghton 1922).

---

7. Copper or copper alloy was also found at the Alhart site.

One version of the origin narrative, transcribed by James E. Seaver on the basis of an account by Mary Jemison, and then related by Frederick Houghton is as follows:

> The tradition of the Seneca Indians, in regard to their origin is that they broke out of the earth from a large mountain near the head of Canandaigua Lake; and that mountain they still venerate as the place of their birth. Thence they derive their name, "Ge-nun-de-wah," or "Great Hills," and are called "The Great Hill People," which is the true definition of the word Seneca.
>
> The great hill at the head of Canandaigua Lake, from whence they spring, is called Genundewah, and has for a long time past been the place where the Indians of that nation have met in council, to hold great talks, and to offer up prayers to the Great Spirit, on account of its having been their birthplace; and, also, in consequence of the destruction of a serpent at that place in ancient time, in a most miraculous manner, which threatened the destruction of the whole of the Senecas, and barely spared enough to commence replenishing the earth.
>
> The Indians say that the fort on the big hill, or Ge-nun-de-wah, near the head of Canandaigua Lake, was surrounded by a monstrous serpent, whose head and tail came together at the gate. A long time it lay there, confounding the people with its breath. At length they attempted to make their escape some with their hominy blocks, and others with different implements of household furniture; and in marching out of the fort walked down the throat of the serpent. Two orphan children, who had escaped this general destruction by being left on this side of the fort were informed, by an oracle, of the means by which they could get rid of their formidable enemy—which was, to take a small bow and a poisoned arrow, made of a kind of willow, and with that shoot the serpent under its scales. This they did, and the arrow proved effectual; for, on penetrating the skin, the serpent became sick, and, extending itself, rolled down the hill, destroying all the timber that was in its way, disgorging itself, and breaking wind greatly as it went. At every motion a human head was discharged, and rolled down the hill into the lake where they lie at this day in a petrified state, having the hardness and appearance of

stones; and the Pagan Indians of the Senecas believe, that all the little snakes were made of the blood of the great serpent, after it rolled into the lake. (Houghton 1922, 31–32)

Other versions of the story relate that some of the disgorged heads were revitalized with new bodies and became living humans again (Converse 1908, 114). Common knowledge ascribes the site of these events to Bare Hill, a treeless hilltop located near Vine Valley, New York, on the east side of Canandaigua Lake. Houghton, however, disputes the exact location saying that "there seems then every reason to suppose that the great mountain of the tradition was not Bare Hill, but one of the hills that encircle the valley at the head of Canandaigua Lake" (1922, 36).

The human effigy pipes discussed here seem to embody several critical elements of this origin legend. First they exhibit a "lifeless-looking" human face emerging from, or encircled by, a band or hood that may plausibly be interpreted as a highly stylized version of a serpent or snake. The series of incised, spade-shaped, punctate, or circular markings on the band or hood encircling the head or face are informed by four other, realistically portrayed artifacts from Iroquois sites. One is a tiny antler maskette (fig. 12) from the Tram site depicting a figure with the same hollow, vacant expression portrayed on the pipes—and wrapped around the head is a realistically depicted snake, complete with eyes, mouth, and short incised markings, conceivably indicating scales (Sempowski 2004b). A steatite pipe from Allegany County, similar in some ways to the pipes discussed here (Parker 1922, plate 146), a Mohawk smoking pipe (Beauchamp 1898, fig. 188), and a St. Lawrence Iroquois pipe (Mathews 1981, fig. 7) also provide realistic depictions of similar serpent encirclements of a human head or face. Thus, it seems reasonable that the so-called headgear surrounding the faces on the pipes studied here represents a serpent or snake. Furthermore, it is conceivable that the "lifeless" human figures emerging from the serpent-surround may depict the disgorgement, or emergence, of the ancestral Seneca people after the snake is killed and they are freed from their imprisonment.

12. Antler maskette, RMSC AR 18451, Tram site. Approximate height = 3.6 cm. Object courtesy of the Rochester Museum & Science Center, Rochester, New York. Image used with permission of the Rock Foundation Inc. and artist Gene Mackay.

Thus, it is proposed that these distinctive effigy pipes circulating in western Iroquoia during this complex period represent a very special case of material expression for the people of the region, in that they relate to the Seneca narrative of origins in the very heart of the western Finger Lakes region. As the heterogeneous group from that area grew in size and power—either through peaceful coalescence or forcible accretion—smoking and exchanging these highly symbolic pipes in diplomatic encounters across the wider region may represent a visible assertion of common origins, identity, and affiliation with the

"Great Hill People" and their homeland, even if the reality may have been quite different.

Another common feature of the pipes is the presence of rectangular slots or cavities, some of which have been found to include traces of marine shell, suggesting that these were openings that accommodated insertions of marine shell inlay. In light of the highly charged symbolic nature of marine shell and its apparently recent accessibility to groups in the western Finger Lakes area, these inlays may have added validity and weight to any political negotiations in which the pipes were used.

A less prevalent feature of the pipes, the long-bodied, long-tailed animals that appear to be crawling up the back of some of the pipes, also carry symbolic value and add to an understanding of the potential complexity conveyed by these pipes. According to George Hamell, rattlesnakes, symbolizing the underworld of darkness and death, pair with the Underwater Panther, Ontarraoura, a long-bodied animal with a long, spiral tail who represents the sky world of light and life, to symbolize movement from death to life (1980, 1998; Tooker 1991, 102). This would seem consistent with the postulated theme of emergence from the serpent world into the world of life.

Finally, the relative abundance of freshwater shell, particularly perforated gastropods, in these early sites may also be of significance relative to symbolic associations with the Iroquois League's beginnings, although this interpretation is vigorously debated. Reviewing accounts of the Deganawida story in chapter 1, my co-author refers us to the "gathering and stringing" of an ancient form of wampum called *Ote-ko-ä* (Morgan 1962), which, according to Tooker (1994, 215) consisted of spiral-shaped freshwater shells. Morgan explicitly identified *Ote-ko-ä* as an early form of wampum consisting of freshwater rather than marine shell (1852; 1962, 120n1). Two other accounts, which may have been derivative from Morgan (Gibson and Newhouse, see chapter 1), provide a similar interpretation of the original wampum as freshwater shell. This attribution may have found its origin in the account of Jacques Cartier's 1534 encounter with Native people along the St. Lawrence River, in which he describes white beads, *esurgny* (or *esnoguy*), which were considered to be very precious. Over the years, the identification of *esnoguy* as freshwater shell was repeated by many scholars (Woodward 1880, 12; Converse 1908; Ceci 1986, 6; Tooker 1994, 215). Pendergast (1989, 101) asserts most definitively that Cartier's account leaves little doubt as to the nature of this early form of white bead as freshwater shell. More recently, however, Tremblay (2006, 91–93) argues vehemently that what Cartier received from the St. Lawrence Iroquois in 1534 were tubular beads made of marine shell, such as those he illustrates from the Mandeville site.

Summary and Conclusions

In sum, discrete lines of archaeological evidence, Native oral traditions, and symbolic interpretations of this distinctive set of ceramic smoking pipes combine to pose a deeper understanding of social and political processes occurring during the mid-1500s in western Iroquoia. They suggest that the fledgling consolidations and alliances that formed laid the groundwork for the growth of the Seneca tribe in the latter half of the century, and the eventual inclusion of the Seneca in the League of the Iroquois around AD 1600 (Kuhn and Sempowski 2001; see chapter 6).

Initially, there appears to be a movement of a splinter group from Cayuga territory, or a region to the west of it, into the western Finger Lakes area and, subsequently, a coalescence with local populations. Consequently, amidst a climate of violence and internecine warfare throughout the region, perhaps spurred by competitive pressures from larger and more organized groups surrounding them, some individuals or groups from along the Genesee River apparently joined with the group growing in the western Finger Lakes area, either as captives or possibly refugees (Niemczycki 1987, 36–37). Perhaps somewhat later in time, it seems feasible that there may have been population input from west of the Genesee River, given the dearth of late sixteenth-century sites in that region and the known historic location of Wenro settlements further to the west (White 1978b, 407).

It has been postulated here that the Harscher, Hilliard, Belcher, and Richmond Mills sites represent a temporal sequence of village sites moving from northeast to southwest within a relatively small area in the Mud Creek and Honeoye Creek watersheds (see map 4). The settings of the first two sites in the series, Harscher and Hilliard, do not seem to offer a high degree of natural defensibility, as do those of the Belcher and Richmond Mills sites, set on narrow terraces high above the creeks with steep ravines on two sides. The choice of more fortifiable site locations at the two latest sites, together with disproportionate numbers of adult females in the burial populations of all but the earliest site in the series, would appear to argue for increasing threats and warfare during this time, as well as for the incorporation of a substantial number of female captives or refugees in these western Finger Lakes village groups.

Other important changes were also taking place, both in the focal western Finger Lakes area later dominated by the Senecas, and within a region about fifty to sixty miles to the west and northwest. Mortuary rituals intensify across the entire region, as does the use of marine shell, virtually nonexistent in the western Finger Lakes area during the preceding period. It seems conceivable that groups closer to and west of the Genesee River in ancestral Wenro territory had enjoyed access to long-distance exchange networks supplying shell and other exotic materials for some time, and that this may have been one source of conflict with their neighbors east of the river. While the evidence is slim, at least some of the marine shell found on many of these sites comes from southerly sources that do not appear to have been accessed during subsequent years in the region.

Coinciding with all of these social and cultural changes, the distinctive set of human effigy smoking pipes highlighted here—or at least the symbolic concepts underlying them—begin to appear throughout the region. It is proposed that this phenomenon reflects political or diplomatic interactions involving pipe smoking among adult males in the region. These interactions seem most likely to represent attempts to forge small-scale population consolidations and alliances for greater strength or protection within the region.

A widely recognized oral tradition regarding the Seneca's ancestral origins on a great hill in the western Finger Lakes area offers us an inroad into the symbolism expressed in the pipes, and how they may have fit into the larger picture of Seneca growth and alliance-building during this period. It is suggested that the pipes—with themes of a powerful serpent, human emergence, and transformation—illustrate in highly stylized ceramic imagery the tale of where and how the Senecas originated on a great hill near Canandaigua Lake. Thus, in their apparent reference to tribal origins, these "identity" pipes are thought to provide an archaeological marker for the initial processes of Seneca tribalization. Identification, fictive or not, with that origin narrative may have helped to bind together an ethnically diverse group of people and allowed for greater social cohesion.

4

War along the St. Lawrence, Early to Mid-1500s

Anthony Wonderley

An interaction sphere of distinctive pipes in the late 1400s to earliest 1500s probably reflected interregional diplomacy and peaceful relations among the eastern Iroquois and a Jefferson County group. In addition to cooperation of this sort, however, a model of contentious confederacies brings the expectation that, while structurally dedicated to making peace among themselves, tribes in alliance outwardly manifested what Bradley called a "state of generalized belligerency" (1987, 108). That directs one's attention to conflict, and the fighting probably of most concern to Mohawks, Oneidas, Onondagas, and to the people of Jefferson County involved St. Lawrence Iroquoians during the 1500s.

The early pre–Iroquois League alliance mentioned by David Cusick in chapter 2 apparently came to a bad end. His last words on the subject suggest that life on the St. Lawrence got pretty rough:

> About this time, a great horned serpent appeared on Lake Ontario, the serpent produced diseases and many of the people died, but by the aid of thunder bolts the monster was compelled to retire. A blazing star fell into a fort situated on the St. Lawrence and destroyed the people; this event was considered as a warning of their destruction. After a time a war broke out among the northern nations which continued until they had utterly destroyed each other, the island again become in possession of fierce animals. (Beauchamp 1892, 9–11)

Perhaps this passage expresses some distant memory of violence during the sixteenth century. At any rate, the St. Lawrence Iroquoians ceased to exist at that time and their disappearance, by 1603 or earlier, has been a topic of considerable speculation. The introduction of European diseases and climate deterioration are cited as possible explanations (Jamieson 1990b). However, warfare almost certainly contributed to the outcome because St. Lawrence Iroquoian villages were consistently fortified and manifest other indications of violence (Chapdelaine 2004, 67; Engelbrecht 1995, 49; Jamieson 1990b, 81–82; Pendergast 1990, 24). "This was a veritable human tragedy" affecting at least ten thousand people, according to Roland Tremblay, who also stressed that it was more a dispersal than a disappearance (2006, 118). There is, in fact, widespread scholarly acknowledgment that St. Lawrence Iroquoians were displaced and scattered in war.[1]

Where did the survivors of these people go? In 1642 several Indians told the French:

> That they belonged to the nation of those who had formerly dwelt on this [Montreal] Island. Then, stretching out their hands towards the hills that lie to the East and South of the mountain, "There," said they, "are the places where stood Villages filled with great numbers of Savages. The Hurons, who then were our enemies, drove our Forefathers from this country. Some went towards the country of the Abnaquiois [Abenakis], others toward the country of the Hiroquois [Iroquois], some to the Huron themselves, and joined them. And that is how this Island became deserted." (Thwaites 1896–1901, 22:215)

Recent discoveries confirm the presence of St. Lawrence Iroquoian pottery (and presumably St. Lawrence Iroquoian makers of the pottery) in Abenaki country of northern New England (Peterson et al.

---

1. Among those believing the St. Lawrence Iroquoians were dispersed in war are Brandão (1997, 64–66); Engelbrecht and Jamieson (2016b, 96); Parmenter (2010, 14–15, 72); Snow (1994, 75); Trigger (2000, 218); and Warrick (2008, 201–3).

2004). Other archaeological investigations have demonstrated a high incidence of stylistically Laurentian pottery (more than 10 percent) on certain sites of the Hurons and of their close neighbors, the Petuns.[2]

There also seems to be a St. Lawrence Iroquoian presence among the eastern Iroquois. The evidence for this is chiefly ceramic, detected in the form of such attributes as reed-produced "annular punctuates" considered typical of Laurentian ceramics. It is also reported in terms of types—that is, congeries of form and design recurring on pottery from sites believed to be from the same tribe. Defined by Richard MacNeish from St. Lawrence Iroquoian stations, types such as Durfee Underlined, Lanorie Crossed, and Roebuck Low Collar are regarded as typical of St. Lawrence Iroquoian pottery (1952).[3] However, the ceramic evidence for Laurentians among the Iroquois is less than that present among the Hurons. Only about 2 percent of the relevant Mohawk assemblages, for example, manifest St. Lawrence Iroquoian characteristics (Funk and Kuhn 2003, 157; Kuhn et al. 1993, 85). That suggests that fewer St. Lawrence Iroquoians ended up among the Onondagas, Oneidas, and Mohawks than went to Huronia.

Women, almost certainly, were the potterymakers in all these societies (Allen 1992, 135, 141; Wonderley 2002, 37). Yet, the ceramic evidence for St. Lawrence Iroquoians among the eastern Iroquois is consistently interpreted as indicating intertribal conflict because foreign pottery is often regarded as the work of prisoners. Researchers reason from a series of plausible assumptions often called the "captive bride" scenario (Engelbrecht 1974, 61). The argument is that male

2. High incidences of St. Lawrence Iroquoian sherds among Huron and Petun ceramic assemblages are reported by Engelbrecht (1995, 52); Kuhn (2004, 150–52); Kuhn et al. (1993, 78); Ramsden (1990a, 382–83, 1990b, 90); Robertson and Williamson (1998, 147–48); and Williamson (2016, 108, 116).

3. MacNeish originally regarded pottery from such St. Lawrence Iroquoian sites as Durfee, Roebuck, and Lanorie as belonging to an Onondaga-Oneida series (1952, 56–64). The attribution was later corrected as it became clear the St. Lawrence Iroquoians were historically distinct from the Onondaga and the Oneida tribes (MacNeish 1980, 3–4).

prisoners of war, being generally unpromising as candidates for reso-
cialization and relatively unimportant for producing future offspring,
were not brought back to the captors' villages (Brandão 2003, 73).
In consequence, artifacts associated with them are absent from the
archaeological record of the victors' villages. Women, for the opposite
reasons, were more likely to be seized in the raids characteristic of Iroquoian societies and retained for adoption. This, pretty clearly, is the
scenario indicated in the archaeological record of the Seneca Adams
site as discussed in chapter 6.

"Female captives often made pottery from local clays in their
native styles," Dean Snow explained, "so that although pots did not
travel far, pot types did" (2001, 23). Hence, If one finds that the basic
elements of St. Lawrence Iroquoian culture on a site involve "female
technology" (e.g., pottery) but not "male technology" (e.g., pipes, say,
or bone projectile points), then the archaeologist is, as James Wright
put it, "likely dealing with the products of captive women" (1990, 500;
see also Finlayson 1998, 20, 30; Jamieson 1990a, 402–3; Kuhn 2004,
150; Pendergast 1991b, 58–59; Ramsden 1990a, 382–83). A caveat is
that a few female captives make small amounts of pottery whereas
high percentages of foreign ceramics imply whole groups of adoptees
who may have been captives or refugees (Kuhn 2004, 146–53; Warrick
2008, 194–96). Hence, much of the record of Iroquoian war is read
from Iroquoian potsherds.

Examples of the effigy pipes characteristic of the earlier interaction
sphere are all but absent from the archaeological record after about
1520. A single figure-in-arch pipe is known from the Mohawk Garoga
site and a bone in the Dougherty style is reported from Smith-Pagerie,
another Mohawk site (Snow 1995b, 155, 173). These may be survivals
or carry-overs, of course, but they might also be heirlooms, curated
and valued, and suggestive of oral tradition preserved and recounted.

What happened during the first half of the sixteenth century,
subsequent to the interaction sphere of symbolically charged pipes,
seems to have involved war. Certainly that was so in southern Ontario
where, in 1500–1550, violence was pervasive to judge by heightened

concern with defensive measures visible nearly everywhere (Jamieson 1992, 77; Dermarkar et al. 2016, 87). The same situation pertained among the eastern Iroquois. To get at that and to apprehend the character of the evidence, I survey the archaeological record of the three Iroquois members of the earlier interaction zone of pipes. Although the ceramic assemblages will not be described in detail, it should be remembered that the pottery of the Mohawks, Oneidas, and Onondagas was similar. More generally, these three tribal entities were closer to one another in their material culture than they were to that of the Cayugas and Senecas (Engelbrecht 1985, 178; MacNeish 1952, 57; Snow 1995b, 91).

Onondaga

During approximately the first half of the sixteenth century, the center of Onondaga residence was shifted about six miles east from the Burke site to the western shore of Cazenovia Lake (Bradley 1987, 34–35). In making this move, the Onondagas abandoned exposed hilltop locations in favor of "secondary elevations such as platforms, ridges, or the promontories that flank broad glacial valleys" (Bradley 1987, 35). The result was four new villages of unprecedented size (three to eight acres), the largest being the Barnes site. James Tuck perceived the four sites as comprising a pair of villages over time—the Barnes and McNab sites, followed by Temperance House and Atwell Fort—the latter two estimated to date to 1525–50 (1971b, 169, 216).

At least three of the sites were fortified and the circumstances of the two later settlements radiate fear. Access to them "would have been quite restricted and surprise attack difficult" (Bradley 1987, 50). Similarly, it was clear to Tuck that the Temperance and Atwell locations were selected for maximum defensive advantage. The impression of heightened concern with defensibility at these sites is reinforced by the extraordinary massiveness of some of the upright poles (up to fifteen inches in diameter) set in palisade lines protecting the villages (Ricklis 1963, 2). This was the period, in short, during which

Onondagas "seem to have been the most concerned with defense" (Tuck 1971b, 162).[4] Two pieces of human bone showed up in the refuse of the Barnes site, evidence it is supposed of ritual cannibalism suggestive, in turn, of interpersonal violence (Bradley 1987, 37; Gibson 1968, 8).

Eric Jones thinks the tribe numbered five hundred to one thousand individuals (2010, 400). Onondaga mortuary practices prior to this time are almost completely unknown because only one burial locus has been reported. Immediately outside the village palisade at Barnes were two small burial plots containing bodies that had been interred flexed and unaccompanied by offerings in very shallow ground. The impression, Tuck remarked, "is one of disposal burials" (1971b, 150; Bradley 1987, 214n4, 217n25).

The most dramatic change in the inventory of early sixteenth-century Onondaga is the appearance of materials that had been absent from the archaeological record for many centuries. The new "exotics" comprise Native materials from distant regions including copper but, far more frequently, artifacts and pieces of marine shell. The examples from the Barnes site include ten shell beads, of which seven are discoidal and three are tubular, all apparently drilled biconically—that is, with tools not made of iron (Gibson 1968, 3; Tuck 1971, 160; Bradley 1987, 42, 213n44). The influx of exotics also includes trace amounts of European items (Bradley 1987, 5, 69, 79; Tuck 1971b, 160, 168).

European material appears across Iroquoia at about the same time, a pattern of distribution suggesting that "some sort of cooperative arrangement" must have been in place (Bradley 1987, 104). Further, both European and Native exotics were viewed by the Onondagas as materials/objects of great spiritual power, the acquisition of which was necessary for the performance of League ritual (Bradley 1987, 43,

4. Another indication of defensibility, Eric Jones suggests, is that contemporaneous villages tended to be mutually visible, a circumstance that would have been "beneficial for communication and defense" (2006, 537).

110).[5] Therefore, the appearance of the exotics signaled the formation or early development of the League of the Iroquois at the Barnes site.[6]

Onondaga contacts with other groups are inferred from the presence of foreign pottery, especially ceramics identified as St. Lawrence Iroquoian. Tuck believed the relevant evidence amounted to little more than a handful of Laurentian sherds with stamped, low collars found at Atwell and Temperance House, presumably Roebuck Low Collar; (1971b, 168, 170). The sporadic nature of these remains, Tuck concluded, "suggests the presence of a few people from the North" at Onondaga, "probably refugees from disease or disaster in the St. Lawrence Valley, perhaps occasioned by the arrival there of the Europeans" (1971b, 207).

Bradley thought that a St. Lawrence Iroquoian presence, specifically from Jefferson County, was first detectable in the pottery of the Barnes, Atwell, and Temperance House sites as a few sherds of Laurentian type supplemented by Laurentian traits in pots that looked otherwise Onondagan ("ceramic miscegenation") (1987, 56–57, 85). Laurentian traits may have included examples of a St. Lawrence Iroquoian diagnostic called "corn-ear" pottery discussed at greater length later (Bradley 1987, 215–16n115). The totality of the St. Lawrence Iroquoian ceramic package was numerically minor (1–2 percent of the total assemblages), the work perhaps of "captive brides" (Bradley 1987, 58). But there were other Laurentian artifacts (e.g., pipe stems with circular incisions and bone projectile points) suggestive of St. Lawrence Iroquoian men being present (Bradley 1987, 61, 64, 216n22). This northern influence was showing up at Onondaga at approximately

5. Bradley's notion of "power" objects drew heavily on the insights of George Hamell, who argued that certain substances, especially those such as marine shell coming from a great distance, were highly charged with symbolic significance to the Iroquois (Bradley 1987, 222n23; see Hamell 1987a-b, 1992).

6. Bradley later dated the beginning of the Iroquois League to about the mid-sixteenth century and regarded the appearance of foreign materials as evidence, more generally, of shock experienced from first contact with Europeans (2001, 28–29, 32–33).

the time occupation was ending in Jefferson County—ca. 1515–50 (Bradley 1987, 61, 64, 216n22; Abel 2018). Hence, "it now seems certain that a portion of the St. Lawrence Iroquois of Jefferson County were adopted and eventually assimilated by the Onondaga" (Bradley 1987, 85; Bradley 2001, 31). James Bradley visualized a "sizable group," or perhaps several smaller groups, of refugees fleeing from the north (1987, 85–87). Reaffirming close links of some sort, a recent study of ceramic decoration identified unusually close ties between Onondaga's Atwell station and several sites in Jefferson County (Hart and Engelbrecht 2017, 209).

Another change in the Onondaga archaeological record, but one that has attracted far less wonderment than the exotics or foreign pottery, is the beginning of a long tradition of decorating pottery with humanoid representations. Such effigies first appear at the Barnes and McNab sites in the form of human faces, 2–3 cm high, modeled into the vessel fabric or modeled separately then applied to the pot (Gibson 1963, 6; Gibson 1968, 3, 17; Tuck 1971b, 155, 164, 168; Bradley 1987, 38, 55). Such depictions were placed at or directly underneath a castellation—the upward flaring point at the top of a vessel's collar.

Oneida

After Nichols Pond and Dougherty (chapter 2), Oneida occupation moved east toward the drainage of Cowaselon Creek as inferred from a series of small sites (an acre or less in extent) and one larger one (Buyea, perhaps three to four acres) (Bennett 2006; Gibson 1971a, 1971b, 1986; Pratt 1976, 96–100; Whitney 1970). Next, two enormous sites appear on the gentle slope of a high east-west trending ridge overlooking Cowaselon Creek. One, Olcott, is the largest in the Oneida sequence (about ten acres). The other, Vaillancourt, is very nearly so (roughly five acres). Vaillancourt has a precipitous drop on its east side but the overall topography of both sites does not impress as obviously defensive in nature (Pratt 1961b). Nevertheless, both had heavy vertical members in their palisades with enormous girths (up to two feet in diameter) not seen in the Oneida sequence prior to this time.

Archaeologists who dug these features regarded them as evidence of a preeminent concern with warfare, which they also inferred from the presence of human bone in the refuse (Pratt 1976, 100; Peterson 1958). Based on this and many other similarities to Temperance House and Atwell Fort in the Onondaga area and to the Garoga/Klock/Smith Pagerie sites in the Mohawk Valley, the dates of the Oneida stations are thought to be about the 1520s (Olcott) and circa 1525–55 (Vaillancourt) (see the introduction).

Estimates of Oneida population range widely, from one thousand to four thousand (Jones 2010, 403; Starna 1988, 16). Little is known of their mortuary customs up to and during this time. A few burials were exhumed within the site area of Nichols Pond but the circumstances are not known in any detail (Pratt 1966, 169). At Olcott, a farmer reportedly dug up a cemetery of some forty graves just west of the site area. Except for one ceramic vessel, no objects were interred with the burials (Pratt 1963, 62).

European material probably appears for the first time in the Oneida sequence at Vaillancourt and, perhaps, at Olcott as well.[7] And, while one seashell artifact was documented at Nichols Pond, the first substantive presence of marine shell is a characteristic of Olcott (four discoidal beads and a shell pendant) and Vaillancourt (two tubular beads of what is classified as "early wampum," and four shell fragments) (Pratt 1963, 80; Wonderley 2006, 12).

Foreign connections at the Oneida sites are visible in the plastic decoration of the pottery: symbolically meaningful elements coming from the St. Lawrence Iroquoian region. The most easily recognizable trait from that area is corn-ear pottery diagnostic of St. Lawrence Iroquoian subregions from Montreal (Hochelaga area) west to the Prescott and Summerstown clusters and, to a lesser extent, Jefferson

---

7. For metal at Vaillancourt, see Gibson (1966) and Wonderley (2006, 8). In 2002 a portion of the Wednesday afternoon digging group of the Chenango Chapter—Dick Hosbach, Alex Neill, Ed Gibson, and Francis Hailey—found what they thought was a metal projectile point in a postmold at Olcott (Richard Hosbach, personal communication).

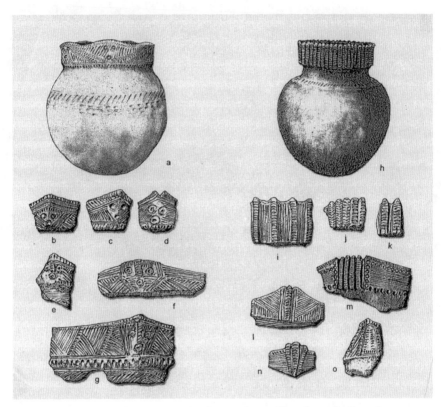

13. St. Lawrence Iroquoian pottery decoration: effigy faces (left) and corn ears (Wonderley 2009, figs. 4a–b and 7). Examples l–n show the corn-ear motif featured at a castellation. Sherds (l) and (m) are from the Glenbrook site (Summerstown cluster); the others are from the Roebuck site (Prescott cluster).

County (Chapdelaine 2004, 65, 68–70; Engelbrecht 2004, 128; Tremblay 2006, 130) (see map 2). The corn ear is a distinct kind of ceramic vessel, a type characterized by a series of raised, vertically oriented ridges applied around a vessel's exterior rim. Each ridge is indented with horizontal slashes, incised lines, or punctates usually lined up in a single column. Each vertical ridge is one corn-ear motif. The name corn ear derives from a perceived resemblance to "ears of corn, the rows of transverse linear impressions being intended to represent the kernels" (Wintemberg 1936, 113) (fig. 13h–o).

The design as both type and motif, in other words, is regarded as naturalistic because it looks like an ear of corn (Kuhn, Funk, and Pendergast 1993, 80; Tremblay 2006, 82). At Vaillancourt the corn ear appears to be part of the local Oneida ceramic assemblage because it looms large in a small sample and is physically indistinguishable from other local pottery.

Earlier, St. Lawrence Iroquoian influence was manifest in the appearance of human-like depictions at or under vessel castellations. An effigy art of anthropomorphic faces, modeled and applied, first appeared in the Oneida area about 1500 (Bennett 2006, 86; Pratt 1976, 100). Very likely it was derived from or inspired by northern antecedents. Pottery of that area had been decorated with tripunctate faces as early as the 1300s (Clermont, Chapdelaine, and Barré 1983) (fig. 13a–g). A modeled and applied variant of the face apparently also was developed earlier in the St. Lawrence Iroquoian area. Sometime about 1450, such three-dimensional faces occurred alongside the tripunctate examples in the Prescott and Summerstown clusters northeast of Jefferson County (Pendergast 1968, plate 4, nos. 2, 5–6; Wintemberg 1936, plate 9, nos. 25–26). Among the earliest Oneida examples (at the Buyea site) is a tripunctate face in the St. Lawrence Iroquoian style (Whitney 1970, plate 4).

The face tradition, as it continued at Olcott and Vaillancourt (fig. 14a), included human-like visages to which bodies were added. Depictions of possible arms and legs appeared at the Olcott site in the form of applied bands of clay marked with parallel indentations or hash marks. At the succeeding Vaillancourt site, such appliquéd ribbons occasionally were attached to the faces to show the first clearly recognizable anthropomorphic figure (Wonderley 2005b, fig. 7; Wonderley 2006, fig. 11).

The Laurentian corn ear is circumstantially implicated in this symbolic synthesis because the fully evolved figure has a body literally consisting of two elongated corn-ear elements. If we are justified in recognizing corn in the corn ear, then corn meaning is being added to the face. That hypothesis is strengthened by the fact that other

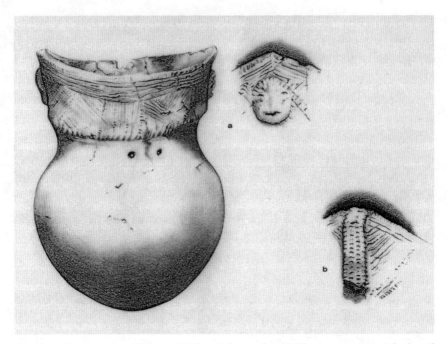

14. Oneida ceramic effigies. (a) Vessel from the Vaillancourt site with detail of face; (b) apparent depiction of corncob from the Olcott site (Wonderley 2004, figs. 15, 17d). Vessel shown in (a) is about 28 cm high.

elements placed at the castellation about this time really do resemble cobs of maize (fig. 14b).

Corn meaning also seems appropriate from contextual clues. Here it must be posited that, in the absence of any overarching theory of reification explaining why and when specific things came into being, one can only assume that the meaning(s) of material symbols had to have been consistent with the contexts in which they were employed. How meaning was constituted therefore requires looking at how the objects were situated in social practice (Hodder 1986, 1987).

Pots, as previously noted, probably were made by women for cooking. Historically, the ceramic vessels were placed over the fire primarily to boil water for cooking corn (Harrington 1908, 581–82). The most common dish was a corn soup, a mush or gruel the French call sagamité, brought to a boil in the pot (Waugh 1916, 90–95, 116). "The ordinary sagamité," Father Gabriel Sagard said in a passage describing the Hurons but applicable to the Iroquois, "is raw maize ground into meal. . . . with a little meat or fish if they have any. . . . It is the soup, meat, and dessert of every day, and there is nothing more" (Wrong 1939, 107). "Every morning," Father Joseph François Lafitau wrote of the Iroquois in the early 1700s, "the women prepare the sagamité and bring it a boil for the nourishment of the family" (Fenton and Moore 1977, 60). It seems very likely, then, that ceramic vessels at Olcott and Vaillancourt, including those with effigies, reflect the domestic activities of women in the home and were used mainly for cooking maize gruels. Assuming that symbolism had something to do with how effigy pottery was employed in daily life, one would guess the imagery related to domestic, feminine, and maize-related concerns.[8]

Aside from one possible bone projectile point from Vaillancourt, the traces of St. Lawrence Iroquoians on these Oneida sites are ceramic and, inferentially, feminine (Wonderley 2006, 12). Although the relevant pottery comprises a small proportion of the whole, it testifies to an important chapter of cultural assimilation. What we see in the corn ears and effigies is the start of a symbolically resonant trend in Oneida pottery that endures for a hundred years (fig. 15). It looks like a substantial St. Lawrence Iroquoian contribution to Oneida culture.

The appearance of corn-ear pottery and the development of the full-figure humanoid imagery occur against the archaeological backdrop

8. Elsewhere, Wonderley elaborates the interpretation that these effigies connoted corn and possibly made reference to mythological corn-husk people associated with bountiful crops (2002, 2005b, 2012).

The tradition of humanoid effigies discussed here is characteristic of Oneida and Onondaga pottery and present—though rarely—in Mohawk country. Stylistically different effigies showing a human-like figure are also reported in the ceramics of the Senecas and Susquehannocks (Wonderley 2002, 27).

For the Seneca examples of anthropomorphic effigy figures, see Sempowski and Saunders (2001, 159, 430–31, figs. 3–81g-h, 7–83f); Wray, Sempowski, and Saunders (1991, 274, fig. 7-54d); and Wray et al. (1987, 76–78, fig. 3-3b). For Susquehannock examples, see Kent (1980, fig. 3); Skinner in Morehead (1938, plates 20–21).

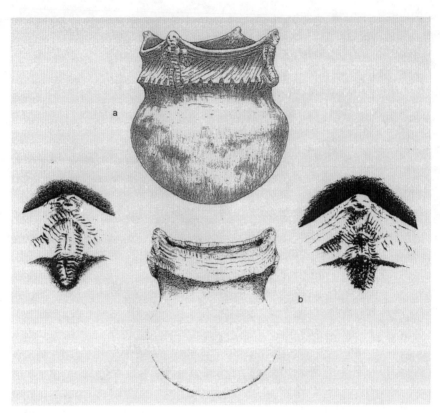

15. The full-figure effigy in Oneida ceramic art. (a) Vessel probably of the type Wagoner-Syracuse incised with four humanoid figures (ca. 1620–34), 23 cm high; (b) vessel of the type Thurston Horizontal with two humanoid figures (ca. 1634–55), 16 cm high (Wonderley 2004, fig. 16).

of defensive precautions implied by the enormous palisade uprights. A possible tradition of war in the north was asserted in 1784 by an Oneida who said the land along the St. Lawrence River was theirs by right of conquest because, "a long time ago," they had taken an enemy fort there (Hough 1861, 46). All in all, the makers of foreign pottery from Vaillancourt are more likely to have been captive brides than refugees, adoptees who haled from one of the corn-ear rich subregions of the St. Lawrence Iroquoians (the Prescott cluster or further east).

But there may be something else going on. In his pioneering study of the Oneida archaeological record, Peter Pratt detected a St. Lawrence Iroquoian presence in Oneida pottery, chiefly in the form of sherds belonging to Durfee Underlined and Roebuck Low Collar. These materials have not been recognized among the Olcott and Vaillancourt assemblages but, instead, show up at sites later in the Oneida sequence: Bach (ca. 1560–80), Diable (ca. 1570–1600), and Cameron (ca. 1605–20) (Pratt 1976, 173, 175, 242, 245).

In a subsequent comparison of ceramic types from Jefferson County and the eastern Iroquois area, William Engelbrecht found that the closest connections to one of the last sites to be occupied in Jefferson County were with pottery from the Oneida Bach and Diable stations. Presumably detecting the same phenomenon noted by Pratt, Engelbrecht suggested that some portion of the Jefferson County population remaining at that point (Dry Hill cluster) "was incorporated into the eastern nations of the Iroquois Confederacy" (2004, 133).

Mohawk

Otstungo, mentioned earlier as the possible birthplace of the Mohawk tribe, initiated a new pattern of settlement in the Mohawk Valley focused on defense (Bond 1985, 37). Even greater concern with protection is manifested in the later sites of Cayadutta (ca. 1525–45), and of Garoga, Klock, and Smith-Pagerie—the latter three dated 1525–80 by Snow (1995b, 146, 165, 171, 181), and from the late 1400s into the 1580s by Hart (2018). About 2.5–5 acres in extent, all were located along steep cliffs and further protected by earthworks and palisades containing enormous upright posts up to twenty-seven inches in diameter (Ritchie and Funk 1973, 315; Funk and Kuhn 2003, 9, 56, 98). The concentration of people within these villages was, Snow reasoned, yet another defensive measure: "Simple arithmetic shows that by doubling the length of a village defensive perimeter, they could increase village area four times. A village that doubled its perimeter quadrupled not only its area but also, consequently, its population. This economy in scale reduced the amount of perimeter that had to be maintained and defended by each warrior" (1994, 52).

All of this implies a violent age. "Severed finger bones and other evidence of torture and cannibalism turn up in village refuse middens from this time forward" (Snow 1994, 53). It is apparent, Funk and Kuhn agreed, "that the sixteenth century was a time of dramatically increased warfare and that the Mohawk were extremely concerned about attack and the village defenses" (2003, 156–57). Snow thought the fortified villages testified to an impulse to end strife, which led to the formation of the League of the Iroquois by 1525 (1994, 49). "We take the highly defensive settlements of the sixteenth-century Mohawk," Funk and Kuhn rejoined, "to be a good indication that the formidable Five Nations Confederacy . . . had not been established" (2003, 157).

Snow estimated there were about 1,500 Mohawks at this time (1995b, 45, 90). Knowledge of their mortuary practices is limited to the observation that burials tended to be flexed primary interments with few or no burial offerings. Cayadutta reportedly had a cemetery similar, perhaps, to what was described for the Onondaga site of Barnes (Bamann 1993, 123). Although other burial areas apparently are known, a general absence of them from fifteenth- and sixteenth-century village sites led Snow to wonder whether a "specialized central cemetery" remains to be discovered (2001, 23).[9]

Effigy faces on pottery occur rarely; only two each were documented among the enormous ceramic samples from the Klock and Smith-Pagerie sites (Funk and Kuhn 2003, 34, 73). From an Oneida perspective, the tradition of humanoid representation is not characteristic of the Mohawk Valley.

9. Evidently, there has been little advance in mortuary knowledge among the eastern Iroquois since William Ritchie's summary of state archaeology: "The burial customs of the late prehistoric Iroquois are not well known. The cemeteries often seem to have been located quite a distance from the villages, [and] . . . consequently most of them have so far escaped discovery. Flexed burial without mortuary goods was the rule in the graves that have been found" (1980, 321).

Marine shell seems to appear rather suddenly in the archaeological record at sites presumed to date to the 1500s: Cayadutta (twelve objects, including four discoidal and two tubular beads), Garoga (two tubular beads and four other pieces), Klock (twelve fragments, including eight discoidal and two tubular beads), and Smith-Pagerie (two, including one tubular bead) (Kuhn and Funk 1994, 78; Funk and Kuhn 2002, 44, 79; Snow 1995b, 160–61). Seashells, it is thought, were reaching the Mohawk area via a trade route stretching south from the Susquehanna River to the Chesapeake Bay area of the Atlantic coast (Kuhn and Funk 1994, 80–82; Snow 1995b, 154). At precisely the same archaeological moment shell appears, European material makes its first appearance in the Mohawk Valley about 1525–30 (Snow 1995b, 28; Funk and Kuhn 2003, 132; Hart 2018).

A significant increase in beaver hunting took place in the early sixteenth century. Older faunal assemblages of the Mohawk Valley have very small amounts of beaver remains, rarely more than 2 percent. In contrast, beaver remains make up 10 percent of the faunal assemblages from the Garoga and Klock sites and almost 20 percent from the Smith-Pagerie site. "There appears to be little doubt that the Mohawk were already changing their traditional hunting practices in order to accommodate trade for European goods" (Funk and Kuhn 2003, 156; Lenig 1977, 73–74).

Here, as elsewhere, contacts with nearby groups are inferred from the presence of exotic ceramic material and here, as elsewhere, most of the exotic pottery is characterized by St. Lawrence Iroquoian traits (Kuhn 2004, 148). The St. Lawrence Iroquoian component was defined from a small number of sherds belonging to Laurentian types (Roebuck Low Collar, Durfee Underlined, Lanorie Crossed) and attributes characteristic of St. Lawrence Iroquoian pottery (chiefly annular punctuates and crisscrossed lines and, from a single vessel, the corn-ear motif) (Kuhn 2004, 150). This Laurentian package appears in low percentages at sites believed to be from the sixteenth century: Cayadutta (0.4 percent), Klock (2.6 percent), Smith-Pagerie (2.9 percent), and Garoga (0.9 percent) (Kuhn 2004, 151). In addition to the potsherds, there are several artifacts of LeRay chert from Jefferson

County, which imply the presence of a few males—or, perhaps, of a Mohawk man curious about the lithic potential of a distant place (Kuhn et al. 1993, 84–85). Overall, the St. Lawrence Iroquoian materials are believed to represent the work of female captives (Funk and Kuhn 2003, 157). Since the apparently foreign potterymakers show up on Mohawk sites as the St. Lawrence Valley is abandoned, their ceramics imply "conflict between Mohawk and St. Lawrence Iroquoian groups leading to the capture and assimilation of St. Lawrence Iroquoian people into Mohawk communities" (Kuhn 2004, 149).

Snow argued for the existence of another St. Lawrence Iroquoian phenomenon based on the belief that a rise in population at this time, particularly at the Rice's Woods and England's Woods sites (perhaps 1560–80), resulted from an influx of people from Jefferson County (1995b, 198, 216). Artifactual evidence lending support to that hypothesis apparently exists in the high percentage of pottery from England's Woods (8.3 percent) manifesting northern Iroquoian attributes (Kuhn 2004, 151). The idea of Jefferson County refugees also accords with Engelbrecht's results in another comparative study of Jefferson County ceramics with those of the three eastern Iroquois areas. In a statistical examination not of types but of attributes, he found that pottery from the last Jefferson County villages to be occupied, Dry Hill cluster, resembled ceramic material coming out of Mohawk sites of the early 1600s (Engelbrecht 1995; Engelbrecht 2004, 126). The implication was that some Jefferson County Iroquoians joined the Mohawks.

The indications of violence in conjunction with the increase in beaver remains, the appearance of European material, and evidence for involvement with St. Lawrence Iroquoians—these circumstances suggest to Kuhn "that during the second quarter of the sixteenth century the conflict between the Mohawk and Northern Iroquoian groups was stimulated by the fur trade" (2004, 161; see also Snow 1994, 75). Some commerce with Europeans had been occurring along the lower reaches of the St. Lawrence River since the early 1500s (Garrad 2014, 12–15; Parmenter 2010, 7; Trigger 2000, 7–8).

Conclusions

As confederacies coalesced, the culturally engendered militancy of the young was likely to be directed outward. A logical consequence of alliance would be to increase and pool manpower, which, dispatched outward, would intensify interpolity warfare beyond any clan- or village-level act of proximate blood revenge. Hence, to forge alliance was to escalate war. Such would be an expectation drawn from the model of contentious confederacies.

We have seen an interaction sphere of symbolically resonant pipes linking the three eastern Iroquois tribal areas with at least some portion of Jefferson County in the late fifteenth to early sixteenth centuries. In this chapter we have reviewed what came after for the culturally similar Onondaga, Oneida, and Mohawk regions. In all three, signs of heightened defensiveness are registered in the living arrangements. Extremely defensive-looking topographic situations were evident among the Onondagas and Mohawks. Huge palisade poles evocative of extraordinary protective concerns characterized all areas. There were, in all three, large concentrations of settlement suggestive of defense and of manpower pooling as Snow speculated. Human bone in the refuse of all areas implies that ritual cannibalism of prisoners was being practiced as it was in later historic times.

Sensing in these circumstances a climate of pervasive fear, archaeologists frequently remark that this was a time of violence precisely as described in the Deganawida epic. Oral traditions of the Iroquois League's founding, however, convey a variety of views about an age of internecine war. Gibson and, to a lesser extent, Newhouse paint a Hobbesian picture in which every man's hand is raised against everyone else's. The Iroquois fought one another intertribally is what Cusick, Morgan, and Hale imply. No, say others, the Iroquois were contending with external foes, either western tribes (Webster), or enemies from the north (Clark, Johnson). Sometimes the emphasis is on the source of violence as coming, for example, from vengeance-seeking (Norton), from the tyranny of a despot (Buck), or from the rivalry of brothers (Brant). The legendary perspectives are diverse and sometimes irreconcilable. So, while they are a wonderful font for metaphorical or poetical expression, clues about who was fighting whom come from the archaeological record and not the other way around.

The evidence suggests that the primary enemies of the eastern Iroquois were St. Lawrence Iroquoians (Warrick 2008, 201, 203). Their settlements disappear about the time their material traces register among the eastern Iroquois as the chief foreign presence. Investigators of all three areas, noting the feminine nature of the ceramic evidence as well as its relative paucity, lean toward the idea that these are residues of captive brides—that is, female captives taken in war and brought home to become integrated into the lives of the eastern Iroquois villages. Such a case seems clearest at Oneida sites in which a distinctive St. Lawrence Iroquoian trait, the corn-ear motif, probably derived from St. Lawrence Iroquoian villages on the Canadian side of the St. Lawrence River, shows up in the local pottery. The corn-ear motif then apparently contributes to the development of a full-figure humanoid depiction. It looks like a set of feminine- and corn-associated material symbols that come to be expressed in Oneida pottery. The process most likely illustrates incorporation of former captives and the assimilation of their values into the cultural life of the home village.

Investigators commonly identify Jefferson County as the source of St. Lawrence Iroquoian material among the eastern Iroquois. In the Oneida and Mohawk cases, such a phenomenon may have occurred a little later in time than that of the Oneida captive brides with their preference for corn ears. And, bearing in mind the earlier pipe interaction sphere, people from Jefferson County may have come not so much as individual captives but as small groups of refugees seeking help from confederates or former friends.

The disappearance of the St. Lawrence Iroquoians is a complicated subject involving several village clusters, each with its own history and, overall, a number of different actors (Tremblay 2006, 124). Focusing, however, on contentious confederacies and on the eastern Iroquois, the big picture, as Bruce Trigger discerned, was that "as more tribes joined the Huron and Iroquois confederacies and ceased to fight with one another, the young men of these confederacies would have found it necessary to direct their hostilities farther afield. Increasing warfare between these confederacies would have been an additional factor promoting their internal consolidation" (2000, 244). The St. Lawrence Iroquoians fell victim to nascent confederacies of the Iroquois and the Hurons developing on either side of them (Engelbrecht 1995; Tremblay 2006, 124).

However, one must go beyond that simple paradigm to understand what happened in upstate New York in the early 1500s because archaeology reveals the existence of other variables demanding consideration. One of them is that European material first shows up at this time in all three eastern Iroquois areas. We know, furthermore, that the Mohawks greatly increased the processing of beaver after 1525. Obviously, European presence and fur trade should be taken into account when considering the events of this period.

Trigger thought it likely that the fur trade was a motive for Iroquois conflict with St. Lawrence Iroquoians (2000, 223). To all the Indigenous peoples, European materials, especially those made of metal, were highly desirable because they were functionally superior to Native-made counterparts (2000, 409). European goods were obtainable at trading locations which, by 1580, had advanced up the St. Lawrence River as far as Lachine. The St. Lawrence Iroquoians blocked Iroquois access to these sites and goods, and especially to those items useful in war. "Such a situation would have put the Mohawk at a serious disadvantage and made obtaining European knives and hatchets seem a matter of life and death to them. The desire for unrestricted access to trading stations on the St. Lawrence, or to secure iron tools in war, may have led to an all-out attack on the Hochelagans [St. Lawrence Iroquoians of the Montreal region] resulting in their destruction not long before 1600" (Trigger 2000, 221). More generally, Trigger concluded, "It seems likely that Iroquois attacks led to the dispersal of the St. Lawrence Iroquoians late in the 16th century" in order to gain access to European goods (1978, 345).

Tremblay, likewise, was impressed by the coincidence of war dispersing the St. Lawrence Iroquoians just as Europeans arrived and the fur trade began. "The St. Lawrence Iroquoians were ideally placed to maintain direct economic relations with the foreigners, and to profit from European innovations more than other groups," he reasoned. "We can imagine that their role as middlemen aroused the envy of their neighbours and that they might have come under increasingly heavy and more frequent attack as a result" (2006, 121).

However, evidence on this score is inconclusive. Tremblay noted a paucity of datable, physical Laurentian material bearing on the problem. Certainly in New York State at the time of concern here, there are no iron tools of the sort Trigger emphasized. "For the time being, then, the role played in this tragedy by Europeans in particular must be approached with caution, while the blame cannot be laid directly at their door, they could certainly have acted as catalysts—probably unwittingly, given how difficult it was for them to understand Native traditions and customs" (Tremblay 2006, 25, 27).

Of course it is not only European items that show up in the Onondaga, Oneida, and Mohawk regions. For the first time in centuries, foreign exotics from Indigenous sources—chiefly marine material—appear at about the same time. Why these phenomena are related in time and what that might mean to Iroquois cultural development is another recurrent interpretive concern among Iroquoianists. Several have sensed that exotics, especially marine shells, must be bound up with emergent ritual and symbolic expression. George Hamell pointed out that the presence of marine shells in large quantities, in tandem with the availability of European goods, stimulated burial ceremonialism and demand for more goods associated with such rituals (Hamell 1987a, 64–65; Hamell 1998, 271). It is pointed out in chapters 5 and 6 that the material correlates of burial ceremonialism—foreign exotics—were much the same as those of condolence and requickening. It is possible, therefore, that mortuary forms of condolence gave rise to or contributed to the development of condolence protocol as historically and ethnographically attested. In any event, the funerary use of exotics surely intensified the desire to acquire those goods. And, when mortuary behavior is tracked into the 1600s, it becomes clear that burial-related rites intensified, presumably to strengthen the social fabric as the number of losses and adoptees added up (chapter 6).

Trigger thought that European goods would have preceded and encouraged the appearance of Native exotics.

> The introduction of iron tools frequently reduces the time required to perform certain important routine tasks, and permits energies to be redirected elsewhere. The result is not a disruption of the indigenous culture or a breakdown in existing social relationships, such as may occur when direct European intervention is involved. Instead, this period witnesses the realization of potentials that existed in the native culture. Particularly, one finds the elaboration of social status, increasing emphasis on ceremonialism (especially involving conspicuous consumption), greater artistic endeavours, and heightened competition to control scarce resources. (Trigger 2000, 408–9)

Bradley, as noted earlier, emphasized that both Native and European exotics were equated in the Iroquois view as objects/substances of high spiritual value that were necessary for enacting the ceremonies of the Iroquois League. The appearance of European and Native exotics, he argued, signals the formation or early development of the League (2001, 32). And, although internal application to ceremony and ritual was peaceful, the desire for such substances impelled the Iroquois to war in order to obtain them (1987, 104–9).

In the next chapter, the archaeological issue of European and Native exotics is reconsidered with reference to the internal dynamics of confederacy stressing peacekeeping.

5

Wampum, Seashells, and Peace

Anthony Wonderley

The effigy pipes discussed in chapters 2 and 3 as indicating intertribal diplomacy dropped out of the archaeological record in the early 1500s in eastern Iroquoia and a little later in western Iroquoia. In the east, marine shell and, later, beads made from marine shell appeared about the time effigy pipes disappeared from the archaeological record. Why seashell should be regarded as another material correlate of peaceful activity, and why such behavior was chiefly directed inwardly, intra-tribally, is the subject of this chapter

Not shell alone, but several kinds of nonlocal material appeared and increased over time during the sixteenth century. The presence of exotics coincided with increasing village nucleation and, in all likeli-hood, with tribal alliance. Archaeologists suspect that exotics in gen-eral and marine shell in particular signal increased ceremonialism pertaining to the birth or early development of the Iroquois League.[1] In the Seneca area, where most exotics derive from graves, the amount of burial furnishings also rises with the passage of time. That suggests an intensification of mortuary ritual in which marine shell figured prominently.

1. Among those perceiving foreign exotics, especially marine shell, as indi-cating increased ceremonialism reflecting, in turn, the beginning or early develop-ment of the Iroquois League are Ceci (1989, 63, 72); Bradley (1987, 179); Engelbrecht (2003, 132); Kuhn and Funk (1994, 77); and Snow (1995a, 154).

Settlement change, group alliance, and burial ceremonialism are all likely to be related as archaeologically detectable residues of peacekeeping activity. As hostilities were directed outward from tribal coalitions, mechanisms for discouraging violence among the constituent members of an alliance had to be deployed within. Pacific behavior involved the exchange of highly valued substances, the most important of which was marine shell. Such at least was the case later in time when tubular shell beads called wampum were, as Lewis Henry Morgan thought, the material correlate of the operation of the Iroquois League (Morgan 1962, 120). Usages of wampum are well documented from the 1600s on. How this later kind of marine shell material was used is reviewed here to elucidate how marine shell probably was employed earlier.

The Importance of Shell

People often use things to underline and sanction their actions. There is nothing surprising in this. Gifts, Marshal Sahlins emphasized, have always served as little peace treaties. The material flow of presents, often fashioned of foreign material, "underwrites or initiates social relations" (1972, 186; see also Sahlins 1968, 10). Words backed by presents speak more forcibly than lips (Axtell 1985, 88).

But why marine shell? Within the full set of exotics appearing in the 1500s, why not some other nonlocal material? All foreign substances may have been, as George Hamell (1987a, 64–65) and James Bradley (1987, 104, 110) suspected, highly valued and highly suitable for gifting activities connected with peacekeeping rituals.[2] But if, on the one hand, European materials were equated conceptually with Native substances, most tended to be downgraded to routine functional status with the passage of time in Bradley's opinion (2001, 32–33; see also Bradley 1987, 130–34). On the other hand, the largest category of Native exotics of nonlocal derivation was white marine shell.

2. See also Snow (2001, 23); Tooker (1991, 52); and Wolf (1982, 95, 165).

Such items, according to archaeologist Robert Hall, belonged to a class of materials customarily employed in acts of greeting and peacemaking throughout a large region because they had "mythological associations with saliva and other body effluvia" (1997, 58). Or, perhaps white shell represented the sea conceived as a life-giving fluid. Maybe, as Hewitt thought, it represented peace, health, welfare, and prosperity (Ceci 1982, 100). White shell, in Hamell's view, carried the highest and most positive valence of the foreign materials as something connoting physical, spiritual, and social well-being (1987b, 76). It was "a material metaphor for the biological continuity of life, especially human life" (1992, 457).

Whatever the specific symbolic content, however, the high value placed on the material is beyond question. Indeed, the power of that belief is documented in some of the earliest writings pertaining to Iroquoians. Jacques Cartier was impressed by a substance called *esnoguy* in use along the St. Lawrence River during the 1530s. Described as "a sort of bead," it was made of white shell possibly fashioned in tubular form from columella of sea whelks, at least some of which derived from New England (Tremblay 2006, 92–93; see also Trigger 2000, 198). *Esnoguy*, Cartier observed, was "the most precious article they possess in this world" (Tremblay 2006, 91). By 1634, a similar kind of bead dominated Iroquois relations with Europeans. What the Oneidas and Onondagas wanted from the Dutch—more than axes, kettles, "or anything else"—was the shell bead called wampum (Gehring and Starna 1988, 13–19).

True wampum was new to the Iroquois world in the 1600s when it first began to appear in a standardized form with narrow diameter (Ceci 1986). Tubular beads of marine shell—as opposed to disks or other forms—became the preferred bead shape among the Senecas only by about 1600.[3] From then comes "the earliest example of tubular shell

3. It should be noted that the conceptually prominent role of tubular beads could never have been predicted from the archaeological evidence. That is because, during the early 1500s, the marine shell artifact predominant among the eastern Iroquois

beads made into a multiple row 'wampum belt,'" implying that the historic culture of wampum use was familiar at the start of the seventeenth century (Sempowski and Saunders 2001, 686). Such marine shell beads, however, do not become abundant in the archaeological record until the 1630s among the Mohawks and the 1640s among the Senecas.[4]

Preference for the tubular shape owed something to the disruption, in the 1580s, of the Senecas' Susquehanna River trade network. That artery of goods was characterized by different shell and, possibly, a greater emphasis on the discoidal form of bead (Sempowski and Saunders 2001, 686; Bradley 1987, 92–93, 179; Hamell 1992, 460). Almost immediately, outsiders sensed an opportunity to profit from the new circumstances. By the late sixteenth century, Native Americans of the Long Island Sound area were ramping up the making of shell beads with metal tools to supply the new market (Ceci 1982, 97; Kuhn and Funk 1994, 81–82; Snow 1995a, 300). By about 1630, control of wampum production was in Euro-American and, especially, Dutch hands.[5]

Wampum in Diplomacy and Ritual

How was wampum actually used? Historically, it was the material most frequently displayed in formal greetings with strangers. The initiator of the interchange assumed that his interlocutor—the parties almost always being male—had recently suffered the loss of someone close.

---

assemblages was not, it will be recalled, the tubular but the discoidal bead. Lenig and Bradley thought the discoidals must have been the original wampum (Lenig 1977, 79; Bradley 1987, 67, 179–80). A good reason to suspect discoidals were important to the Iroquois is that the disk form inspired a foreign industry responding to Native American demand. In Paris, in the 1590s, shell beads of this type were being manufactured for, presumably, an Iroquois market (Garrad 2014; Turgeon 2001).

4. See Kuhn and Funk (1994, 78, 81); Sempowski (1989, 87–90); Sempowski and Saunders (2001, 671, 686); and Snow (1995a, 300).

5. See Ceci (1989); Dennis (1993, 136); Fenton (1998, 227–29, 298–99); Jennings (1988, 52, 78); D. Lenig (1977, 79–80); W. Lenig (1999, 55); Tooker (1978, 421–23); and Trelease (1997, 48).

Accordingly, the speaker sympathized by expressing his own sorrow. Next, he extended condolences for the other's grief and proffered gifts. The interlocutor then reciprocated. Wampum so offered testified to the truth and strength of the spoken sentiments. The material gift of strings of wampum helped to assuage the other's bereavement and served to encourage the other's return to a state of normal existence.

This interchange is familiar to scholars as the Three Bare Words, which usually alluded to drying tears, clearing the ears, and removing obstructions from the throat. A similar standardized presentation was delivered at every interethnic political meeting for at least a century and a half. William Fenton found it recorded in writing about eighty times between the 1640s and early 1800s (1998, 181). The Three Bare Words, therefore, are easily the best documented ritual element in Iroquois history.

Aside from such diplomatic contexts, the Three Bare Words are a well-known component of the primary ceremony of the Iroquois League—the Condolence Council held to raise up or appoint new sachems. In the course of that rite, the Three Bare Words are performed in segments of the overall ritual called the Wood's Edge Greeting and the Requickening Address (Fenton 1998, 137–39; Tooker 1978, 438).

The ritualized exchange of sympathies could also preface or be part of another ceremony, one which combined procedures of formalized condolence with the concept of symbolic resurrection. Among the Hurons and Iroquois, condolence and resuscitation underwrote political ties linking tribes within an alliance. In both confederacies, the most important leadership positions were hereditary offices. In both, an important ritual identified a new chief with his deceased predecessor "symbolically drawn from the grave by the assembled chiefs" (Trigger 1969, 85, 70; Trigger 2000, 84–85). For the League of the Iroquois, the business of symbolic resuscitation was accomplished in an indoor segment of the Condolence Council often called the Requickening Address. As known ethnographically, this ceremony of raising up a new sachem is performed with thirteen to fifteen strings of wampum (Fenton 1998, 180–81; Tooker 1978, 438; Woodbury 1992, xl–xliii).

Counteracting Vengeance

Wampum was employed, perhaps most of all, as wergild—blood money—payment offered to avert the threat of reprisal for a killing. The danger of revenge killing was, in fact, woven into the fabric of daily life. Some of the most vivid accounts of the fear Iroquois people suffered from the constant threat of vengeance come from Samuel Kirkland's descriptions of Oneida village life during the 1790s and early 1800s. Kirkland discussed several instances in which the kin of a deceased person held the relatives of the presumed killer accountable. Anyone closely related to the perpetrator was considered to be a just target for reprisal.

Kirkland also indicated how revenge killing could be averted if, instead of seeking vengeance, the aggrieved party would accept a payment of valuable goods in compensation for the death. All of this was accomplished in a ceremony that opened with the familiar condolence greeting. Then, the payment supposed to settle the matter was enumerated. In one instance, the compensation consisted of two large belts of wampum supplemented by other goods. The ceremony concluded with the affirmation that the injury would be everlastingly forgotten and forgiven in the metaphorical act of pulling up a:

> pine tree by the roots, casting the hatchet with all its blood into the hole or vault, which would sink down into the lower part of the earth till it reached a subterranean rapid stream of water which would hurry it along with its precipices till it should sink into the unfathomable gulf and never more rise to the sight of the human eye, but forever be buried in oblivion. (Pilkington 1980, 345)

That was how one attempted to quash revenge killings between members of different kin groups. However, the threat of violence never really ended. In the case of the aforementioned Oneida ritual, the ceremony failed to take because, it was said, the speaker left out a key portion of the speech. The same situation—not attaining peace—was well-known throughout Iroquoia. Among the Senecas in the early 1800s, for example:

If murder is committed, the relatives of the murderer go immediately to those of the deceased and offer them a belt of wampum, to
signify their acknowledgement of guilt and a profession of sorrow
in behalf of the murderer—and it is optional with the friends of the
deceased to accept or reject it. In case of a refusal they take revenge
by killing a relative of the murderer, but the broil does not cease
here always, but instances are known where alternate retaliation is
carried on for a long time. (Fenton 1969, 120)

Two centuries earlier, Father Joseph François Lafitau remarked on the
uncertainty of this process in averting blood feud. "Even though these
presents are accepted, if the omens are not favorable for taking complete vengeance for the assassination just at that time," the guilty party
"should not flatter themselves that the insult is entirely forgotten. The
dressing put on this wound only covers, without curing it" (Fenton
and Moore 1977, 102).

Obviously, forming and maintaining tribal partnerships required
that feuds between tribes be discouraged. Hence, the avoidance, sup-
pression, and containment of violence were important duties of the
Iroquois League. The earliest firsthand description of the League's
business implies as much. "They hold every year a general assembly,"
explained the Jesuit François Le Mercier in 1668. "There all the deputies from the different nations are present, to make their complaints and
receive the necessary satisfaction in mutual gifts—by means of which
they maintain a good understanding with one another" (Thwaites
1896–1901, 51:237). The first extensive account of the League's function states this peacekeeping function explicitly. The basic purpose of
the Iroquois Confederacy, as John Norton understood it in the early
1800s, was to suppress internal violence by regularizing wergild payments between and among the Iroquois tribes.

The laws and regulations of the confederacy were few and simple. A
man that should spill the blood of another, it was required of him, or
of his relations, to appease the kindred of the deceased, with wampum, to a considerable amount, which they were at liberty either to

receive or to reject, and remain free to take vengeance. (Klinck and Talman 1970, 111)

Norton's version of the Deganawida epic, it will be recalled, is the earliest and perhaps only account to relate the origin of the Iroquois League to a policy of avoiding the exaction of vengeance for the murder of one's own. Anthony Wallace picked up on this as the central point of the Deganawida epic: "The strategic innovation is the prohibition of blood-revenge by members of one of the five tribes against members of their own tribe or of any of the other four" (1958, 124). In emphasizing the achievements of the Peacemaker, contemporary tellers of the Deganawida epic underline the same point (see chapter 1).

Conclusion

Anthropologists say the same thing: avoiding revenge violence among the Iroquois tribes probably was *the* fundamental reason for the Iroquois League.[6] A keystone of confederacy policy, Robert Hall observed, "Was avoiding the destructive force of blood revenge among League members. Relatives of homicide victims were encouraged at all costs to settle grievances by accepting wergeld in the form of wampum belts, twenty for a man and thirty for a woman" (1997, 176n14). "Vengeance killing," Hall elaborated,

> was especially disruptive within a village, or tribe, so there was the greatest of pressure to settle such affairs by negotiation. The League of the Iroquois became known to its members as the Great Peace because the original five participating nations extended the same attitude toward the League as a whole. The five nations were

6. According to Dean Snow, "The League of the Iroquois formed as a political innovation designed to cut the cycle of revenge, at least between the Mohawks and the four other nations that composed the league" (2001, 23). See also Bradley (1987, 104); Fenton (1998, 247); Dennis (1993, 104); Tooker (1991, 52); and (Wolf 1982, 95, 165).

conceived to be the equivalents of five families occupying compart-
ments in a longhouse of five fires, and all were encouraged to settle
homicides in negotiation and compensation rather than by blood
revenge. (Hall 1997, 39)

The Iroquois League, Wallace stated flatly, was "explicitly designed
to prevent the proliferation of blood feuds within and among the various member nations" and to replace vengeance-taking with reparation
payments for murder (1972, 44, 98). The same was true of their rivals.
"The Huron," Bruce Trigger emphasized, "were well aware that no
tribal organization and no confederacy could survive if internal blood
feuds went unchecked. One of the basic functions of the confederacy
was to eliminate such feuds among its members" (2000, 60). Within
both confederacies, order was maintained by encouraging reparation
payments in lieu of vengeance for murder.

Showing little interest in the implications of wergild for wampum
use, archaeologists have focused on the ways wampum is employed
in the Condolence Ceremony. Given that marine shell is the pre-
wampum wampum, researchers hypothesize that the appearance of
shell signals the early development of that Iroquois League ritual. In
the case of the Huron Confederacy, for example, a few seashell objects
are present prior to about 1580. After that point, substantial quantities appear at about the time (1590–1610) the confederacy attained its
full growth (Lennox and Fitzgerald 1990, 429–30; Trigger 1978, 347;
Trigger 2000, 244).

The appearance of marine shell probably is connected, in some
fashion, with ceremonial activity pertaining to tribal alliance.[7] It is

---

7. The interpretation of seashell signaling tribal alliance might also hold for
the Neutral Confederacy. There an increase in shell correlates approximately with
the gathering together of the constituent tribes in the late sixteenth and early seventeenth centuries (Fitzgerald 2001, 38). Then, coinciding perhaps with some final
event of alliance, the quantity of marine shell material increases dramatically in the
last quarter of the sixteenth century or, perhaps, a few years later in 1607–8 (Fitzgerald 2001, 44; Crerar 1994, 40, 45; Pendergast 1989, 98, 102).

difficult to imagine, however, that actual performances of say, the Three Bare Words, resulted in much that survives archaeologically. Nor does the correlation as proposed explain why, in the case of the eastern Iroquois, the seashell increase is registered mostly as village debris; or why, in the Seneca area, it is detected mostly in grave furnishings (see the introduction).

Our model of contentious confederacies provides a better framework for clarifying several categories of wampum/marine shell use and relating them to several kinds of archaeological context. Words of condolence, rites of symbolic resuscitation, payments of blood money, and probably other applications of shell/wampum were all instances of peacemaking behavior mostly practiced within tribal alliances. As belligerence increased outwardly, more effort was applied to suppress it inwardly.[8] The archaeological record registers a greater investment in dampening violence because, interiorly, the League of the Iroquois was a league of peace.

8. If peace and war are different sides of the same coin, perhaps they are necessary correlates of each other. Some, at any rate, have emphasized that one tendency presupposes and demands the other. The Iroquois League, as Wolf saw it, "attempted to curb internal conflicts by directing energies outward against common enemies" (Wolf 1982, 95). It seemed to Bradley that the League stressed peace *because* it was so committed to war (1987, 104).

6

The Longhouse Metaphor

Its Role in the Growth of the League of the Iroquois

Martha L. Sempowski

Introduction

Metaphors can be powerful. By providing a graphic and coherent set of cultural understandings of fundamental aspects of human experience, firmly entrenched cultural metaphors can exert an enduring influence on the beliefs and behavior of a group of people over many generations. For anthropologists, understanding a society's metaphors may offer valuable insights into the cognitive principles and mechanisms underlying the social dynamics of that group. Father Le Jeune's "Jesuit Relation" of 1636 speaks of the importance of metaphors to an understanding of Huron behavior:

> Metaphor is largely in use among these Peoples; unless you accustom yourself to it, you will understand nothing in their councils, where they speak almost entirely in metaphors. They claim by this present to reunite all hearts and wills, and even entire Villages, which have become estranged. (Thwaites 1896–1901, 10:219)

In keeping with our goal of better understanding the underpinnings and early development of the League of the Iroquois, this chapter examines the potential implications of the "longhouse metaphor," considered by Fenton (1978a) to be the primary symbolic metaphor of the Iroquois. While abstract metaphors leave no archaeological residue, it seems a reasonable assumption that this particular metaphor is quite ancient, given its deep entrenchment as a cultural symbol of the Haudenosaunee—"the people of the longhouse," and therefore likely to be relevant to our investigation of the Iroquois League's beginnings. Furthermore, there is good archaeological evidence for the occupation of longhouses at sixteenth-century Seneca sites such as the Richmond Mills site discussed in this chapter (RMSC Site Records), and elsewhere in Iroquoia.

Archaeological patterning from a temporal series of sixteenth- and seventeenth-century Seneca sites provides on-the-ground evidence for some potential behavioral implications of the longhouse metaphor. It reveals an increase in mortuary ceremonialism as the size of village settlements grew throughout that period. It is assumed that the parallel trajectories of those two processes suggest a possible relationship between them, leading to the hypothesis that the execution of mutual mortuary responsibilities prescribed by the longhouse metaphor may have helped facilitate social integration and group cohesion as the Senecas were expanding in size and heterogeneity during the sixteenth and seventeenth centuries.

As the peoples of the Genesee River Valley region of present-day New York State began to coalesce in the western Finger Lakes area in the early to mid-sixteenth century (see map 5), they adopted material symbols of common identity, which are interpreted in chapter 3 as indicating the initial stages of the process of Seneca tribalization. Over the course of the next century, the Senecas transited from a fledgling, local tribal amalgamation to a large and powerful member of the League of the Iroquois—a political entity whose reach extended throughout much of eastern North America. During that period, they underwent profound alterations in their way of life and their interactions with the world around them. This chapter examines the question of whether the longhouse metaphor may have served to facilitate adaptation to those changes, particularly the growth of social complexity.

Several lines of theory underpin this question concerning the role of the longhouse metaphor in facilitating social growth: William Fenton's discussions of the central role of the longhouse metaphor in

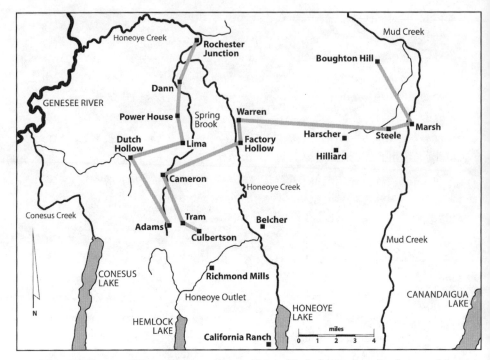

Map 5. Western Finger Lakes region of New York State showing late prehistoric and historic Seneca sites discussed in this chapter. Gray lines indicate dual sequences of historic Seneca sites. Map adapted from Sempowski and Saunders 2001, fig. Intro-2.

the structure of the Iroquois League (1965, 1978a, 1998); Anthony Wallace's insights into revitalization movements (1958), particularly in reference to the League's origins; and Daniel Richter's thoughts on the essentially ceremonial functioning of the League in its early stages (1992).

The Longhouse Metaphor

According to William Fenton (1965, 1978a, 1998), the longhouse metaphor constitutes the primary symbol of group identity for the Iroquois, or Haudenosaunee ("the people of the longhouse"). With reference to the League of the Iroquois, the metaphor entails a symbolic bark longhouse stretching across present-day New York State and accommodating the five "family" fires of Mohawks, Oneidas, Onondagas, Cayugas, and Senecas.[1] Inherent in the model are all the concomitant kinship and affinal relationships represented by the occupants of the longhouse. The tribes are bifurcated into two mutually exclusive "sides," or moieties, with the Mohawks, Onondagas, and Senecas conceived as the three "Elder Brothers" on the father's side, and the Oneidas and Cayugas as the "Younger Brothers" on the mother's side (Fenton 1998, 54–55, citing Hanni Woodbury). According to Fenton, this is essentially a kinship model derived from the most fundamental level of Iroquoian social structure—the nuclear, or "fireside," family of husband, wife, and children (1978a, 311). He explains that the basic structural principles of that unit are progressively extended from the nuclear family, to the lineage, to the clan, to the moiety, to the tribe, and ultimately to the League itself (Hewitt 1944, 82; Fenton 1978a, 309–14; 1998, 54–55). Fundamental principles of duality and reciprocity derive from recognition of the roles of the two sexes and their mutual obligations to one another. The concepts of clan and probably moiety exogamy, Fenton says, follow from the mutually exclusive opposition between the "male" and "female" entities. Herein, we also find the basis for the kinship terminology used between tribes on "the father's side" and those on "the mother's side," respectively (i.e., fathers and father's brothers on the "Elder Brothers' side" and sons or nephews on the "Younger Brothers' side") (Fenton 1978a, 311).

This opposition, however, is partially mitigated by the reciprocity inherent in the very model itself. The prescribed duties that one side performs for the other are well defined and obligatory. Perhaps the most fundamental bifurcated responsibility within families and clans is that of mourning the dead and offering condolence for the opposite side, or moiety. The father's family, clan, or moiety mourns for and helps to condole the mother's family, clan, or moiety following the

---

1. The Tuscaroras, Delawares, and others were incorporated in the eighteenth century on the "Younger Brothers' side" (Fenton 1978a, 311).

death of one of its members, and the reverse (Shimony 1994, 236; Fenton 1978a, 1998). This pattern is reiterated right up to the Iroquois League level, where members of the Elder Brothers condole the Younger Brothers at the death of their respective chiefs. It is suggested that, as Iroquoian groups became larger and more complex, elementary kinship principles, embodied in the basic longhouse model, were progressively applied to larger and larger units of social organization—a process widely recognized by Iroquoian scholars (Fenton 1978a; Tooker 1978, 428). Beyond that, however, it is hypothesized here that the longhouse metaphor may have actually enabled and facilitated the growth of social complexity among sixteenth- and seventeenth-century Iroquoian groups (Wray et al. 1987, 247–48; Sempowski et al. 1988).

The following two assumptions underlie this thesis. First is that a key behavioral correlate of the principles of condolence reciprocity embodied in the longhouse metaphor, is activity associated with mortuary ritual or ceremonialism, and that archaeologically such activity is most tangibly manifest in the material goods presented to the grieving members of the "other side" at the time of the death of one of their kin. We know from ethnographic accounts that at least some of these gifts were buried with the deceased. The second is that evidence of an increase in the quantities of material goods in graves may reasonably be assumed to indicate an intensification of these reciprocal mortuary behaviors associated with death and interment.

Daniel Richter argues that "clans had reciprocal obligations centering on ceremonial gift giving and mutual ritual duties—particularly involving mourning and funerals—analogous to those of families on opposite sides of the longhouse" (1992, 21). Further, Richter says that the Iroquois League rites that took place at the death of a sachem "represent an extension of the duties one clan owed another in village rituals" (1992, 39).

Le Jeune's "Jesuit Relation" of 1636 describes the extraordinary significance of material offerings or gifts in mortuary rites among the seventeenth-century Hurons:

You might say that all their exertions, their labors, and their trading, concern almost entirely the amassing of something with which to honor the Dead. They have nothing sufficiently precious for this purpose; they lavish robes, axes, and Porcelain in such quantities that, to see them on such occasions, you would judge that they place no value upon them; and yet these are the whole riches of the Country. You will see them often, in the depth of winter, almost entirely naked, while they have handsome and valuable robes in store, that they keep in reserve for the Dead; for this is their point of honor. (Thwaites 1896–1901, 10:265)

Intensification of Mortuary Ceremonialism

Bruce Trigger points to "a growing interest in mortuary ceremonialism" among both the Hurons and the Iroquois during the late prehistoric period, citing "the inclusion of trade goods and other valued items" in burials and ossuaries as evidence (2000, 243–44). William Fitzgerald (2007, 260) also indicates an explosion in quantities of marine shell and other exotic goods on late sixteenth-century Neutral sites, signaling, he says, an intensification of mortuary ceremonialism. While timing and causality are debatable, Trigger points to the incorporation of European goods into Native belief systems, saying that "European goods fitted into a pre-existing structure of religious beliefs, and that growing access to them stimulated a florescence of a series of mortuary cults throughout the Iroquoian region" (1986, 219).

Indeed, the archaeological record from New York Iroquoian sites is replete with reports of increasingly larger and more complex grave assemblages beginning in the mid- to late sixteenth century (Wray 1985; Bradley 1987, 110, 214n4; Snow 1995b, 197). Nowhere is that phenomenon better documented than in the Seneca region, for which mortuary data are abundant and site occupation dates seem reasonably secure (Wray et al. 1987, 1991; Sempowski and Saunders 2001). Even well into the eighteenth century, when many of the Iroquois peoples had scattered far beyond their original geographic homelands, Richter reports that burial customs remained essentially intact. In addition to other enduring aspects of mortuary protocol, "the dead continued to be buried not just symbolically but literally with presents" (1992, 276).

Heightened emphasis on condolence behaviors, including the burial of material goods with the dead, appears to have been part of a widespread revitalization of mortuary behaviors (Wallace 1958) that manifests itself across Iroquoia (including present-day New York State and Ontario) during the sixteenth century. Although obviously differing in scale, the fundamentals of reciprocal mortuary ceremonies were replicated at all levels of society—from common village funerals to those at the highest level of Iroquois League functioning—involving the passing of League sachems. The source of this widespread renewal of mortuary ceremonialism—whether internally or externally generated—is open to question and debate. Further, the source of its behavioral linkage to a fundamental Iroquoian cognitive construct like the longhouse metaphor bears further in-depth investigation beyond the scope of this chapter.

For now, however, Seneca archaeology represents a fruitful area with which to examine, more specifically, the relationship between growing social complexity and intensifying mortuary ceremonialism. Evidence relating to several periods of Seneca Iroquois development is brought to bear. It includes oral tradition as well as trends in mortuary, demographic, osteological, and archaeological evidence pertaining to early to mid-sixteenth-century population coalescence, probable tribal consolidation later in the century, Seneca incorporation into the League of the Iroquois around the turn of the seventeenth century, and historically known League expansion during the mid-seventeenth century.

Seneca Sequence of Sites: Relevant Archaeology

Early to Mid-Sixteenth-Century Sites: Population Coalescence

During the early sixteenth century, scattered populations throughout northeastern North America began consolidating into increasingly larger residential and political groups. Several factors have been hypothesized as underlying those amalgamations, including warfare and greater defensibility (Trigger 1969, 17; Trigger 1981, 33; Wright 1966, 99) and increased access to trade (Hayden 1979).

Regarding western New York, Mary Ann Palmer Niemczycki cites ceramic data indicating early to mid-sixteenth-century village population consolidation in the Genesee Valley region (1984, 93). In chapter 3, I discussed the probable consolidation of some of those regional populations into a series of four village sites—the Harscher, Hilliard, Richmond Mills, and Belcher sites—located in the Mud Creek and Honeoye Creek drainages of the western Finger Lakes area (map 5). A distinctive set of human effigy pipes at three of those sites, and their likely symbolic relationship to a Seneca origin narrative involving ancestral emergence from a large hill in the area, led to the conclusion that the pipes represented archaeological markers of the earliest stages of Seneca tribal formation. The Belcher and Richmond Mills site occupations, the latest in this series of prehistoric villages, are thought to be the immediate predecessors of the earliest major village sites in the historic sequence of Seneca sites—the Adams and Culbertson sites—located several miles to the west and north (map 5). It is not clear whether the Belcher and Richmond Mills sites were occupied simultaneously, as Wray originally conceived (1973), or consecutively.

Concomitant with the larger village size of these prehistoric sites, relative to other earlier sites in the region, is a striking disparity in the demographic ratios of females to males in the burial populations. Although sex ratios were nearly equivalent at the Harscher site, the earliest in the series, females accounted for nearly 70–85 percent of the adult burials at the Hilliard, Belcher, Richmond Mills, and California Ranch sites (see chapter 3, table 4). This pattern suggests the incorporation of substantial numbers of captive or refugee women in the groups, and therefore greater diversity in the population. There is corresponding evidence for a slight intensification of mortuary ritual in these sites, relative to earlier sites in the area, as demonstrated by increasing numbers of graves associated with material offerings (e.g., from 10 percent to nearly 18 percent at three sites in the series—the Harscher, Belcher, and Richmond Mills sites—versus virtually no grave goods in preceding sites in the immediate area; see chapter 3). Exotic marine shell also began appearing at Seneca sites of this period, with discoidal beads predominating. Other "foreign" commodities, such as blue glass beads, catlinite, native and European copper, and iron appear for the first time in the area, albeit with great rarity.

In these larger groups, then, there are tentative indications of increased emphasis on condolence behaviors and the acquisition and use of valued goods with which to conduct those rites. I suggest that these mortuary patterns provide preliminary hints of the importance of the duties associated with kinship reciprocity, as embodied in the longhouse metaphor, as these groups became larger and more heterogeneous.

Late Sixteenth-Century Sites: Tribal Formation

The Adams site, hypothesized as an immediate successor to the late prehistoric Harscher/Hilliard/Belcher/Richmond Mills sequence of village sites, provides a very informative archaeological case in several regards (map 5). It and the Culbertson site, located less than two miles to the east, have been identified as the earliest large aggregated Seneca villages recognizable in the historic Seneca sequence of sites (Wray and Schoff 1953; Wray 1973; Wray et al. 1987). William Engelbrecht suggests that "typically, historic Iroquois tribes were composed of two or more villages located not more than about ten miles apart" (1985, 165; 1997, 2). His thoughts regarding the founding of the Onondaga tribe in the late fifteenth century follow those of James Tuck and Bruce Trigger. They point to a pattern of village fusion and movement of the two resulting villages into close proximity (Tuck 1971a, 214–16; Trigger 2000, 153–54), although Trigger cautions that linguistic and cultural commonalities may have been the basis of an earlier political grouping.

It has generally been assumed that these two closely situated Seneca villages, with a combined estimated population of around 1,600–2,000, represented the emergence of the Seneca as a tribal entity (Wray et al. 1987, 255). I have argued that the initial processes of Seneca tribal formation may have taken place a generation or so earlier, as signaled by the occurrence and distribution of the distinctive "identity" smoking pipes discussed in chapter 3. The possibility that the Richmond Mills and Belcher sites, located in close proximity to one another, may have been occupied simultaneously would lend weight to that argument. Nevertheless, what seems clear is that by the time the Adams and Culbertson sites were first occupied, ca. AD 1570–75, the Senecas had established themselves as a large and powerful tribal entity, worthy of notice and perhaps fear, by the growing tribes and emerging alliances surrounding them.

Evidence for the heterogeneity of the Senecas at this time goes far beyond the demographic disparities of males and females cited for the preceding period. First, Lorraine Saunders (Wray et al. 1987; Sempowski et al. 1988) compared osteological data based on forty-six discrete, nonmetric skeletal traits, considered to be genetically transmitted, from the Adams site population, with those of the contemporary Culbertson site and earlier local sites. Coefficients of divergence (see Saunders 1986) provided the first indications of atypical levels of genetic diversity in the Adams site population. Even more intriguing were comparisons in light of demographics, indicating that the divergence and genetic distance from other local populations noted at the Adams site was primarily due to the females in the burial population, not to the males (Saunders 1986; Wray et al. 1987, 25–26; Sempowski et al. 1988, 97–98, 103–4). While not as dramatic as the disproportionate number of females in the sites of the immediately preceding period, demographic data from the Adams site indicated nearly twice as many adult females relative to adult males in the general population. Even more informative is the fact that the ratio was three females to one male among the adults buried in two of the three burial or cemetery areas.[2] Furthermore, the females in one of these two exceptional

2. A similar, but less dramatic, disproportion of females is also noted in the burial population at the subsequent, and partially chronologically overlapping, Seneca Tram site in the eastern sequence of Seneca sites (Wray et al. 1991, 388).

cemeteries showed the greatest biological distance from males buried at the site, and from earlier populations in the area (Sempowski et al. 1988, 97–98, 103–4). Second, an analysis of pottery designs from the Adams site, while indicating the presence of local and nonlocal types of decoration, showed that the pottery with the greatest divergence from earlier local traditions was included in graves in the two cemeteries noted earlier (Wray et al. 1987, 62–97; Sempowski et al. 1988, 101–3). Finally, several changes were noted in mortuary customs, including a greatly increased incidence of westerly (rather than easterly) heading burials, multiple graves, and inclusion of grave goods, along with different types of grave-covering techniques, as compared with earlier sites in the area (Wray et al 1987, 167–78, 247; Sempowski et al. 1988, 99–101). Interestingly, those burials with the smallest quantities of European grave goods were those in the two cemeteries that were divergent in other ways.

At the large Adams site, then, there is strong, multilayered evidence for a genetically and culturally diverse group of inhabitants, primarily women, who, one might speculate, were incorporated through the consolidation of peoples from across a wide region. The source of at least some of the cultural diversity appears to have been from west of the Genesee River, reflecting influences from the Niagara frontier, or from the intervening area between Niagara and the Genesee River, one of the regions in which the distinctive smoking pipes discussed in chapter 3 were found. I suggest that such a scenario might reflect the incorporation of significant numbers of female captives or war refugees from that region (see evidence from the Alhart site, located about thirty miles west of the Adams site; see Hamell 1976; Wray et al. 1987, 247–48; Sempowski et al. 1988, 104–6). A similar hypothesis

---

Demographic mortuary data gathered by the author from the entire early historic sequence of Seneca sites—dating from the mid-1500s through 1687—illustrates the uniqueness of this anomalous pattern. Later sites consistently show more typical, nearly 50/50, ratios of males and females in the burial populations (Sempowski 1975–83).

was posed by William Finlayson for the formation of the Draper site in Ontario (Finlayson 1985, 439).

These early stages of social amalgamation could not have been easy. The larger, more ethnically diverse groups, with their linguistic and cultural differences, must have been fraught with tensions and potential strife. It is proposed that the longhouse metaphor, with its kinship terminology, its basic duality, and the prescribed ritual obligations of one side toward the other, may have helped to mitigate the potential for conflict and disruption. Kinship conceptualizations and related responsibilities were consistent throughout northern Iroquoia (Fenton 1978a), and would have embodied a common "language"— a set of understandings that provided everyone a prescribed place in the system, even if only fictively. Along with that place came a well-defined list of prescribed behaviors and ceremonial obligations, including those related to rites of condolence.

Archaeological evidence for alterations in mortuary practices at these first, very populous Seneca sites—Adams, Culbertson, Tram, and Cameron—appears to support such a scenario. Some of these changes were noted in nascent form at sites of the preceding late prehistoric period. In sum, they are thought to reflect elaboration of and heightened emphasis on mortuary ceremonialism in these late sixteenth-century Seneca sites. Table 5 summarizes those patterns of mortuary change that are most evident in the archaeological record: a noticeable rise in the number of individuals interred with material grave goods, increases in the numbers of individuals interred with exotic goods (European-manufactured items and marine shell), and a marked shift in the prevailing pattern of grave orientation (i.e., increasing percentages of graves oriented to the west versus the east).[3] While it is a challenge to understand or explain the shift in burial orientation in terms of a heightened emphasis on mortuary ritual, as

---

3. Data from sites of the preceding period suggest westerly orientation percentages ranging from 12.1 percent at the Harscher site and 13.3 percent at the Belcher site, to 27.8 percent at the Richmond Mills site.

Table 5
Mortuary data: Seneca sites (ca. AD 1570–1610)*

SITES	ADAMS	CULBERTSON	TRAM	CAMERON
Number of graves	250	16	114	118
Percent graves w/associated artifacts	56.0	50.0	53.5	55.9
Percent graves w/European goods	24.0	18.8	17.5	26.3
Percent graves w/marine shell	12.8	12.5	14.0	19.5
Percent graves w/smoking pipes	1.6	—	1.8	0.9
Number of individuals for whom burial orientation is known (some graves included multiple individuals)	354	28	126	139
Percent westerly oriented graves	36.7	42.9	50.0	46.8

* Adapted from Wray et al. 1987, 1991.

suggested by the other two patterns, the coincidence of the change in burial orientation with the other trends noted earlier is too striking and too consistent over time to be ignored as merely serendipitous. Seventeenth-century Iroquoian groups such as the Hurons are well-known to have favored westerly orientation in the burial of their dead. An account recorded in the "Jesuit Relations" of 1636 attests to that cultural preference and the reasons for it: "They bury their dead in such a way that the head of the departed one faces the West, in order that the soul may know the place whither it is to go. They believe, as I have said, that it goes to the place where the Sun sets" (Thwaites 1896–1901, 16:207). Furthermore, Seneca mortuary data from subsequent seventeenth-century sites shows a clear pattern of preference for westerly burial orientation (see note 3).

It is proposed that this entire set, or complex, of relatively abrupt mortuary changes among the Seneca may well be part of a more widespread religious revitalization movement, as described by Anthony Wallace (1958). As such, it may reflect new or renewed emphasis on reciprocal condolence responsibilities, which, in turn, would have affirmed tenuous relationships, thus helping to solidify the newly formed amalgamated groups (see Sempowski et al. 1988).

It is tempting to suggest that a rather quiescent period may have followed Seneca tribalization, at least relative to interactions with outsiders, perhaps because of the substantial numbers and power that the Senecas now represented. During the preceding period, there is osteological evidence of trauma and signs of fire on village sites indicating probable warfare, as well as the positioning of villages on high, defensible ridges surrounded by steep cliffs. By contrast, all four of the late sixteenth-century sites—the Adams, Culbertson, Tram, and Cameron sites—are situated on relatively low, flat, not easily defensible terrain. The flow of European-made goods and marine shell, thought to have been from the mid-Atlantic coastal region, seems substantial, and suggests peaceful trade relations with the Susquehannocks—sufficient to fill Seneca ceremonial needs (Wray et al. 1991, 393–95).

Interestingly, in contrast to the preceding period in the proto-Seneca homeland, during which smoking pipes, particularly the distinctive human effigy pipes highlighted in chapter 3, were present in such abundance, smoking pipes of any kind are all but nonexistent at this time, either in burials or in refuse on the sites. Might this suggest the absence of the pipe-smoking negotiations and diplomatic interactions associated with the preceding period, when assertions of group identity were so crucial to amalgamation and alliance-building? It may be telling that the inexplicable dearth of smoking pipes of this period would be significantly reversed in subsequent early seventeenth-century Seneca sites.

Early Seventeenth-Century Sites: Iroquois League Affiliation

It is widely recognized that the League of the Iroquois came into being gradually, the culmination of a series of small local alliances between individual tribal groups (Fenton 1961; Tooker 1978; Engelbrecht 1985; Snow 1991). Estimates of the time frame during which this process occurred vary widely. "Precise dates for complicated social institutions are at best spurious," Fenton observes. "Rather than a single event, the formation of the Iroquois League was a process that occupied the lifetimes of its founders" (1998, 72).

Regardless of the exact timing of that process, there is general agreement that the earliest alliances involved the easternmost groups (see chapter 2), and that the Senecas were the last to join (Heckewelder 1991). Several lines of evidence from Seneca sites suggest that this final alliance with the Iroquois League occurred sometime around the turn of the seventeenth century, resulting in the classic Five Nations form of the Iroquois League.

First, is the observation that the Senecas do not appear to have fully established themselves as a sizeable tribal entity until the second half of the sixteenth century. At that time, there is evidence for population nucleation (1,600–2,000 persons) in two large villages— the Adams and Culbertson sites—located in close proximity to one another, or possibly at two sites of the preceding period (see the previous discussion of the Richmond Mills and Belcher sites earlier in the chapter). Tuck (1971a) and Engelbrecht (1985; 1997, 2) point to this pattern of two closely situated villages as a likely archaeological indicator of tribal consolidation. Prior to that time, it seems unlikely that the smaller Seneca village groups in the western Finger Lakes region would have attracted the attention of, or posed a serious threat to, their Iroquoian neighbors to the east.

Second, late sixteenth-century artifactual assemblages—particularly ceramics, exotic marine shell, and European-made trade goods such as glass beads and copper alloy objects—from Seneca and Mohawk sites look distinctly different from one another, suggesting little, if any, direct contact between these two groups at the eastern and western extremities of the "eventual League" (Bradley and Childs 1989; Sempowski and Saunders 2001, 609; see Rumrill 1991; Snow 1995b). That contrast in assemblages changes abruptly around 1600–1610, when Seneca and Mohawk assemblages begin to show a resemblance to one another. Particularly relevant are the abundant quantities of Dutch-made goods on the Seneca Dutch Hollow and Factory Hollow sites (Sempowski and Saunders 2001, 689), suggesting that the Senecas' access to Dutch trade along the Hudson River was in relatively full swing. It seems highly unlikely that that access could have been realized without the approval, or at least acquiescence, of the Mohawks and their allies.

Finally, there is an extraordinary increase in the prevalence of ceramic smoking pipes in refuse and burial contexts on Seneca sites dating to the early seventeenth century (Sempowski and Saunders 2001, 712–13; see table 6 for increased frequency in burials). Robert Kuhn reports a similar increase in Mohawk sites of the same period (personal communication, 1997). In light of the well-documented role played by pipe smoking in diplomatic and ceremonial activities associated with the Iroquois League, this phenomenon seems likely to be relevant to the timing of the classic Five Nations League formation.

Nearly one hundred smoking pipes from mid-sixteenth-century to early seventeenth-century Seneca sites were subjected to analysis using X-ray fluorescence (XRF) and X-ray emission (PIXE) spectrometry (Kuhn 1985, 1989) to discriminate any smoking pipes that may

Table 6
Mortuary data: Seneca sites (ca. AD 1605–1625)*

SITES	DUTCH HOLLOW	FACTORY HOLLOW
Number of excavated graves	318	220
Percent graves w/associated artifacts	70.8	65.9
Percent graves w/European goods	45.3	45.5
Percent graves w/marine shell	6.0	1.8
Percent graves w/smoking pipes	6.3	5.5
Number of individuals for whom burial orientation is known (some graves included multiple individuals)	343	151**
Percent westerly oriented graves	52.5	65.6**

* Adapted from Sempowski and Saunders 2001.
** Due to an unusually large number of burials for which orientation was unreported at the Factory Hollow site, only known cases were included in this calculation (see Sempowski and Saunders 2001, 575–76, table 8.8).

have been made from Mohawk Valley clays (Kuhn and Sempowski 2001; Sempowski and Saunders 2001, 712–13;).[4] Results showed that none of the pipes sampled from earlier sites (pre-1595) were identified as deriving from the Mohawk Valley, while five samples from post-1595 sites were identified as such—one from the Cameron site, two from the Dutch Hollow site, and two from the Factory Hollow site. Although samples are small and need to be bolstered by further studies of other Iroquoian site assemblages, this initial evidence suggests a "heightened level of interaction" between the Senecas and the Mohawks around the turn of the seventeenth century. Kuhn and Sempowski (2001) interpreted these multiple lines of evidence as a likely indication of Seneca incorporation into the League of the Iroquois at that time, thereby signaling the coalescence of the Iroquois Confederacy in its classic Five Nations form.[5]

This important, archaeologically based conclusion brings some closure to the long-standing historical and anthropological debate with regard to the timing and causative factors involved in the formation of the League of the Iroquois. It seems clear that while earlier, smaller alliances to the east preceded the incorporation of the Seneca by some decades (see chapter 2), this early seventeenth-century "finalization" represents an important time marker for the Iroquois League. It also puts to rest the argument that the formation of the League was precipitated by competition for European trade goods, since the seeds of the League had been laid almost a century earlier with warfare and alliance-building among competing Native groups, who had only scant knowledge of European-made trade goods.

4. Baseline data provided by pottery samples from each area.

5. At present, little is known regarding a possible earlier Seneca/Cayuga alliance and when that may have occurred, or whether the Cayugas had previously allied themselves with their neighbors to the east, becoming the second to last tribe to join the Iroquois League. Inquiries, along the lines of the Mohawk/Seneca investigation, would appear to offer promise in tracing the outlines of the Cayugas' involvement in the Iroquois League.

I suggest that the familiar longhouse metaphor, which had reinforced earlier, smaller-scale alliances, would have been extended to the complex union of these more or less ethnically distinct five tribal groups. Once again, as a conceptual model, the metaphor would have helped define the relative place of each nation and dictate the ritual obligations of that role within an elaborate, formalized system of reciprocal condolence rites and gift exchange. Indeed, according to Daniel Richter, maintaining the peace through mourning ceremonies and gift-giving constituted the essential function of the Iroquois League in its earliest stages (1992, 40).

Furthermore, several lines of archaeological evidence suggest continued elaboration of local mortuary behavior at the two major early seventeenth-century Seneca sites, the Dutch Hollow and Factory Hollow sites, (see table 6): a far greater number of burials associated with grave goods; an enormous escalation in the quantity of material goods, particularly European-made trade goods, in graves; and a substantial increase in the percentage of burials oriented to the west versus the east.[6] These particular trends in mortuary behavior first showed themselves faintly in mid-sixteenth-century sites occupied some fifty years earlier, and then more strongly twenty to thirty years later, as the Senecas became more populous in the late sixteenth century, but they greatly intensify sometime after 1600, as the Senecas took their place as members of the Five Nations League (Sempowski and Saunders 2001, 706–8).

It is proposed that, again, these behavioral indices at the local level may reflect a more pervasive emphasis on condolence rituals at all societal levels—a true revitalization movement in Wallace's sense of the term (1958). Performance of reciprocal funerary rituals, such as gift-giving at the tribal level, would have provided active, visible validation of the fictive kin relationships that were being asserted among these

---

6. It should be noted that there is a significant decline in the numbers of graves that contain marine shell at the Dutch Hollow and Factory Hollow sites, reversing an earlier trend (Sempowski 1989, 96).

newly allied tribal groups. In doing so, I suggest that they bound the Iroquois Confederacy together by repeated reinforcement in a language that everyone understood—the vocabulary, the grammar, of kinship. In a sense, this whole process helped weave together a fabric of kinship across the Five Nations, just as it had facilitated social integration on a more limited scale during earlier times.

Mid-Seventeenth-Century Sites: Iroquois League Expansion

During the mid-seventeenth century (ca. 1620–75), continued escalation is evident in the types of mortuary behaviors that have been characterized as possible signs of a religious revitalization movement. Table 7 provides mortuary data from five Seneca sites—the Warren, Steele, Power House, Marsh, and Dann sites—occupied between approximately 1620 and 1675. These data show the continuing elaboration of local mortuary ritual throughout this period: an ever-increasing number of graves associated with material goods, especially European-manufactured goods and other exotics; and a continued rise in the proportions of westerly versus easterly heading burials (Wray 1985; Wray et al. 1987; Wray et al. 1991; Sempowski and Saunders 2001).[7] It seems highly likely that these now-customary mourning behaviors, based on the kinship paradigm embodied in the longhouse metaphor, would have continued to facilitate integration and help to maintain peaceful relations among the members of the Iroquois Confederacy.

Ironically, of course, the successful alliance for peace that was forged among the Five Nations Iroquois did not extend to those outside the fold. By the second quarter of the seventeenth century, an ever-spiraling cycle of hostilities was underway between the Iroquois and neighboring groups, due to both demographic and economic causes.

---

7. Marine shell continues to be very sparse at the outset of this period, but becomes much more abundant around mid-century at the Power House and Steele sites.

Table 7
Mortuary data: Seneca sites (ca. AD 1620–1675)*

SITES	WARREN	STEELE	POWER HOUSE	MARSH	DANN
Number of excavated graves **undisturbed	42**	101**	87**	39**	42**
Percent graves w/associated artifacts	78.6	78.2	89.7	89.7	88.1
Percent graves w/European goods	33.3	64.4	74.7	82.1	85.7
Percent graves w/marine shell	4.8	30.7	52.9	41.0	33.3
Percent graves w/smoking pipes	11.9	9.9	23.0	15.4	19.0
Number of individuals for whom burial orientation is known (some graves included multiple individuals)	15	160	167	71	150
Percent westerly oriented graves	73.3	71.9	84.4	85.9	65.3

* Adapted from Sempowski, mortuary data 1975–83.
** An unusually large number of graves at these sites had been disturbed by ancient and/or modern looting of artifacts. The calculations are based only on undisturbed graves, far fewer than total number of graves excavated at the sites.

European diseases had begun taking a huge toll on all of the Native peoples of the Northeast; access to the highly valued European goods and other exotic materials needed for the obligatory condolence gifts was uneven among northeastern peoples; and the populations of fur-bearing animals needed to acquire the necessary goods were declining in some regions more than others. The combination of these factors led to continuous attacks and raids in pursuit of captives to replace lost family members, obtain high-quality furs that were more readily available in distant territories, and in turn to acquire the valued booty required for performance of condolence rituals (Richter 1992, 50, 57–66).

Most of the Iroquoian-speaking neighbors of the Five Nations
League also had complex and populous political confederacies similar
to that of the Iroquois. Nevertheless, between 1638 and 1656, groups
to the west, southwest, and north—Wenros, Hurons, Petuns, Neutrals, and Eries—were defeated and dispersed by a relentless series of
raids and expeditions carried out by Senecas in concert with some or
all of their League allies (White 1978a, 412–17; White 1978b, 407–11;
Heidenreich 1978, 368–78; Garrad and Heidenreich 1978, 394–97;
Richter 1992, 50–74). Even after distancing themselves earlier in the
century, Susquehannocks to the south were eventually "submerged
politically among the Iroquoians and Delawares by 1675" (Jennings
1978, 366). While casualties of this ongoing warfare were significant,
and groups of survivors sometimes migrated to other regions for ref-
uge with neighbors, many captives—especially women and children—
were taken back to the Iroquois homeland, adopted, and incorporated
into the ever more diverse Iroquois society, a process presumably facilitated by the kinship principles described earlier. Yet, the role of the
longhouse metaphor in fueling seventeenth-century League expansion appears to be far more complicated and nuanced than that discussed for earlier periods.

Daniel Richter (1992) points to the other face of the Iroquois
League's model of peace, kinship, and reciprocal mourning. On one
hand are the peaceful, friendly relations of diplomacy (i.e., kin-like relations) that are maintained by reciprocal condolence and the exchange
of valued goods as gifts, resulting in an ever-growing demand for the
kinds of goods appropriate to these rituals. But on the other hand we
have the opposite—hostile, warlike relations between enemies, characterized by a failure to condole and exchange gifts, and leading to
the means by which to satisfy the demand for goods and furs—raiding
and warfare (Richter 1992, 50–74). In other words, people bound by
ties of kinship and marriage (i.e., those within the longhouse) condole
one another; those outside do not. Any group with whom the requisite
relations associated with peace do not prevail are viewed as the enemy,
potentially in a state of warfare with the Iroquois (see chapter 5, note 8).

Another key factor was the devastating population loss brought on by the epidemic diseases that were raging among all of these Native societies through the early to mid-seventeenth century, combined with deaths due to intertribal warfare. A heightened need for captives to compensate for the continuing loss of population among all of these groups fed a growing cycle of violence. Replacement of deceased family members by adoption of captive prisoners in elaborate requickening ceremonies was designed "to cleanse sorrowing hearts and to ease the survivors' return to normal life" (Richter 1992, 33). Indeed, it was only the incorporation of foreigners that allowed the Senecas to maintain viable populations throughout the seventeenth century.

So we have a young Iroquois League, immersed in the context of these two opposing dynamics. A Dutch trading post on the Hudson River meant access to an abundant supply of exotic goods—the very kinds of symbolically charged goods considered appropriate for ceremonial use by the Mohawks and their allies in these sacred mourning rituals. It seems certain that, initially, League members would have utilized this new resource to great advantage in reinforcing old and cementing new diplomatic ties. But as the scale of mortuary condolence practices grew, so too did the escalating requirement for the kinds of goods necessary for these crucial rites. That was viable as long as the supply of new trade items, and the furs to acquire them, kept pace with the steadily rising demand. But in fact, the numbers of fur-bearing animals diminished drastically in New York during this period. Efforts to acquire the needed furs became increasingly difficult, which inevitably led to an escalation of Iroquois warfare and raiding against neighboring groups (Richter 1992, 57). As the Iroquois League grew more aggressive and outwardly expansive, its members vied with those outside the longhouse for furs, exotic goods, and captives.

During the seventeenth century, then, the deeply entrenched longhouse metaphor and its implications, in terms of reciprocal kinship mourning and condolence requirements, served an even more significant role than it had in earlier periods by fueling a powerful, self-amplifying feedback system involving escalating mortuary rituals, a need for exotic goods and captives, population losses due to warfare and epidemics, and raiding and warfare.

Summary

As others have observed, the richly nuanced longhouse metaphor, with all that it implied, was deeply entrenched in Iroquoian thought. What is proposed here on the basis of archaeological data pertaining to the Senecas is that, from at least the mid-sixteenth century (and probably earlier elsewhere), the metaphor actually helped to facilitate the integration of the larger and progressively more heterogeneous social units that were forming as local groups coalesced, amalgamated with neighboring groups, and eventually allied themselves politically in the League of the Iroquois. In essence, this was a familial metaphor that implied kin-like relationships among individuals and groups who were unrelated or even antagonistic to one another. The metaphor carried with it the basic principles of duality, reciprocity, and mutual obligations, particularly the responsibilities for conducting condolence rites for the dead of the "other side." At higher levels of social integration, where these fictive relationships would have been most tenuous, condolence rites reinforced the fragile bonds that held these coalitions together. Serendipitously, the heightened demand for exotic goods that followed coincided with the abundant new supply of Dutch-made goods that fed the early growth of the Iroquois League—visible symbols of peaceful, kin-like relationships. Once the demand outstripped the supply of the quality furs needed to acquire the valued goods, however, the Iroquois were compelled to push outward, resulting in the pattern of expansion associated with the later seventeenth-century League of the Iroquois.

Examining the role of the traditional longhouse metaphor as a symbolic paradigm underlying, reinforcing, and propelling the growth of the Seneca Iroquois tribal group, its incorporation into the Iroquois League, and the expansion of the League itself, provides meaningful insights into this critical period of Iroquois prehistory and history. There is no question that external economic and political circumstances played significant roles affecting these processes, and they are not to be discounted as irrelevant, but an explication of the longhouse metaphor and its ceremonial ramifications moves us closer to an understanding of the underlying Native cultural constructs and social dynamics that appear to have been at play during this period.

7

Summary and Conclusions

The Deganawida Epic

The Deganawida epic is a body of oral narrative telling how the League of the Iroquois came about. Archaeologists frequently make reference to it in order to bolster or flesh out interpretations of the past, especially those concerning indications of violence in the archaeological record. They also, not surprisingly, are attracted to details in the epic that seem to offer help in dating long-ago events.

However, when archaeologists project the Deganawida epic into the past, they are positing that the plot or details of the plot are true; that the epic faithfully, or, in some important measure, documents something that took place long before. That assumption is, to date, an unexamined assertion advanced without evidence. Claims of factuality have not been based on historical inquiry into the age, content, and development of the oral narrative.

Accordingly, chapter 1 surveyed founding traditions of the Iroquois League's origin with a view toward understanding their relevance to archaeological interpretation. We charted the content of the epic across space from its first documented appearance up to the time it assumed definitive expression in written form. Having established what the facts are in multiple narratives, we then tried to understand them by relating narrative content to social context and to the archaeological record.

Our major findings are these. First, there is no consensus within the body of the epic about when the Iroquois League was formed. Estimates of dating are disparate and should not be taken as historical fact without outside corroboration. Second, the documented oral narrative is relatively recent. Prior to the mid-eighteenth century, no one mentioned anything about a tradition of the Iroquois Confederacy's origins. Third, the Deganawida epic is really many different versions setting forth different details and emphases, not a few of which are mutually contradictory. Within this complex body of variable material, there is no consensus about who formed the Iroquois League or why.

The latter point—the simple fact of multiple versions—raises serious problems for applying this material to the past. That is because an archaeologist working with the direct historical approach should justify the choice of one particular version as being more useful or truer than another. In general, one would suppose, archaeologists projecting oral narrative into the past would favor older material as being closer in time to the phenomena being interpreted.

It turns out that the oldest documented strain of Iroquois League tradition looks like two storylines—one Onondaga, the other Mohawk—joined together to comprise a single narrative. By the early 1800s, an Onondaga tale introduced Hiawatha as a lawgiver promoting tribal union, an initiative thwarted by the evil wizard Thadadaho. When Thadadaho murdered one of Hiawatha's offspring, Hiawatha did not retaliate. Instead, he dealt with his grief by removing himself to Mohawk country in the east. There he encountered a leader named Deganawida. Thereafter, Deganawida became the leading actor in a Mohawk-centered drama in which the Onondaga shaman was overcome and tribal union was achieved.

Now it is certainly true that some versions describe the formation of the Iroquois League as a prolonged process of overcoming obstacles and resistance to achieve tribal alliance. Some seem to emphasize the peacekeeping role of reciprocal mourning and condolence. In several, a kind of value-laden bead (reed, freshwater shell, or marine shell) plays a critical role in legitimating or strengthening Hiawatha's condolence sentiments. Several convey the spiritual power of wampum in validating rituals and alliances. All of these concepts could very well be old and all could be important for understanding the early development of the League via the archaeological record.

Setting aside questions of age, the Deganawida epic is, with equal certainty, the story of establishing the League's peacekeeping mechanisms. The Deganawida epic is a political parable about achieving alliance not by force, but by offering consolation (condoling with wampum) to assuage grief and turn aside vengeance. In this narrative sense and inwardly, the League of the Iroquois was very much a league of peace.

Tribalization and Alliance-Building

Prior to addressing these subjects, we begin with a genre of oral narrative that holds promise as supplement to other sources of information: localized traditions referring not to the origin of confederations but to the beginnings of other social formations, most obviously tribes. Mythical vignettes describing people coming out of caves, rising up out of the ground, or emerging from a snake's mouth, supply an interpretive tack clarifying why identical imagery is present on smoking implements of different groups at certain times. Pipes illustrating such themes of emergence make sense as material correlates of tribalization and alliance-building in both eastern and western Iroquoia—arguably the earliest archaeologically detectable markers of these processes in both regions.

Eastern Iroquoia

An early pre–Iroquois League alliance among the eastern Iroquois has long been suspected by scholars. If it was a reality, what about the process of tribal coalition might register materially in the archaeological record? In a markedly austere material culture, what stands out is fired-clay smoking pipes incised with pictorial representations. Identical and emotionally resonant images are found on pipes in areas known as the homelands of the eastern Iroquois tribes—the Mohawk, Oneida, and Onondaga—and in the St. Lawrence Iroquoian province of Jefferson County, New York, during the late 1400s and early 1500s.

To the extent Iroquois behavior as historically known can be projected into a recent past, the most likely reading is that pipes belonged to men, and the distribution of pipes reflects male engagement with diplomacy. Finding identical pipes in several areas implies interactions reflecting interregional diplomacy among groups from those areas. Iconographically, what is depicted on the pipes seems to show scenes of human emergence from a place associated, in the case of the Dougherty pipe, with snakes. Referencing myths of tribal-ethnic origin presumably fostered notions of kinship and relatedness in a diplomatic setting.

In answer to a long-standing question in Iroquoian studies, the development of this eastern coalition was pre-Columbian. Evidently the proto-League came to be a four-tribe union in which, very possibly, the principal member was the St. Lawrence Iroquoian group of Jefferson County. One type of pipe—the Dougherty—actually shows three or four figures joined together, lending support to the notion of a three- and, subsequently, a four-tribe alliance. While an early alliance of three eastern tribes could be inferred from some versions of the Deganawida epic, no version mentions a Jefferson County group as one of them.

As confederacies coalesced, the culturally engendered militancy of young males was directed toward distant others. Tribal alliances increased manpower, which, dispatched outward, intensified interpolity warfare beyond any clan- or village-level act of proximate blood revenge. To forge alliance was to escalate war.

During the early to mid-1500s, violent conditions are implied by heightened defensive measures apparent in all three of the tribal areas of the eastern Iroquois. Their primary enemies must have been St. Lawrence Iroquoians, whose settlements to the north disappear about the same time their material traces register among the ceramic assemblages of Mohawks, Oneidas, and Onondagas. Foreign elements appear in pottery because—again projecting historically attested patterns back in time—most captives taken in war and brought back to assimilate into the home villages were women, and it was women who made the pottery. The process is most clearly signaled by a distinctive

St. Lawrence Iroquoian trait, the corn-ear motif, which shows up in Oneida pottery, then apparently contributes to the development of a full-figure humanoid depiction. The result was an emotionally resonant set of symbols that endured for a century.

The Oneida effigy tradition most likely derived from villages on the Canadian side of the St. Lawrence River, where the corn-ear motif was particularly popular. Archaeologists, however, commonly identify Jefferson County as the source of Laurentian material among the eastern Iroquois. In the Oneida and Mohawk cases, such a phenomenon may have occurred a little later than that of the Oneida captive brides, with their preference for maize imagery. Bearing in mind the earlier pipe interaction sphere, people from Jefferson County may have come south not as prisoners but as refugees seeking help from former confederates.

Western Iroquoia

In an intriguing parallel, a genre of ceramic smoking pipes—distinct from those in eastern Iroquoia but also bearing motifs suggestive of emergence from a place of serpents or snakes—appears in sites throughout the Genesee River Valley during the early to mid-1500s. Though regional in distribution, the pipes are most concentrated in a sequence of proto-Seneca villages sited on defensible ridges surrounded by steep cliffs in the western Finger Lakes—sites that immediately precede the earliest in the well-known sequence of historic Seneca sites. The pipes feature a lifeless-looking human face framed or encircled with details suggestive of snakish symbols that some analysts associate with an underworld of darkness and death. Further imagery, depicting a long-bodied animal on many of the pipes, may signal emergence into a world of light and life—an allusion that may have been symbolically reinforced or materialized by putative traces of white shell found in the rectangular slots on some of these pipes. That thematic complex is reasonably interpreted in the light of Seneca oral traditions of tribal origin—tales that describe people emerging from a mountain or out of the imprisoning jaws of a serpent, and being revitalized in this particular geographic locale in the western Finger Lakes.

As in eastern Iroquoia, the distribution of the pipes is believed to reflect intergroup interactions associated with the process of Seneca tribal formation. It appears that as Senecas consolidated themselves demographically and geographically, smaller-scale alliances were formed with previously hostile neighboring groups throughout the region. A striking disparity in the ratios of females to males becomes evident in the village cemeteries of the latest of these sites. Up to 75 percent of the adult burials were female—a startling preponderance strongly implying the incorporation of foreign captive or refugee women, not unlike the interpretations of "foreign" pottery motifs made by captive or refugee women in Oneida sites. In both east and west, the "common origins" messages of the pipes could have reinforced social cohesion by helping to bind together ethnically heterogeneous groups of people.

While there is ceramic evidence suggesting a possible link to the Cayuga at one of these mid-sixteenth-century Seneca sites, thus far none of the characteristic "origin" smoking pipes have been found in sixteenth-century Cayuga sites.[1] Despite traditional wisdom that Senecas and Cayugas were the last to join the Iroquois League—suggesting a likely pre-League alliance between them—the absence of these origin pipes from Cayuga sites makes it impossible to confirm such a union here. This question warrants further intensive study of archaeological collections from Cayuga sites of this period.

Symbolic Underpinnings of the Iroquois League

Mourning and Condolence

On sixteenth-century Seneca sites, and elsewhere in the northeast, there is rich evidence of a growing emphasis on mortuary ceremonialism, as indicated by ever-increasing numbers of the dead buried

---

1. One such pipe dating to the early 1600s does appear at the Cayuga Genoa Fort site.

with grave goods, and ever-increasing quantities of goods buried with each individual. These ceremonial trends first appear in the early to mid-1500s and continue to escalate steadily through the mid-1600s.

The pattern of gradually intensifying mortuary practices coincides with evidence for growing social complexity—from small, scattered villages to two large villages in close proximity to one another to affiliation with the Five Nations League. These parallel and contemporaneous archaeological trends would certainly seem to suggest that the sixteenth-century intensification of mortuary ceremonialism may have foreshadowed, or provided a template, for the elaborate condolence rituals associated with the death and replacement of sachems of the classic Five Nations League during the seventeenth and eighteenth centuries (see Foley 1973).

Nucleation of population into two large and closely situated villages initiates the historically known configuration of the Seneca tribe sometime around the mid-sixteenth century. Burials from the sites show a disproportionate majority of females as they do at the succeeding Adams site, where they have been identified—from skeletal analysis and artifactual evidence—as foreigners, at least some of whom appear to have derived from the west side of the Genesee River.

These larger new villages, then, were ethnically and culturally diverse and, on that account, were presumably tense places in which to live. Heightened anxiety and potential conflicts needed to be salved and disputes avoided by promoting and reinforcing assertions of common origins, familial ties, and unity through the exercise of funerary ritual with its reciprocal responsibilities.

Wampum and Other Exotics

The mid-sixteenth century also witnessed an influx of materials from distant sources, including marine shells and the earliest European goods to reach Native peoples in present-day upstate New York. Whether the introduction of these new materials is related to the forging of early pre–Iroquois League alliances and what that might mean to Iroquois cultural development is a recurrent interpretive concern among Iroquois archaeologists. Our interpretive tack is to consider the issue of the exotics with reference to the internal dynamics of confederacy that stressed peacekeeping and mortuary ritual.

The exotic substances new to the eastern Iroquois were also entering the archaeological records of Iroquoian groups in western New York and southern Ontario. It is worthy of note that marine shell appears to have been more accessible to neighboring groups on the periphery of Iroquoia earlier. For example, we know that groups located to the west of the emerging Seneca tribe—groups later either absorbed by Senecas or pushed out of the region—appear to have had access to a relative abundance of sinistrally whorled species of marine shell that derived from southerly sources distinct from those that supplied later Senecas with exclusively dextrally whorled species. Only during this initial period of alliance-building does the more distantly sourced shell appear, albeit in small quantity, in sites in the Seneca homeland of the western Finger Lakes. It would be of great interest to know whether this might also be true of the St. Lawrence Iroquoians, including the Jefferson County group with whom the Oneida, Onondaga, and Mohawk tribes formed an early alliance. If so, we might then speculate about access to marine shell being a possible motivating factor.

Marine shell, it seems likely, represents but one of a special class of value-laden materials carrying the power to validate words, agreements, and treaties. The substance of this kind most commonly known historically is, of course, wampum. Having said that, it is not unusual to observe seventeenth- and eighteenth-century Iroquois wampum belts that include similarly sized white and dark tubular glass beads right alongside those made of marine shell. In an earlier example, we note that for a brief period in the late sixteenth century in western Iroquoia (e.g., at the Seneca Cameron site), short wampum-like tubular white and dark blue glass beads (Ontario Glass Bead Period II) dominated glass bead assemblages (Sempowski and Saunders 2001,

825–31, appendix C).[2] Traditional Native accounts also hint at other, perhaps earlier or alternative, forms of wampum, such as beads of jointed rushes, or twisted elderberry, sumac, or basswood (see chapter 1; see also Woodbury 1992), or freshwater snail shells either as specified in the accounts or inferred from their contextual association with freshwater lakes (see chapter 1).

The new European items probably also had strong ideational associations, although, with the notable exception of glass beads, many European-derived items, such as brass kettles and iron knives tended, over time, to be downgraded to routine functional status. Among native exotics of nonlocal derivation, the most abundant was white marine shell—a commodity known historically to have been employed in acts of greeting and peacemaking, and archaeologically in rituals associated with burials. The latter pattern of mortuary use of marine shell continues to occur, and in ever-increasing quantities.

Later in time, wampum—marine shell in the form of tubular beads—was, as Lewis Henry Morgan thought, the material correlate of the operation of the Iroquois League (1962, 120). In ritual context, wampum was employed in formal greetings with strangers. Much the same exchange of sympathies could also preface or be part of another ceremony, one that combined procedures of condolence with the concept of symbolic resurrection. For the League of the Iroquois, that was accomplished in an indoor segment of the Condolence Council often called the Requickening Address. Finally, wampum was used as wergild— blood money—payment offered to avert the threat of reprisal for a killing.

Although condolence, requickening, and wergild were all instances of peacemaking behavior, the activity most obviously and directly applied to that end was blood-money payment. One of the basic functions of the Iroquois League was to eliminate such feuds among its

2. Marine shell artifacts also seem to occur in a greater variety of forms during this period, just prior to a sharp drop in marine shell in seventeenth-century Seneca sites.

members. Order within the League was maintained by encouraging reparation payments in lieu of vengeance for murder. The Norton version of the Deganawida epic, it will be recalled, relates the beginning of the Iroquois League to a policy of avoiding the exaction of vengeance for the murder of one's own. The anthropologist Anthony Wallace picked up on this as the central point of the Deganawida epic: "The strategic innovation is the prohibition of blood-revenge by members of one of the five tribes against members of their own tribe or of any of the other four" (1958, 124). In emphasizing the achievements of the Peacemaker, contemporary tellers of the Deganawida epic underline the same point (see chapter 1).

Earlier in time, the pre-wampum wampum—that is, marine shell—was, in all likelihood, similarly employed. Our model of contentious confederacies provides the conceptual framework for relating the later categories of wampum use to several kinds of archaeological context. Words of condolence, rites of symbolic resuscitation, payments of blood money, and probably other applications of shell/wampum were all instances of peacemaking behavior mostly practiced within tribal alliances. Intergroup alliance was possible only to the extent that revenge killings and blood feuds could be suppressed among participant members. As belligerence increased outwardly, more effort was applied to discourage feuding inwardly. During the sixteenth century, the archaeological record registers more seashell because a greater investment in dampening violence between tribes became necessary. Interiorly, let it be said again, the nascent and developing confederacy was a league of peace.

Formation of the Classic Five Nations League

As the seventeenth century dawned, the artifact assemblages of the Mohawks and Senecas—the members of the League of the Iroquois most distant from each other—become similar. Abruptly and for the first time, both not only look the same, they contain the same abundance of Dutch-derived, manufactured goods. Among both Mohawk and Seneca assemblages, an extraordinary increase in smoking pipes is evident, presumably related to an upswing in diplomatic and ceremonial activities. Overall, the heightened Mohawk-Seneca interaction strongly suggests the establishment of direct and friendly ties between the two tribes around 1600–1610. That is the archaeological footprint of Seneca involvement in the Iroquois League and the completion of the confederacy in its Five Nations form. This event occurs in the context of the fur trade, and it certainly looks, as William Fenton remarked, as if the Iroquois Confederacy formed out of frustration to get at European goods (1998, 243; see also Engelbrecht 2003, 134–35; Parmenter 2010, 16–18, 32).

In the bigger picture, however, this represents just the final spurt of confederacy growth, a continuation of a process set in motion long before Europeans and their goods were present (Trigger 2000, 163). Seeking the causes of tribal formation and tribal alliance, we were led back to an earlier climate of anthropological interpretation. We find, as have archaeologists before us, that increasing social complexity resulted most obviously from cultural valorization of feuding with distant nonrelatives; the subsequent absorption of unrelated captives/refugees in localized villages and tribes; and the mutual peacekeeping mechanisms—mortuary and otherwise—that facilitated integration of the heterogeneous new groups.

While the origins of endemic violence in Iroquoia are obscure, its presence, James Tuck noted:

Is well attested to before the fourteenth century; and the fear of reprisals in this never-ending pattern of blood revenge was probably a major factor in the formation of large villages, tribal units, and ultimately the several historic confederacies. It is interesting to note that the formation of alliances to regulate aggression succeeded only in suppressing blood revenge within a league and as a result made even more intensive the raiding among the various confederacies. The blood revenge patterns of a single lineage segment or village of the thirteenth century were transferred to tribal units and finally to allied tribes. For instance, when the Iroquois or Hurons ceased to acquire their victims from among their own respective peoples, they were even more likely to conduct long-distance raids on each other or some other neighboring tribe. The demise of the Saint Lawrence Iroquoians in the sixteenth century may be in some way related to their position between the Iroquois and the Huron confederacies. (Tuck 1978, 330–31)

Ultimately, the Iroquois and Huron Confederacies—and other alliances in the region—brought each other to life, eliminated intervening and neighboring groups, such as the St. Lawrence Iroquoians, and continued to enlarge in parallel fashion as they competed and fought. The chronology of the Iroquois League is, in fact, the same as that of the Huron Confederacy. The latter began in the alliance of two tribes occurring, according to historical tradition (recorded in 1639) in the fifteenth century. The Huron Confederacy was completed in its historically known form with the joining of its final member in about 1610 (Trigger 1969, 14, 21, 76; Trigger 2000, 58, 156, 163, 174–75, 445n20; Tooker 1991, 10; Warrick 2008, 11, 185–92). The time frames for Iroquois and Huron confederation are the same for a good reason also presciently laid out by Bruce Trigger. War forced groups to band together for mutual defense. A successful coalition left neighboring villages at a disadvantage, unless they too managed to consolidate themselves into larger groupings (2000, 158). This led to the development of defensive alliances that routinely sent their men out to wage war. Internally, they devoted themselves to making peace among kith and kin—as described in the Deganawida epic and expressed in the Iroquois longhouse metaphor.

A Brief Overview

The sixteenth century witnessed the transformation of life in Iroquoia—not so much materially or technologically, because those aspects seem largely intact at the beginning of the seventeenth century—but socially, politically, and ceremonially. Spurred by endemic regional hostilities and the competitive advantages of larger numbers, political tribes and alliances challenged one another into existence.

Internal peacekeeping mechanisms emerged that foreshadowed the validation power of wampum and the highly ritualized condolence and requickening rites characteristic of the historically known Haudenosaunee.

Early on and apparently quite independently, in both eastern and western Iroquoia, distinctive forms of ceramic effigy smoking pipes, depicting and reinforcing themes of local "emergence" and common ethnic origins, played a role in authenticating the formation of localized tribal groups and the small-scale alliances that underlay them. Indeed, these pipes appear to represent the earliest archaeological markers of these initial processes in the evolution of the classic Five Nations League of the Iroquois.

The more heterogeneous social groupings resulting from the assimilation of nonkin members were further reinforced by ceremonial mechanisms that required the acquisition and use of value-laden exotic goods: beads of marine shell, native copper, and presumably other native materials that have not survived. By the mid-sixteenth century, as the occasional European items—especially glass and copper alloy beads—found their way into the system, they took on a similar role in these ceremonial contexts. As access to these exotic foreign goods increased during the latter half of the sixteenth century, we see rising trends in both quantities of material goods in graves and the proportion of individuals buried with them. This pattern of growth continues unabated well into the seventeenth century, attesting to the long-term relevance and significance of these funerary behaviors for the Iroquois.

Was competition for access to the valued European trade goods a motivating factor in the formation of the League of the Iroquois, as many have asserted? This seems unlikely. The developmental processes of early alliances that culminated in the union of the classic Five Nations League early in the seventeenth century were well underway a century or more before regularized European presence in the region, long before manufactured goods had become a significant factor. Rather, the roots of tribalization and alliance-building that led to the emergence of the Iroquois League lie in pre-European patterns of warfare and blood revenge, and in the Native peacekeeping mechanisms that were devised to hold them in check within newly formed social and political groups.

What about the peacekeeping procedures, particularly the reciprocal mortuary rituals that reinforced the integration of increasingly complex social and political groups during the sixteenth century? Do they represent newly introduced ritual behaviors from outside the region, or rather an elaboration of deeply entrenched familial responsibilities for reciprocal mourning as embodied in the Iroquois longhouse metaphor? It is difficult to say with almost exclusively negative mortuary evidence from the preceding century.

Several lines of thought discussed here may be worth considering in answer to that question. First, is the relatively abrupt and widespread occurrence of an intensified emphasis on mortuary ceremonialism among sixteenth-century New York and Ontario Iroquoians. Second are suggestions raised by Susan Jamieson and Robert Hasenstab that some northern Iroquoian ceremonial practices, including aspects of mortuary treatment, may have been moving northward with exotic goods along the upper Ohio River drainage from "Mississippified" polities to the south. Third is the seemingly deep-seated nature of familial longhouse principles of reciprocal condolence practices in Iroquoian thought and metaphor.

In sum, we propose that, at least in western Iroquoia, the revitalization of mortuary ritual may represent a local manifestation of a small body of newly introduced ritual concepts and practices, interpreted and contextualized within a long-standing and familiar kinship model. As access to marine shell and later European goods grew in the latter half of the sixteenth century, it fueled the escalation of these local funerary practices and the demand for exotic material goods.

These altered dynamics, then—social, political, and ceremonial—constitute the somewhat challenging new environment within which the classic Five Nations League of the Iroquois was finalized early in the seventeenth century.

References | *Index*

References

Abel, Timothy. 2001. "The Clayton Cluster: Cultural Dynamics of a Late Prehistoric Village Sequence in the Upper St. Lawrence Valley." PhD diss., State Univ. of New York at Albany.

——. 2002. "Recent Research on the St. Lawrence Iroquoians of Northern New York." *Archaeology of Eastern North America* 30:137–54.

——. 2016. "The Iroquoian Occupations of Northern New York: A Summary of Current Research." *Ontario Archaeology* 96:65–75.

——. 2018. "Radiocarbon Dating the Iroquoian Occupation of Northern New York." Paper presented at the 102nd Annual Meeting of the New York State Archaeological Association, Syracuse, NY.

Abler, Thomas S. 2004. "Seneca Moieties and Hereditary Chieftainships: The Early-Nineteenth-Century Political Organization of an Iroquois Nation." *Ethnohistory* 51 (3): 459–88.

Allen, Kathleen M. S. 1992. "Iroquois Ceramic Production: A Case Study of Household-Level Organization." In *Ceramic Production and Distribution: An Integrated Approach*, edited by George J. Bey III and Christopher A. Pool, 133–54. Boulder, CO: Westview Press.

Andrews, William. 1716. Letter to the Society, October 11. Records of the Society for the Propagation of the Gospel, Letter Books, series A, vol. 12, 239–43, London, Ontario.

Aquila, Richard. (1983) 1997. *The Iroquois Restoration: Iroquois Diplomacy on the Colonial Frontier, 1701–1754*. Reprint, Lincoln: Univ. of Nebraska Press.

Axtell, James. 1985. *The Invasion Within: The Contest of Cultures in Colonial North America*. New York: Oxford Univ. Press.

Bamann, Susan E. 1993. "Settlement Nucleation in Mohawk Iroquois Prehistory: An Analysis of a Site Sequence in the Lower Otsquago Drainage of the Mohawk Valley." PhD diss., State Univ. of New York at Albany.

Barbeau, C. Marius. 1915. *Huron and Wyandot Mythology*. Canada Department of Mines, Geological Survey, Memoir 80, Anthropological Series 11. Ottawa: Government Printing Bureau.

———. 1951. "The Dragon Myth and Ritual Songs of the Iroquoians." *Journal of the International Folk Music Council* 3:81–85.

———. 1952. "The Old-World Dragon in America." In *Indian Tribes of Aboriginal America: Selected Papers of the XXIXth International Congress of Americanists*, edited by Sol Tax, 155–22. Chicago: Univ. of Chicago Press.

Barnouw, Victor. 1977. *Wisconsin Chippewa Myths and Tales and Their Relation to Chippewa Life*. Madison: Univ. of Wisconsin Press.

Beauchamp, William M. 1891. "Hi-a-wat-ha." *Journal of American Folk-Lore* 4:295–306.

———. 1892. *The Iroquois Trail, or Foot-Prints of the Six Nations*. Fayetteville, NY: H. C. Beauchamp.

———. 1895a. "Mohawk Notes." *Journal of American Folk-Lore* 8:217–21.

———. 1895b. "Onondaga Notes." *Journal of American Folk-Lore* 8:209–16.

———. 1898. *Earthenware of the New York Aborigines*. New York State Museum Bulletin 5, no. 22. Albany: Univ. of the State of New York.

———. 1905. *A History of the New York Iroquois, Now Commonly Called the Six Nations*. New York State Museum Bulletin 78, Archeology section 9, 126–461. Albany: Univ. of the State of New York.

———. 1907. *Civil, Religious and Mourning Councils and Ceremonies of Adoption of the New York Indians*. New York State Museum Bulletin 113. Albany: Univ. of the State of New York.

Bennett, Monte. 1983. "Glass Trade Beads from Central New York." In *Proceedings of the 1982 Glass Trade Bead Conference*, edited by Charles F. Hayes III, 51–58. Research Records no. 16. Rochester, NY: Rochester Museum & Science Center.

———. 2006. "A Brief Look at the Brunk Site, a Mid to Late Prehistoric Oneida Village: Field Work Report 1997–2001." *Chenango Chapter Bulletin* 29 (1): 79–109.

Bennett, Monte, and Anthony Wonderley. Forthcoming. "An Overview of Oneida Archaeology." In *The Archaeology of New York State Revisited*, edited by Susan E. Maguire and Lisa M. Anselmi. Albany: New York State Museum Record. E-book.

Biggar, Henry P., ed. 1993. *The Voyages of Jacques Cartier*. Introduction by Ramsay Cook. Toronto: Univ. of Toronto Press.

Birch, Jennifer. 2012. "Coalescent Communities: Settlement Aggregation and Social Integration in Iroquoian Ontario." *American Antiquity* 77 (4): 646–70.

———. 2015. "Current Research in the Historical Development of Northern Iroquoian Societies." *Journal of Archaeological Research* 23 (3): 3–63.

———. 2016. "Geopolitics and Dimensions of Social Complexity in Ancestral Wendake c. A.D. 1450–1600." *Ontario Archaeology* 96:35–46.

Birch, Jennifer, and John P. Hart. 2017. "Social Networks and Northern Iroquoian Confederacy Dynamics." *American Antiquity* 83 (1): 13–33.

Birch, Jennifer and Sturt Manning. 2016. "Bayesian Modeling and Refinement of Iroquoian Regional Settlement Histories." Paper presented at the 81st Annual Meeting of the Society for American Archaeology, Orlando, FL.

Blau, Harold, Jack Campisi, and Elisabeth Tooker. 1978. "Onondaga." In *Northeast*, edited by Bruce Trigger, 491–99. *Handbook of North American Indians*, vol. 15. Washington, DC: Smithsonian Institution.

Bond, Jr., Stanley C. 1985. "The Relationship between Soils and Settlement Pattern in the Mohawk Valley." In *The Mohawk Valley Project: 1982 Field Season Report*, edited by Dean R. Snow, 17–40. Albany: Institute for Northeast Archaeology, State Univ. of New York at Albany.

Boyce, Douglas W. 1973. "A Glimpse of Iroquois Culture History through the Eyes of Joseph Brant and John Norton." *Proceedings of the American Philosophical Society* 117 (4): 28–94.

Bradley, James W. 1987. *Evolution of the Onondaga Iroquois: Accommodating Change, 1500–1655*. Syracuse, NY: Syracuse Univ. Press.

———. 2001. "Change and Survival among the Onondaga Iroquois since 1500." In *Societies in Eclipse: Archaeology of the Eastern Woodlands Indians, A. D. 1400–1700*, edited by David S. Brose, W. Wesley Cowan, and Robert C. Mainfort Jr., 27–47. Washington, DC: Smithsonian Institution Press.

———. Forthcoming. *Onondaga and Empire*. Albany: New York State Museum. E-book.

Bradley, James W., and Terry S. Childs. 1989. "Spirals and Rings: Analysis of Two 16th Century Artifact Forms." Paper presented at the World Archaeology Conference, Baltimore, MD.

Brandão, José António. 1997. *"Your Fyre Shall Burn No More": Iroquois Policy toward New France and Its Native Allies to 1701*. Lincoln: Univ. of Nebraska Press.

————. 2003. *Nation Iroquoise: A Seventeenth-Century Ethnography of the Iroquois*, edited by José António Brandão, translated by José António Brandão with K. Janet Rich. Lincoln: Univ. of Nebraska Press.

Brandão, José António, and William A. Starna. 1996. "The Treaties of 1701: A Triumph of Iroquois Diplomacy." *Ethnohistory* 43:209–44.

Brasser, Ted J. 1980. "Self-Directed Pipe Effigies." *Man in the Northeast* 19:95–104.

Braun, Gregory Vincent. 2015. "Ritual, Materiality, and Memory in an Iroquoian Village." PhD diss., Univ. of Toronto.

Bricker, Victoria Reifler. 1981. *The Indian Christ, the Indian King: The Historical Substrata of Maya Myth and Ritual*. Austin: Univ. of Texas Press.

Brinton, Daniel G. (1868) 1974. *Myths of the New World: The Symbolism and Mythology of the Indians of the Americas*. Reprint, New York: Multimedia, Blauvelt.

Bruner, Jerome. 1991. "The Narrative Construction of Reality." *Critical Inquiry* 18 (Autumn): 1–21.

Caldwell, Joseph R. 1964. "Interaction Spheres in Prehistory." In *Hopewellian Studies*, edited by Joseph R. Caldwell and Robert L. Hall, 133–43. Scientific Papers 12. Springfield: Illinois State Museum.

Campbell, William J. 2004. "Seth Newhouse, the Grand River Six Nations and the Writing of the Great Laws." *Ontario History* 96 (2): 183–202.

Canadian Museum of Civilization. 1998. "Canadian Museum of Civilization Repatriates Human Remains to Akwesasne Mohawks." Communiqué of the Museum, Hull, Québec, November 10, online.

Canfield, William W. 1902. *The Legends of the Iroquois, Told by "The Cornplanter."* New York: A. Wessels.

Cantine, John, and Simeon DeWitt. ca. 1793. Report of a Council Held to Purchase Lands, n.d., Assembly Papers (Petitions, Correspondence and Reports Relating to Indians, 1783–1831), vol. 40, 119–48. Albany: New York State Archives.

Ceci, Lynn. 1982. "The Value of Wampum among the New York Iroquois: A Case Study in Artifact Analysis." *Journal of Anthropological Research* 38 (1): 97–107.

————. 1986. "The Origins of Wampum among the Seneca Iroquois." On file at the Rochester Museum & Science Center, Rochester, NY.

————. 1989. "Tracing Wampum's Origins: Shell Bead Evidence from Archaeological Sites in Western and Coastal New York." In *Proceedings of the 1986 Shell Bead Conference: Selected Papers*, edited by Charles F. Hayes III, Lynn Ceci, and Connie Cox Bodner, 63–80. Research Records no. 20. Rochester, NY: Rochester Museum & Science Center.

Chapdelaine, Claude. 2004. "A Review of the Latest Developments in St. Lawrence Iroquoian Archaeology." In *A Passion for the Past: Papers in Honour of James F. Pendergast*, edited by James V. Wright and Jean-Luc Pilon, 63–75. Archaeological Survey of Canada, Mercury Series Paper 164. Gatineau, Québec: Canadian Museum of Civilization.

Clark, Joshua V. H. 1849. *Onondaga; Or, Reminiscences of Earlier and Later Times*. Vol. 1. Syracuse, NY: Stoddard and Babcock.

Clark, Lynn. 2004. "Gender at an Early Seventeenth-Century Oneida Village." PhD diss., State Univ. of New York at Binghamton.

Clermont, Norman, Claude Chapdelaine, and Georges Barré. 1983. *Le site Iroquoien de Lanorie: témoignage d'une maison-longue*. Recherches amérindiennes au Québec. Montreal.

Colden, Cadwallader. (1727, 1747) 1988. *The History of the Five Indian Nations Depending on the Province of New-York in America*. Reprint, Ithaca, NY: Cornell Univ. Press.

Converse, Harriet Maxwell. 1908. *Myths and Legends of the New York State Iroquois*. New York State Museum Bulletin 125. Albany: Univ. of the State of New York.

Crerar, Jacqueline E. M. 1994. "Assets and Assemblages: The Neutral Economic Approach to Inter-Cultural Relations." In *Proceedings of the 1992 People to People Conference: Selected Papers*, edited by Charles F. Hayes III, Connie Cox Bodner, and Lorraine P. Saunders, 37–49. Research Records no. 23. Rochester, NY: Rochester Museum & Science Center.

Cruikshank, Julie. 1994. "Oral Tradition and Oral History: Reviewing Some Basics." *Canadian Historical Review* 75:403–18.

Dennis, Matthew. 1993. *Cultivating a Landscape of Peace: Iroquois-European Encounters in Seventeenth-Century America*. Ithaca, NY: Cornell Univ. Press.

Dermarkar, Susan, Jennifer Birch, Termeh Shafie, John P. Hart, and Ronald F. Williamson. 2016. "St. Lawrence Iroquoians and Pan-Iroquoian Social Network Analysis." *Ontario Archaeology* 96:87–103.

Drooker, Penelope Ballard. 1997. *The View from Madisonville: Protohistoric Western Fort Ancient Interaction Patterns*. Memoirs of the Museum of Anthropology 31. Ann Arbor: Univ. of Michigan Press.

———. 2004. "Pipes, Leadership, and Interregional Interaction in Protohistoric Midwestern and Northeastern North America." In *Smoking Culture: The Archaeology of Tobacco Pipes in Eastern North America*, edited by Sean M. Rafferty and Rob Mann, 73–123. Knoxville: Univ. of Tennessee Press.

Druke, Mary A. 1981. "Structure and Meaning of Leadership among the Mohawk and Oneida during the Mid-Eighteenth Century." PhD diss., Univ. of Chicago.

———. 1987. "Linking Arms: The Structure of Iroquois Intertribal Diplomacy." In *Beyond the Covenant Chain: The Iroquois and Their Neighbors in Indian North America, 1600–1800*, edited by Daniel K. Richter and James H. Merrill, 29–39. Syracuse, NY: Syracuse Univ. Press.

Drummond, Lee. 1981. "The Serpent's Children: Semiotics of Cultural Genesis in Arawak and Trobriand Myth." *American Ethnologist* 8:633–60.

Dwight, Timothy. 1822. *Travels in New-England and New-York*. Vol. 4. New Haven, CT: Published by the author.

Earle, Timothy. 2004. "Culture Matters in the Neolithic Transition and Emergence of Hierarchy in Thy, Denmark: Distinguished Lecture." *American Anthropologist* 106:111–25.

Eiseley, Loren. 1957. *The Immense Journey*. New York: Vintage Books.

Engelbrecht, William. 1974. "The Iroquois: Archaeological Patterning on the Tribal Level." *World Archaeology* 6 (1): 52–65.

———. 1985. "New York Iroquois Political Development." In *Cultures in Contact: The Impact of European Contacts on Native American Cultural Institutions, A.D. 1000–1800*, edited by William W. Fitzhugh, 163–83. Washington, DC: Smithsonian Institution Press.

———. 1991. "Erie." *The Bulletin* (Journal of the New York State Archaeological Association) 102:2–12.

———. 1995. "The Case of the Disappearing Iroquois: Early Contact Period Superpower Politics." *Northeast Anthropology* 50:3–59.

———. 1997. "Iroquoian Ethnicity and Archaeological Taxa." In *Taming the Taxonomy: Toward a New Understanding of Great Lakes Archaeology*, edited by Ronald F. Williamson and Christopher M. Watts. Toronto: Eastendbooks, Ontario Archaeological Society.

———. 2003. *Iroquoia: The Development of a Native World*. Syracuse, NY: Syracuse Univ. Press.

———. 2004. "Northern New York Revisited." In *A Passion for the Past: Papers in Honour of James F. Pendergast*, edited by James V. Wright and

Jean-Luc Pilon, 125–44. Archaeological Survey of Canada, Mercury Series Paper 164. Gatineau, Québec: Canadian Museum of Civilization.

Engelbrecht, William, and Bruce Jamieson. 2016a. "St. Lawrence Iroquoian Projectile Points: A Regional Perspective." *Archaeology of Eastern North America* 44:81–98.

———. 2016b. "Stone-Tipped versus Bone- and Antler-Tipped Arrows and the Movement of the St. Lawrence Iroquoians from Their Homeland." *Ontario Archaeology* 96:76–86.

Erickson, Kirstin C. 2003. "'They Will Come from the Other Side of the Sea': Prophecy, Ethnogenesis, and Agency in Yaqui Narrative." *Journal of American Folklore* 116:465–82.

Fenton, William N. 1940. "Problems Arising from the Historic Northeastern Position of the Iroquois." In *Essays in Historical Anthropology of North America*, edited by Julian H. Steward, 159–251. Smithsonian Miscellaneous Collections 100. Washington, DC: Smithsonian Institution.

———. 1946. "An Iroquois Condolence Council for Installing Cayuga Chiefs, 1945." *Journal of the Washington Academy of Sciences* 36 (4): 110–27.

———. 1949. "Seth Newhouse's Traditional History and Constitution of the Iroquois Confederacy." *Proceedings of the American Philosophical Society* 93 (2): 141–58.

———. 1961. "Iroquoian Culture History: A General Evaluation." In *Symposium on Cherokee and Iroquois Culture*, edited by William N. Fenton and John Gulick, 257–77. Bureau of American Ethnology Bulletin 180. Washington, DC.

———. 1962. "Introduction." In *League of the Iroquois*, by Lewis Henry Morgan, v–xviii. Secaucus, NJ: Citadel Press.

———. 1965. "The Iroquois Confederacy in the Twentieth Century: A Case Study in the Theory of Lewis Henry Morgan in 'Ancient Society.'" *Ethnology* 4 (3): 251–65.

———. 1968. "Editor's Introduction." In *Parker on the Iroquois*, edited by William N. Fenton, 1–47. Syracuse, NY: Syracuse Univ. Press.

———. 1969. "Answers to Governor Cass's Questions by Jacob Jameson, a Seneca (ca. 1821–1825)." *Ethnohistory* 16 (2): 113–39.

———. 1978a. "Northern Iroquoian Cultural Patterns." In *Northeast*, edited by Bruce Trigger, 296–321. *Handbook of North American Indians*, vol. 15. Washington, DC: Smithsonian Institution.

———. 1978b. "Problems in the Authentication of the League of the Iroquois." In *Neighbors and Intruders: An Ethnohistorical Exploration of the Indians of Hudson's River*, edited by Laurence M. Hauptman and Jack Campisi, 261–68. National Museum of Man Mercury Series, Canadian Ethnology Service Paper no. 39. Ottawa: National Museums of Canada.

———. 1985. "Structure, Continuity, and Change in the Process of Iroquois Treaty Making." In *The History and Culture of Iroquois Diplomacy: An Interdisciplinary Guide to the Treaties of the Six Nations and Their League*, edited by Francis Jennings et al., 127–53. Syracuse, NY: Syracuse Univ. Press.

———. 1987. *The False Faces of the Iroquois*. Norman: Univ. of Oklahoma Press.

———. 1989. "Introduction." In *Seneca Myths and Folk Tales*, by Arthur C. Parker, xi–xviii. Lincoln: Univ. of Nebraska Press.

———. (1953) 1991. *The Iroquois Eagle Dance: An Offshoot of the Calumet Dance*. Reprint, Syracuse, NY: Syracuse Univ. Press.

———. 1998. *The Great Law and the Longhouse: A Political History of the Iroquois Confederacy*. Norman: Univ. of Oklahoma Press.

———. 2002. *The Little Water Medicine Society of the Senecas*. Norman: Univ. of Oklahoma Press.

Fenton, William N., and Gertrude P. Kurath. 1951. "The Feast of the Dead, or Ghost Dance at Six Nations Reserve, Canada." In *Symposium on Local Diversity in Iroquois Culture*, edited by William N. Fenton, 145–65. Bulletin no. 149, Bureau of American Ethnology. Washington, DC: Smithsonian Institution.

Fenton, William N., and Elizabeth L. Moore, eds. and trans. 1974, 1977. *Customs of the American Indians Compared with Customs of Primitive Times by Father Joseph François Lafitau*. 2 vols. Toronto: Champlain Society.

Finlayson, William D. 1985. *The 1975 and 1978 Rescue Excavations at the Draper Site: Introduction and Settlement Patterns*. Mercury Series 111. Ottawa: National Museum of Man.

———. 1998. *Iroquoian Peoples of the Land of Rocks and Water, A.D. 1000–1650: A Study in Settlement Archaeology*. Special Publications 1. London, Ontario: London Museum of Archaeology.

Fitzgerald, William R. 2001. "Contact, Neutral Iroquoian Transformation, and the Little Ice Age." In *Societies in Eclipse: Archaeology of the Eastern Woodlands Indians, A. D. 1400–1700*, edited by David S. Brose, W. Wesley Cowan, and Robert C. Mainfort Jr., 37–47. Washington, DC: Smithsonian Institution Press.

———. 2007. "Contact, Neutral Iroquoian Transformation, and the Little Ice Age." In *Archaeology of the Iroquois: Selected Readings and Research Sources*, edited by Jordan E. Kerber, 251–68. Syracuse, NY: Syracuse Univ. Press.

Foley, Denis. 1973. "The Iroquois Condolence Business." *Man in the Northeast* 5:47–53.

Funk, Robert E., and Robert D. Kuhn. 2003. *Three Sixteenth-Century Mohawk Iroquois Village Sites.* New York State Museum Bulletin 593. Albany: Univ. of the State of New York.

Garrad, Charles. 2014. *Petun to Wyandot: The Ontario Petun from the Sixteenth Century.* Edited by Jean-Luc Pilon and William Fox. Mercury Series, Archaeology Paper 174. Ottawa: Univ. of Ottawa Press and Canadian Museum of History.

Garrad, Charles, and Conrad E. Heidenreich. 1978. "Khionontateronon (Petun)." In *Northeast*, edited by Bruce G. Trigger, 394–97. *Handbook of North American Indians*, vol. 15. Washington, DC: Smithsonian Institution.

Geertz, Clifford. 1973. *The Interpretation of Culture: Selected Essays by Clifford Geertz.* New York: Basic Books.

Gehring, Charles T., and William A. Starna, trans. and eds. 1988. *A Journey into Mohawk and Oneida Country, 1634–1635: The Journal of Meyndertsz van den Bogaert.* Syracuse, NY: Syracuse Univ. Press.

Gibson, Stanford J. 1963. "Iroquois Pottery Faces and Effigies." *Chenango Chapter Bulletin* (New York State Archaeological Association, Norwich) 4, no. 8.

———. 1966. "The Vaillancourt Site." *Chenango Chapter Bulletin* (New York State Archaeological Association, Norwich) 8, no. 2.

———. 1968. "The Oran-Barnes Site." *Chenango Chapter Bulletin* (New York State Archaeological Association, Norwich) 10, no. 1.

———. 1971a. "An Elevation Comparison of Iroquois Sites in Three Valleys of Central New York State." *Chenango Chapter Bulletin* (New York State Archaeological Association, Norwich) 12 (2): 1–8.

———. 1971b. "Vaillancourt Axes." *Chenango Chapter Bulletin* (New York State Archaeological Association, Norwich) 12 (1): 1–7.

———. 1986. "A Report on Two Oneida Iroquois Indian Sites: Ond 12, Ond 16." *Chenango Chapter Bulletin* (New York State Archaeological Association, Norwich) 22, no. 1.

Goldenweiser, A. A. 1916. "Review of *The Constitution of the Five Nations* by Arthur C. Parker." *American Anthropologist* 18:431–36.

Goldschmidt, Walter. 2000. "A Perspective on Anthropology." *American Anthropologist* 102:789–807.

Gramly, Richard Michael. 1977. "Deerskins and Hunting Territories: Competition for a Scarce Resource of the Northeastern Woodlands." *American Antiquity* 42 (4): 601–5.

Grantham, Bill. 2002. *Creation Myths and Legends of the Creek Indians.* Gainesville: Univ. Press of Florida.

Graymont, Barbara. 1988. *The Iroquois.* New York: Chelsea House.

Greer, Allan. 2005. *Mohawk Saint: Catherine Tekakwitha and the Jesuits.* New York: Oxford Univ. Press.

Grumet, Robert S. 1995. *Historic Contact: Indian People and Colonists in Today's Northeastern United States in the Sixteenth through Eighteenth Centuries.* Norman: Univ. of Oklahoma Press.

GRVCAP. 2001. Reports of the Genesee River Valley Cultural Affiliation Project. On file at the Rochester Museum & Science Center, Rochester, NY.

Haan, Richard L. 1987. "Covenant and Consensus: Iroquois and English, 1676–1760." In *Beyond the Covenant Chain: The Iroquois and Their Neighbors in Indian North America, 1600–1800,* edited by Daniel K. Richter and James H. Merrill, 41–57. Syracuse, NY: Syracuse Univ. Press.

Hale, Horatio. 1894. "The Fall of Hochelaga: A Study of Popular Traditions." *Journal of American Folk-Lore* 7:1–14.

———. 1895. "An Iroquois Condoling Council." *Transactions of the Royal Society of Canada* (2nd series) 1:45–65.

———. (1883) 1963. *The Iroquois Book of Rites.* Introduction by William N. Fenton. Reprint, Toronto: Univ. of Toronto Press.

———. (1883) 1969. *The Iroquois Book of Rites.* Reprint, New York: AMS Press.

Hall, Robert L. 1997. *An Archaeology of the Soul: North American Indian Belief and Ritual.* Urbana: Univ. of Illinois Press.

Hamell, George R. 1976. Preliminary Report on the Alhart Site. On file at the Rochester Museum & Science Center, Rochester, NY.

———. 1979. "Of Hockers, Diamonds, and Hourglasses: Some Interpretations of Seneca Archaeological Art." Paper presented at the Annual Conference on Iroquois Research, Albany, NY.

———. 1980. "Sun Serpents, Tawiskaron, and Quartz Crystals." Paper presented at the Annual Conference on Iroquois Research, Rensselaerville, NY.

———. 1987a. "Mythical Realities and European Contact in the Northeast during the Sixteenth and Seventeenth Centuries." *Man in the Northeast* 33:63–87.

———. 1987b. "Strawberries, Floating Islands, and Rabbit Captains: Mythical Realities and European Contact in the Northeast during the Sixteenth and Seventeenth Centuries." *Journal of Canadian Studies* 21 (4): 72–94.

———. 1992. "The Iroquois and the World's Rim: Speculations on Color, Culture, and Contact." *American Indian Quarterly* 16 (1): 451–69.

———. 1998. "Long-Tail: The Panther in Huron-Wyandot and Seneca Myth, Ritual, and Material Culture." In *Icons of Power: Feline Symbolism in the Americas*, edited by Nicholas J. Saunders, 258–91. New York: Routledge.

Harrington, Mark R. 1908. "Some Seneca Corn-Foods and Their Preparation." *American Anthropologist* 10:875–90.

Hart, John P. 2012. "The Effects of Distances on Pottery Assemblage Similarities: A Case Study from Northern Iroquoia." *Journal of Archaeological Science* 39:128–34.

———. 2018. "Resetting the Radiocarbon Chronology for the Late Prehistoric Mohawk Valley." Paper presented at the Annual Meeting of the New York State Archaeological Association, Syracuse, NY.

Hart, John P., and William Engelbrecht. 2012. "Northern Iroquoian Ethnic Evolution: A Social Network Analysis." *Archaeological Method and Theory* 19:322–49.

———. 2017. "Revisiting Onondaga Iroquois Prehistory through Social Network Analysis." In *Process and Meaning in Spatial Archaeology: Investigations into Pre-Columbian Iroquoian Space and Time*, edited by Eric E. Jones and John L. Creese, 189–214. Boulder: Univ. Press of Colorado.

Hasenstab, Robert J. 1987. "Canoes, Caches, and Carrying Places: Territorial Boundaries and Tribalization in Late Woodland Western New York," *The Bulletin* (Journal of the New York State Archaeological Association) 95:39–49.

Hayden, Brian. 1979. "The Draper and White Sites: Preliminary and Theoretical Considerations." In *1979 Settlement Patterns of the Draper and White Sites: 1973 Excavations*, edited by Brian Hayden, 1–28. Department of Archaeology Publication no. 6. Burnaby, British Columbia: Simon Fraser Univ.

Heckewelder, John. (1876) 1991. *History, Manners, and Customs of the Indian Nations Who Once Inhabited Pennsylvania and the Neighboring States.* Reprint, Salem, NH: Ayer.

Heidenreich, Conrad E. 1978. "Huron." In *Northeast*, edited by Bruce G. Trigger, 368–88. *Handbook of North American Indians*, vol. 15. Washington, DC: Smithsonian Institution.

Henige, David. 1999. "Can a Myth Be Astronomically Dated?" *American Indian Culture and Research Journal* 23 (4): 127–57.

Hewitt, J. N. B. 1892. "Legend of the Founding of the Iroquois League." *American Anthropologist* 5:131–48.

———. 1917. "Review of *The Constitution of the Five Nations* by Arthur C. Parker." *American Anthropologist* 19:429–38.

———. 1918. "Seneca Fiction, Legends, and Myths: Collected by Jeremiah Curtin and J. N. B. Hewitt." In *Thirty-Second Annual Report of the Bureau of American Ethnology, 1910–1911*, 37–819. Washington, DC: Smithsonian Institution.

———. 1920. "A Constitutional League of Peace in the Stone Age of America: The League of the Iroquois and Its Constitution." In *Annual Report of the Board of Regents of the Smithsonian Institution [for] 1918*, 527–45. Washington, DC: Government Printing Office.

———. 1944. "The Requickening Address of the Iroquois Condolence Council." Edited by William N. Fenton, *Journal of the Washington Academy of Sciences* 34 (3): 65–85.

Hill, Jonathan D. 1988. "Introduction: Myth and History." In *Rethinking History and Myth: Indigenous South American Perspectives on the Past*, edited by Jonathan D. Hill, 1–17. Urbana: Univ. of Illinois Press.

Hodder, Ian. 1986. *Reading the Past: Approaches to Interpretation in Archaeology.* Cambridge: Cambridge Univ. Press.

Hosbach, Richard E. 1992. "A Gyneco-Android Subset of Native Iroquoian El Rancho Pipes: A New Pipe Designation with the Philosophical Concept of Sexual Duality as Its Basic Motif." In *Proceedings of the 1989 Smoking Pipe Conference: Selected Papers*, edited by Charles F. Hayes III, Connie Cox Bodner, and Martha L. Sempowski, 83–96. Research Records no. 22. Rochester, NY: Rochester Museum & Science Center.

———. 2004. "Carlo I and Carlo II Coins Found on Two New York Iroquois Sites." In *A Passion for the Past: Papers in Honour of James F. Pendergast*, edited by James V. Wright and Jean-Luc Pilon, 193–204. Mercury

Series, Archaeology Paper 164. Gatineau, Québec: Canadian Museum of Civilization.

Hough, Franklin B., ed. 1861. *Proceedings of the Commissioners of Indian Affairs, Appointed by Law for the Extinguishment of Indian Titles in the State of New York*. Albany, NY: Munsell.

Houghton, Frederick. 1922. "The Traditional Origin and Naming of the Seneca Nation." *American Anthropologist*, New Series 24 (1): 31–43.

Jamieson, James Bruce. 1990a. "The Archaeology of the St. Lawrence Iroquoians." In *The Archaeology of Southern Ontario to A.D. 1650*, edited by Chris J. Ellis and Neal Ferris, 385–404. Occasional Publications of the London Chapter, Ontario Archaeological Society no 5.

———. 1990b. "Trade and Warfare: The Disappearance of the St. Lawrence Iroquoians." *Man in the Northeast* 39:79–86.

Jamieson, Susan M. 1992. "Regional Interaction in Ontario Iroquois Evolution." *Canadian Journal of Archaeology* 16:70–88.

———. 1999. "A Brief History of Aboriginal Social Interaction in Southern Ontario and Their Taxonomic Implications." In *Taming the Taxonomy: Toward a New Understanding of Great Lakes Archaeology*, edited by Ronald F. Williamson and Christopher M. Watts, 175–92. Toronto: Eastendbooks.

Jennings, Francis. 1978. "Susquehannock." In *Northeast*, edited by Bruce Trigger, 362–67. *Handbook of North American Indians*, vol. 15. Washington, DC: Smithsonian Institution.

———. 1984. *The Ambiguous Iroquois Empire: The Covenant Chain Confederation of Indian Tribes with English Colonies from Its Beginnings to the Lancaster Treaty of 1744*. New York: W. W. Norton.

———. 1988. *Empire of Fortune: Crowns, Colonies, and Tribes in the Seven Years War in America*. New York: W. W. Norton.

Jennings, Francis, with William N. Fenton, Mary A. Druke, and David R. Miller, eds. 1985. "The Earliest Recorded Description: The Mohawk Treaty with New France at Three Rivers, 1645." In *The History and Culture of Iroquois Diplomacy: An Interdisciplinary Guide to the Treaties of the Six Nations and Their League*, 127–53. Syracuse, NY: Syracuse Univ. Press.

Johnson, Elias. 1881. *Legends, Traditions and Laws of the Iroquois or Six Nations and History of the Tuscarora Indians*. Lockport, NY: Union Printing and Publishing.

Jones, Eric E. 2006. "Using Viewshed Analysis to Explore Settlement Choice: A Case Study of the Onondaga Iroquois." *American Antiquity* 71 (3): 523–38.

———. 2010. "Population History of the Onondaga and Oneida Iroquois, A.D. 1500–1700." *American Antiquity* 75 (2): 387–407.

Judkins, Russell A. 1987. "David Cusick's *Ancient History of the Six Nations*: A Neglected Classic." In *Iroquois Studies: A Guide to Documents and Ethnographic Resources from Western New York and the Genesee Valley*, edited by Russell A. Judkins, 26–40. Geneseo: Department of Anthropology, State Univ. of New York at Genesco.

Kapches, Mima. 2003. "Invisible Women." *Rotunda* 35 (3): 12–19.

Kearsley, Ronald Glen. 1997. "Pinched-Face Human Effigy Pipes: The Social Mechanisms that Conditioned Their Manufacture and Use in Seventeenth-Century Iroquoia." Master's thesis, Trent Univ.

Kelsay, Isabel Thompson. 1984. *Joseph Brant, 1743–1807: Man of Two Worlds*. Syracuse, NY: Syracuse Univ. Press.

Kenyon, Ian T., and William R. Fitzgerald. 1986. "Dutch Glass Beads in the Northeast: An Ontario Perspective." *Man in the Northeast* 32:1–34.

Kinsey, III, W. Fred. 1989. "Susquehannock Zoomorphic Images: Or Why the Seasons Changed." In *New Approaches to Other Pasts*, edited by W. Fred Kinsley III and Roger W. Moeller, 71–88. Bethlehem, CT: Archaeological Services.

Klein, Kevin Lee. 1997. *Frontiers of Historical Imagination: Narrating the European Conquest of Native America, 1890–1990*. Berkeley: Univ. of California Press.

Klinck, Carl F., and James J. Talman, eds. 1970. *The Journal of Major John Norton, 1816*. Toronto: Champlain Society.

Kozuch, Laura. 1998. "Marine Shells from Mississippian Archaeological Sites." PhD diss., Univ. of Florida.

Kuhn, Robert D. 1985. "Trade and Exchange among the Mohawk-Iroquois: A Trace Element Analysis of Ceramic Smoking Pipes." PhD diss., State Univ. of New York at Albany.

———. 1989. "The Trace Element Analysis of Hudson Valley Clays and Ceramics." *The Bulletin* (Journal of the New York State Archaeological Association) 99:25–30.

———. 1999. "Recent Contributions to Iroquoian Archaeology in New York State." *Archaeology of Eastern North America* 21:73–88.

———. 2004. "Reconstructing Patterns of Interaction and Warfare between the Mohawks and Northern Iroquoians during the A.D. 1400–1700 Period." In *A Passion for the Past: Papers in Honour of James F. Pendergast*, edited by James V. Wright and Jean-Luc Pilon, 145–66. Mercury Series, Archaeology Paper 164. Gatineau, Québec: Canadian Museum of Civilization.

Kuhn, Robert D., and Robert E. Funk. 1994. "Mohawk Interaction Patterns during the Long Sixteenth Century." In *Proceedings of the 1992 People to People Conference: Selected Papers*, edited by Charles F. Hayes III, Connie Cox Bodner, and Lorraine P. Saunders, 77–84. Research Records no. 23. Rochester, NY: Rochester Museum & Science Center.

Kuhn, Robert D., Robert E. Funk, and James F. Pendergast. 1993. "The Evidence for a Saint Lawrence Iroquoian Presence on Sixteenth-Century Mohawk Sites." *Man in the Northeast* 45:77–86.

Kuhn, Robert D., and Martha L. Sempowski. 2001. "A New Approach to Dating the League of the Iroquois." *American Antiquity* 66:301–14.

Kurath, Gertrude Prokosch. 1952. "Matriarchal Dances of the Iroquois." In *Indian Tribes of Aboriginal America: Selected Papers of the XXIXth International Congress of Americanists*, edited by Sol Tax, 123–30. Chicago: Univ. of Chicago Press.

Landy, David. 1978. "Tuscarora among the Iroquois." In *Northeast*, edited by Bruce G. Trigger, 518–24. *Handbook of North American Indians*, vol. 15. Washington, DC: Smithsonian Institution.

Lankford, George E. 1987. *Native American Legends; Southeastern Legends: Tales from the Natchez, Caddo, Biloxi, Chickasaw, and Other Nations*. Little Rock, AR: August House.

———. 2007. "Some Cosmological Motifs in the Southeastern Ceremonial Complex." In *Ancient Objects and Sacred Realms: Interpretations of Mississippian Iconography*, edited by F. Kent Reilly III and James F. Garber, 8–38. Austin: Univ. of Texas Press.

Lenig, Donald. 1977. "Dutchmen, Beaver Hats and Iroquois." In *Current Perspectives in Northeastern Archaeology: Essays in Honor of William A. Ritchie*, edited by Robert E. Funk and Charles F. Hayes III, 71–84. Researches and Transactions of the New York State Archaeological Association 17, no. 1. Rochester and Albany, NY.

Lenig, Wayne. 1999. "Patterns of Material Culture during the Early Years of New Netherlands Trade." *Northeast Anthropology* 58:47–74.

Lennox, Paul A., and William R. Fitzgerald. 1990. "The Culture History and Archaeology of the Neutral Iroquoians." In *The Archaeology of Southern Ontario to A.D. 1650*, edited by Chris J. Ellis and Neal Ferris, 405–56. Occasional Publications of the London Chapter, Ontario Archaeological Society no 5.

Lounsbury, Floyd G. 1978. "Iroquoian Languages." In *Northeast*, edited by Bruce G. Trigger, 334–43. *Handbook of North American Indians*, vol. 15. Washington, DC: Smithsonian Institution.

Lounsbury, Floyd G., and Bryan Gick, eds. and trans. 2000. *The Oneida Creation Story: Demus Elm and Harvey Antone*. Lincoln: Univ. of Nebraska Press.

MacNeish, Richard S. 1952. *Iroquois Pottery Types: A Technique for the Study of Iroquois Prehistory*. National Museum of Canada Bulletin 124. Ottawa: Canada Department of Resources and Development.

———. 1980. "Iroquois Pottery Types 32 Years Later." In *Proceedings of the 1979 Iroquois Pottery Conference*, edited by Charles F. Hayes III, George R. Hamell, and Barbara M. Koenig, 1–6. Research Records no. 13. Rochester, NY: Rochester Museum & Science Center.

Malinowski, Bronislaw. 1984. "The Role of Myth in Life." In *Sacred Narratives: Readings in the Theory of Myth*, edited by Allen Dundes, 193–206. Berkeley: Univ. of California Press.

Mason, Ronald J. 2006. *Inconstant Companions: Archaeology and North American Indian Oral Traditions*. Tuscaloosa: Univ. of Alabama Press.

Mathews, Zena Pearlstone. 1976. "Huron Pipes and Iroquoian Shamanism." *Man in the Northeast* 12:15–31.

———. 1981. "Janus and Other Multiple-Image Iroquoian Pipes." *Ontario Archaeology* 35:3–22.

———. 1982. "On Dreams and Journeys: Iroquoian Boat Pipes." *American Indian Art Magazine* 7 (3): 46–51, 80.

McCallum, James Dow, ed. 1932. *The Letters of Eleazar Wheelock's Indians*. Hanover, NH: Dartmouth College.

Michelson, Gunther. 1988. "An Account of an Iroquois Condolence Council." *Man in the Northeast* 38:61–75.

Morgan, Lewis Henry. 1852. *Fabrics, Invention, Implements and Utensils of the Iroquois*. Fifth Annual Report of the Regents of the Univ. of New York, Albany.

———. (1851) 1962. *League of the Iroquois.* Reprint, Secaucus, NJ: Citadel Press.

Morehead, Warren King, ed. 1938. *A Report of the Susquehanna River Expedition Sponsored in 1916 by the Museum of the American Indian, Heye Foundation.* Andover, MA: Andover Press.

Niemczycki, Mary Ann Palmer. 1984. *The Origin and Development of the Seneca and Cayuga Tribes of New York State,* edited by Charles F. Hayes III and William Engelbrecht. Research Records no. 17. Rochester, NY: Rochester Museum & Science Center.

———. 1987. "Late Woodland Settlement in the Genesee." *The Bulletin* (Journal of the New York State Archaeological Association) 95:32–38.

———. 1995. "Ceramics and Ethnicity in West-Central New York: Exploring Owasco-Iroquois Connections." *Northeast Anthropology* 49:43–54.

Noble, William C. 1979. "Ontario Iroquois Effigy Pipes." *Canadian Journal of Archaeology* 3:69–90.

Obamsawin, Elizabeth A. 2005. "Iroquois Government and Religion." In *The Encyclopedia of New York State,* edited by Peter Eisenstadt, 794–97. Syracuse, NY: Syracuse Univ. Press.

O'Callaghan, Edmund B., ed. 1853–87. *Documents Relative to the Colonial History of the State of New York, Procured in Holland, England and France, by John R. Brodhead.* 15 vols. Albany, NY: Weed, Parsons.

Parker, Arthur C. 1916. *The Constitution of the Five Nations.* New York State Museum Bulletin 163. Albany: Univ. of the State of New York.

———. 1918. *A Prehistoric Iroquoian Site on the Reed Farm, Richmond Mills, Ontario County, New York.* Researches and Transactions of the New York State Archaeological Association 1, no. 1, Lewis H. Morgan Chapter, Rochester, NY.

———. 1922. *The Archaeological History of New York.* Parts 1–2. New York State Museum Bulletins 235–38. Albany: Univ. of the State of New York.

———. (1923) 1989. *Seneca Myths and Folk Tales.* Reprint, Lincoln: Univ. of Nebraska Press.

Parmenter, Jon. 2010. *The Edge of the Woods: Iroquoia, 1534–1701.* East Lansing: Michigan State Univ. Press.

Pendergast, James F. 1968. "The Summerstown Station Site." National Museum of Canada Anthropology Paper no. 18, Ottawa.

———. 1989. "The Significance of Some Shell Excavated on Iroquoian Archaeological Sites in Ontario." In *Proceedings of the 1986 Shell Bead Conference: Selected Papers*, edited by Charles F. Hayes III, Lynn Ceci, and Connie Cox Bodner, 97–112. Research Records no. 20. Rochester, NY: Rochester Museum & Science Center.

———. 1990. "Emerging Saint Lawrence Iroquoian Settlement Patterns." *Man in the Northeast* 40:17–30.

———. 1991a. *The Massawomeck: Raiders and Traders into Chesapeake Bay in the Seventeenth Century.* Transactions of the American Philosophical Society 81, no. 2. Philadelphia: American Philosophical Society.

———. 1991b. "The St. Lawrence Iroquoians: Their Past, Present, Immediate Future." *The Bulletin* (Journal of the New York State Archaeological Association) 102:47–74.

Peterson, James B., John G. Crock, Ellen R. Cowie, et al. 2004. "St. Lawrence Iroquoians in Northern New England: Pendergast Was 'Right' and More." In *A Passion for the Past: Papers in Honour of James F. Pendergast*, edited by James V. Wright and Jean-Luc Pilon, 87–123. Mercury Series, Archaeology Paper 164. Gatineau, Québec: Canadian Museum of Civilization.

Pilkington, Walter, ed. 1980. *Samuel Kirkland: 18th-Century Missionary to the Iroquois, Government Agent, Father of Hamilton College.* Clinton, NY: Hamilton College.

Pratt, Peter Paul. 1961a. *Oneida Iroquois Glass Trade Bead Sequence: 1585–1745.* Rome, NY: Fort Stanwix Museum.

———. 1961b. "The Bigford Site: Later Prehistoric Oneida." *Pennsylvania Archaeologist* 31 (1): 46–59.

———. 1963. "A Heavily Stockaded Late Prehistoric Oneida Iroquois Settlement." *Pennsylvania Archaeologist* 33 (1–2): 56–92.

———. 1966. "Archaeology of the Oneida Iroquois as Related to Early Acculturation and to the Location of the Champlain-Iroquois Battle of 1615." PhD diss., Univ. of Michigan.

———. 1976. *Archaeology of the Oneida Iroquois, Vol. I.* Occasional Publications in Northeastern Anthropology 1. George's Mills, NH.

Pratt, Peter Paul, and Marjorie K. Pratt. 1986. Report on 1985–86 Excavations at the Nichols Pond Site, Madison County, New York. Prepared for Crawford and Stearns, Architects and Preservation Planners, Syracuse, NY.

Rafferty, Sean M., and Rob Mann. 2004. "Introduction." In *Smoking Culture: The Archaeology of Tobacco Pipes in Eastern North America*, edited by Sean M. Rafferty and Rob Mann, xi–xx. Knoxville: Univ. of Tennessee Press.

Ramsden, Peter G. 1990a. "The Hurons: Archaeology and Culture History. In *The Archaeology of Southern Ontario to A.D. 1650*, edited by Chris J. Ellis and Neal Ferris, 361–84. Occasional Publications of the London Chapter, Ontario Archaeological Society no 5.

———. 1990b. "Saint Lawrence Iroquoians in the Upper Trent River Valley." *Man in the Northeast* 39:87–95.

Randle, Martha Champion. 1953. "The Waugh Collection of Iroquois Folktales." *Proceedings of the American Philosophical Society* 97 (5): 611–33.

Ray, Keith. 1987. "Material Metaphor, Social Interaction and Historical Reconstruction: Patterns of Association and Symbolism in the Igbo-Ukwu Corpus." In *The Archaeology of Contextual Meanings*, edited by Ian Hodder, 66–77. Cambridge: Cambridge Univ. Press.

Richter, Daniel K. 1987. "Ordeals of the Longhouse: The Five Nations in Early American History." In *Beyond the Covenant Chain: The Iroquois and Their Neighbors in Indian North America, 1600–1800*, edited by Daniel K. Richter and James H. Merrill, 11–27. Syracuse, NY: Syracuse Univ. Press.

———. 1992. *The Ordeal of the Longhouse: The Peoples of the Iroquois League in the Era of European Colonization*. Chapel Hill: Univ. of North Carolina Press.

Ricklis, Robert. 1963. "Excavations at the Atwell Fort Site, Madison County, New York." *The Bulletin* (Journal of the New York State Archaeological Association) 28:2–5.

Ritchie, William A. 1980. *The Archaeology of New York State*. 2nd rev. ed. Harrison, NY: Harbor Hill Books.

Ritchie, William A., and Robert E. Funk. 1973. *Aboriginal Settlement Patterns in the Northeast*. New York State Museum and Science Service Memoir 20. Albany: Univ. of the State of New York.

Rochester Museum & Science Center (RMSC). Digital Artifact Catalogue. Rochester Museum & Science Center, Rochester, NY.

———. Site Records. Rochester Museum & Science Center, Rochester NY.

Robertson, David A., and Ronald F. Williamson. 1998. "The Archaeology of the Parsons Site: Summary and Conclusions." *Ontario Archaeology* 65–66:146–50.

Rooth, Anna Birgitta. 1957. "Creation Myths of North America." *Anthropos* 52:497–508.

Rossen, Jack, ed. 2015. *Corey Village and the Cayuga World: Implications from Archaeology and Beyond.* Syracuse, NY: Syracuse Univ. Press.

Rumrill, Donald. 1991. "The Mohawk Glass Trade Bead Chronology: Ca. 1560–1785." *Beads: Journal of the Society of Bead Researchers* 3:5–45.

Sahlins, Marshall D. 1968. *Tribesmen.* Englewood Cliffs, NJ: Prentice-Hall.

———. 1972. *Stone Age Economics.* New York: Aldine de Gruyter.

Sanft, Samantha M. 2018. "Modeling a Seneca Region Site Sequence." Paper presented at the Annual Meeting of the New York State Archaeological Association, Syracuse, NY.

Saunders, Lorraine P. 1976. "Preliminary Report on the Alhart Site." On file at the Rochester Museum & Science Center, Rochester, NY.

———. 1986. "Biological Affinities among Historic Iroquois Groups and Possible Precursive Populations." PhD diss., Univ. of Texas at Austin.

Schoolcraft, Henry Rowe. (1846) 1975. *Notes on the Iroquois; Or, Contributions to the Statistics, Aboriginal History, Antiquities, and General Ethnology of Western New-York.* Reprint, Millwood, NY: Krauss Reprint.

Scott, Duncan C., ed. 1912. "Traditional History of the Confederacy of the Six Nations, Prepared by a Committee of Chiefs." *Transactions of the Royal Society of Canada* (3rd series) 5:195–246.

Seaver, James E. 1990. *A Narrative of the Life of Mrs. Mary Jemison . . . Carefully Taken from Her Own Words, Nov. 29th, 1823.* Syracuse, NY: Syracuse Univ. Press.

Sempowski, Martha L. 1975–83. Unpublished Mortuary Data. Summaries in possession of the author.

———. 1989. "Fluctuation through Time in the Use of Marine Shell at Iroquois Sites." In *Proceedings of the 1986 Shell Bead Conference: Selected Papers*, edited by Charles F. Hayes III, Lynn Ceci, and Connie Cox Bodner, 81–96. Research Records no. 20. Rochester, NY: Rochester Museum & Science Center.

———. 2004a. "Glass Bead Classification and Analysis." Report prepared for History Section, Oneida Indian Nation. Unpublished manuscript in the author's possession.

———. 2004b. "Spiritual Transformation as Reflected in Late Prehistoric Human Effigy Pipes from Western New York." In *A Passion for the Past: Papers in Honour of James F. Pendergast*, edited by James V. Wright and Jean-Luc Pilon, 263–81. Archaeological Survey of Canada, Mercury Series Paper 164. Gatineau, Québec: Canadian Museum of Civilization.

Sempowski, Martha L., and Lorraine P. Saunders, eds. 2001. *Dutch Hollow and Factory Hollow: The Advent of Dutch Trade among the Seneca.* Charles F. Wray Series in Seneca Archaeology vol. 3, Research Records no. 24. Rochester, NY: Rochester Museum & Science Center.

Sempowski, Martha L., Lorraine P. Saunders, and Gian Carlo Cervone. 1988. "The Adams and Culbertson Sites: A Hypothesis for Village Formation." *Man in the Northeast* 35:95–108.

Seneca Nation of Indians. http://www.sni.org/culture.

Service, Elman R. 1962. *Primitive Social Organization: An Evolutionary Perspective.* New York: Random House.

Shannon, Timothy J. 2000. *Indians and Colonials at the Crossroads of Empire: The Albany Congress of 1754.* Ithaca and Cooperstown, NY: Cornell Univ. Press and New York State Historical Association.

———. 2008. *Iroquois Diplomacy on the Early American Frontier.* New York: Penguin.

Shimony, Annemarie Anrod. (1961) 1994. *Conservatism among the Iroquois at the Six Nations Reserve.* Reprint, Syracuse, NY: Syracuse Univ. Press.

Skinner, Alanson. 1921. *Notes on Iroquois Archaeology.* Museum of the American Indian, Heye Foundation, Indian Notes and Monographs, Misc. Series 18:5–216, New York, NY.

Snow, Dean R. 1991. "Dating the Emergence of the League of the Iroquois." In *A Beautiful and Fruitful Place: Selected Rensselaerswijck Seminar Papers*, edited by Nancy Anne McClure Zeller, 139–43. Albany, NY: New Netherland Publishing.

———. 1994. *The Iroquois.* Cambridge, MA: Blackwell.

———. 1995a. *Mohawk Valley Archaeology: The Collections.* Albany: Institute for Archaeological Studies, State Univ. of New York at Albany.

———. 1995b. *Mohawk Valley Archaeology: The Sites.* Albany: Institute for Archaeological Studies, State Univ. of New York at Albany.

———. 1996. "Mohawk Demography and the Effects of Exogenous Epidemics on American Indian Populations." *Journal of Anthropological Archaeology* 15:160–82.

———. 2001. "Evolution of the Mohawk Iroquois." In *Societies in Eclipse: Archaeology of the Eastern Woodlands Indians, A.D. 1400–1700*, edited by David S. Brose, W. Wesley Cowan, and Robert C. Mainfort Jr., 19–29. Washington, DC: Smithsonian Institution Press.

Speck, Frank Gouldsmith. 1955. *The Iroquois: A Study in Cultural Evolution*. Bulletin 23, 2nd ed. Bloomfield Hills, MI: Cranbrook Institute of Science.

Starna, William A. 1988. "The Oneida Homeland in the Seventeenth Century." In *The Oneida Indian Experience: Two Perspectives*, edited by Jack Campisi and Laurence M. Hauptman, 9–22. Syracuse, NY: Syracuse Univ. Press.

———. 2008. "Retrospecting the Origins of the League of the Iroquois." *Proceedings of the American Philosophical Society* 152 (3): 279–321.

Steward, Julian H. 1942. "The Direct Historical Approach in Archaeology." *American Antiquity* 7:337–43.

———. 1955. *Theory of Culture Change: The Methodology of Multilinear Evolution*. Urbana: Univ. of Illinois Press.

Strong, William Duncan. 1942. "Historical Approach in Anthropology." In *Anthropology Today*, edited by Alfred L. Kroeber, 386–97. Chicago: Univ. of Chicago Press.

Surtees, Robert J. 1985. "The Iroquois in Canada." In *The History and Culture of Iroquois Diplomacy: An Interdisciplinary Guide to the Treaties of the Six Nations and Their League*, edited by Francis Jennings, William N. Fenton, Mary A. Druke, and David R. Miller, 67–83. Syracuse, NY: Syracuse Univ. Press.

Thwaites, Reuben Gold, ed. 1896–1901. *The Jesuit Relations and Allied Documents: Travels and Explorations of the Jesuit Missionaries in New France, 1610–1791*. 73 vols. Cleveland: Burrows Brothers.

Tooker, Elisabeth. 1978. "The League of the Iroquois: Its History, Politics, and Ritual." In *Northeast*, edited by Bruce G. Trigger, 418–41. *Handbook of North American Indians*, vol. 15. Washington, DC: Smithsonian Institution.

———. 1984. "The Demise of the Susquehannocks: A 17th Century Mystery." *Pennsylvania Archaeologist* 54 (3–4): 1–10.

———. (1964) 1991. *An Ethnography of the Huron Indians, 1615–1649*. Reprint, Syracuse, NY: Syracuse Univ. Press.

————. 1994. *Lewis H. Morgan on Iroquois Material Culture*. Tucson: Univ. of Arizona Press.

Trelease, Allen W. (1960) 1997. *Indian Affairs in Colonial New York: The Seventeenth Century*. Reprint, Lincoln: Univ. of Nebraska Press.

Tremblay, Roland. 2006. *The St. Lawrence Iroquoians: Corn People*. Montreal: Pointe à Callière, Montreal Museum of Archaeology and History.

Trigger, Bruce G. 1969. *The Huron: Farmers of the North*. New York: Holt, Rinehart and Winston.

————. 1978. "Early Iroquoian Contacts with Europeans. In *Northeast*, edited by Bruce G. Trigger, 344–56. *Handbook of North American Indians*, vol. 15. Washington, DC: Smithsonian Institution Press.

————. 1981. "Prehistoric Social and Political Organization: An Iroquoian Case Study." In *Foundations in Northeast Archaeology*, edited by Dean R. Snow, 1–50. New York: Academic Press.

————. 1986. *Natives and Newcomers: Canada's "Heroic Age" Reconsidered*. Toronto: McGill-Queen's Univ. Press.

————. (1976) 2000. *The Children of Aataensic: A History of the Huron People to 1660*. Reprint, Montreal: McGill-Queen's Univ. Press.

————. 2001. "The Liberation of Wendake." *Ontario Archaeology* 72:3–14.

Tuck, James A. 1971a. "The Iroquois Confederacy." *Scientific American* 224 (2): 32–49.

————. 1971b. *Onondaga Iroquois Prehistory: A Study in Settlement Archaeology*. Syracuse, NY: Syracuse Univ. Press.

———— 1978. "Northern Iroquoian Prehistory." In *Northeast*, edited by Bruce G. Trigger, 322–32. *Handbook of North American Indians*, vol. 15. Washington, DC: Smithsonian Institution.

Turgeon, Laurier. 2001. "French Beads in France and Northeastern North America during the Sixteenth Century." *Historical Archaeology* 35 (4): 58–82.

Urton, Gary. 1990. *The History of a Myth: Pacariqtambo and the Origin of the Inkas*. Austin: Univ. of Texas Press.

Vecsey, Christopher. 1988. *Imagine Ourselves Richly: Mythic Narratives of North America*. New York: Crossroad.

von Gernet, Alexander D. 1992. "Hallucinogens and the Origins of the Iroquoian Pipe/Tobacco/Smoking Complex." In *Proceedings of the 1989 Smoking Pipe Conference: Selected Papers*, edited by Charles F. Hayes

III, Connie Cox Bodner, and Martha L. Sempowski, 171–85. Research Records no. 22. Rochester, NY: Rochester Museum & Science Center.

Wallace, Anthony F. C. 1957. "Origins of Iroquois Neutrality: The Grand Settlement of 1701." *Pennsylvania History* 24:223–35.

———. 1958. "The Dekanawideh Myth Analyzed as the Record of a Revitalization Movement." *Ethnohistory* 5 (2): 118–30.

———. (1969) 1972. *The Death and Rebirth of the Seneca*. Reprint, New York: Vintage Books.

Wallace, Paul A. W. 1945. *Conrad Weiser, 1696–1760: Friend of Colonist and Mohawk*. Philadelphia: Univ. of Pennsylvania Press.

———. 1948. "The Return of Hiawatha." *New York History* 29 (4): 385–403.

———. (1946) 1986. *The White Roots of Peace*. Reprint, Saranac Lake, NY: Channing Press.

Warrick, Gary. 2008. *A Population History of the Huron-Petun, A.D. 500–1650*. New York: Cambridge Univ. Press.

Waugh, Frederick W. 1916. *Iroquois Foods and Food Preparation*. Ottawa: Canada Department of Mines, Geological Survey, Memoir 86, Anthropological Series 12.

———. n.d. Iroquois Folklore Papers. Canadian Museum of Civilization, Library, Archives, and Documentation, Hull, Québec.

Weaver, Sally M. 1978. "Six Nations of the Grand River, Ontario." In *Northeast*, edited by Bruce G. Trigger, 525–36. *Handbook of North American Indians*, vol. 15. Washington, DC: Smithsonian Institution Press.

———. 1984. "Seth Newhouse and the Grand River Confederacy at Mid-Nineteenth Century." In *Extending the Rafters: Interdisciplinary Approaches to Iroquoian Studies*, edited by Michael K. Foster, Jack Campisi, and Marianne Mithun, 165–82. Albany: State Univ. of New York Press.

Weiskotten, Daniel H. 1995. "The Reexamination of 'A Long Lost Point in History': The Real Battle of Nichols Pond." *EIDOS* (Spring): 18–31.

Wheeler-Vogelin, Erminie, and Remedios W. Moore. 1957. "The Emergence Myth in Native North America." In *Studies in Folklore: In Honor of Distinguished Service Professor Stith Thompson*, edited by W. Edson Richmond, 66–91. Bloomington: Indiana Univ. Press.

White, Marian E. 1978a. "Erie." In *Northeast*, edited by Bruce G. Trigger, 412–17. *Handbook of North American Indians*, vol. 15. Washington, DC: Smithsonian Institution.

———. 1978b. "Neutral and Wenro." In *Northeast*, edited by Bruce Trigger, 407–11. *Handbook of North American Indians*, vol. 15. Washington, DC: Smithsonian Institution.

Whitney, Theodore. 1970. "The Buyea Site, Ond 13-3." *The Bulletin* (Journal of the New York State Archaeological Association) 50:1–14.

———. 1971. "The Olcott Site, Msv-3." *Chenango Chapter Bulletin* (New York State Archaeological Association, Norwich) 12, no. 3.

Williamson, Ronald F. 2016. "St. Lawrence Iroquoians and Pan-Iroquoian Social Network Analysis." *Ontario Archaeology* 96:87–103.

Wintemberg, W. J. 1936. *Roebuck Prehistoric Village Site, Grenville County, Ontario*. Canada Department of Mines, National Museum of Canada, Bulletin 83, Anthropological Series 19. Ottawa.

Witthoft, John. 1959. "Ancestry of the Susquehannocks." In *Susquehannock Miscellany*, edited by John Witthoft and W. Fred Kinsey III, 19–60. Harrisburg: Pennsylvania Historical and Museum Commission.

Wolf, Eric R. 1982. *Europe and the People without History*. Berkeley: Univ. of California Press.

Wonderley, Anthony. 2001. "The Iroquois Creation Story over Time." *Northeast Anthropology* 62:1–16.

———. 2002. "Oneida Ceramic Effigies: A Question of Meaning." *Northeast Anthropology* 63:23–48.

———. 2004. *Oneida Iroquois Folklore, Myth, and History: New York Oral Narrative from the Notes of H. E. Allen and Others*. Syracuse, NY: Syracuse Univ. Press.

———. 2005a. "Effigy Pipes, Diplomacy, and Myth: Exploring Interaction between St. Lawrence Iroquoians and Eastern Iroquois in New York State." *American Antiquity* 70:211–40.

———. 2005b. "Iroquois Ceramic Iconography: New Evidence from the Oneida Vaillancourt Site." *Ontario Archaeology* 79–80:73–87.

———. 2006. "Archaeological Research at the Oneida Vaillancourt Site." *The Bulletin* (Journal of the New York State Archaeological Association) 122:1–26.

———. 2009. *At the Font of the Marvelous: Exploring Oral Narrative and Mythic Imagery of the Iroquois and Their Neighbors*. Syracuse, NY: Syracuse Univ. Press.

———. 2012. "Representational Art of the St. Lawrence Iroquoians and Eastern Iroquois." *Northeast Anthropology* 77–78:139–61.

Woodbury, Hanni, ed. and trans., in collaboration with Reg Henry and Harry Webster. 1992. *Concerning the League: The Iroquois League Tradition as Dictated in Onondaga by John Arthur Gibson.* Winnipeg: Algonquian and Iroquoian Linguistics Memoir 9.

Woodward, Ashbel. 1880. "Wampum." Paper presented to the Numismatic and Antiquarian Society of Philadelphia, Albany, NY.

Wray, Charles F. 1973. *Manual for Seneca Iroquois Archaeology.* Honeoye Falls, NY: Cultures Primitive.

———. 1985. "The Volume of Dutch Trade Goods Received by the Seneca Iroquois 1600–1687 A.D." In *New Netherland Studies Bulletin KNOB* 84 (2–3):100–112.

Wray, Charles F., and Harry L. Schoff. 1953. "A Preliminary Report on the Seneca Sequence in Western New York (1550–1687)." *Pennsylvania Archaeologist* 23 (2): 53–63.

Wray, Charles F., Martha L. Sempowski, and Lorraine P. Saunders. 1991. *Tram and Cameron: Two Early Contact Era Seneca Sites.* Charles F. Wray Series in Seneca Archaeology vol. 2, Research Records no. 21. Rochester, NY: Rochester Museum & Science Center.

Wray, Charles F., Martha L. Sempowski, Lorraine P. Saunders, and Gian Carlo Cervone. 1987. *The Adams and Culbertson Sites.* Charles F. Wray Series in Seneca Archaeology vol. 1, Research Records no. 19, Rochester, NY: Rochester Museum & Science Center.

Wright, James V. 1966. *The Ontario Iroquois Tradition.* Bulletin no. 210. Ottawa: National Museum of Canada.

———. 1990. "Archaeology of Southern Ontario to A.D. 1650: A Critique." In *The Archaeology of Southern Ontario to A.D. 1650,* edited by Chris J. Ellis and Neal Ferris, 493–502. Occasional Publications of the London Chapter, Ontario Archaeological Society no 5.

Wrong, George M., ed. 1939. *The Long Journey to the Country of the Hurons by Father Gabriel Sagard.* Translated by H. H. Langton. Toronto: Champlain Society.

Index

251

Anthropologist **Anthony Wonderley** (PhD, Cornell) worked for the Oneida Indian Nation in its cultural management and preservation programs and for the Oneida Community Mansion House (Oneida, New York) as curator of collections and interpretation. A Fulbright postdoctoral fellow and a fellow of the New York State Archaeological Association, Wonderley publishes widely on Iroquois archaeology and oral narrative and on New York history. His books include *Oneida Iroquois Folklore, Myth, and History* (Syracuse Univ. Press, 2004), *At the Font of the Marvelous* (Syracuse Univ. Press, 2009), and *Oneida Utopia: From Bible Communism to Welfare Capitalism* (Cornell Univ. Press, 2016). The latter was named Book of the Year by the Communal Studies Association. Wonderley and his spouse, Pauline, reside in Oneida, New York.

Martha L. Sempowski (PhD, 1983) completed graduate work in anthropology at the University of Rochester, where she specialized in Mexican archaeology. Her dissertation was published as part 1 of *Mortuary Practices and Skeletal Remains at Teotihuacan, Mexico* (Univ. of Utah Press, 1994). Her analytical focus on mortuary practices as reflections of social processes led to nearly forty years of research at the Rochester Museum & Science Center, where she codirected the Seneca Archaeology Research Project. Sempowski coordinated the publication of three major books in the Charles F. Wray Series in Seneca Archaeology: *The Adams and Culbertson Sites*, *Tram and Cameron: Two Early Contact Era Seneca Sites*, and *Dutch Hollow and Factory Hollow: The Advent of Dutch Trade among the Seneca*. Her Seneca research has included the effects of European contact, refinements in site chronology, glass bead analysis, the social status of women, and the League of the Iroquois. She is a research fellow at the Rochester Museum & Science Center, and a fellow of the New York State Archaeological Association, from whom she received a Lifetime Achievement Award. She and her husband, John, now enjoy spending time with their two sons and daughters-in-law, and four grandchildren.